Masters of Copywriting

Masters of Copywriting

22 of the Worlds Greatest Advertising Writers
Reveal the Secrets of Selling with Words!

Edited by J. George Frederick

WAKING LION PRESS

ISBN 978-1-4341-0276-8

Published by Waking Lion Press, an imprint of The Editorium

The Editorium, LLC
West Valley City, UT 84128-3917
wakinglionpress.com
wakinglion@editorium.com

Contents

Contents

Contents

I Am the Printing Press

I am the printing press, born of the mother earth. My heart is of steel, my limbs are of iron, and my fingers are of brass.

I sing the songs of the world, the oratorios of history, the symphonies of all time.

I am the voice of today, the herald of tomorrow. I weave into the warp of the past the woof of the future. I tell the stories of peace and war alike.

I make the human heart beat with passion or tenderness. I stir the pulse of nations. I make brave men do braver deeds.

I inspire the midnight toiler, weary at his loom, to lift his head again and gaze, with fearlessness, into the vast beyond, seeking the consolation of a hope eternal.

When I speak, a myriad people listen to my voice. The Saxon, the Latin, the Celt, the Hun, the Slav, the Hindu, all comprehend me.

I am the tireless clarion of the news. I cry your joys and sorrows every hour. I fill the dullard's mind with thoughts uplifting. I am light, knowledge, power. I epitomize the conquests of mind over matter.

I am the record of all things mankind has achieved. My offspring comes to you in the candle's glow, amid the dim lamps of poverty, the splendor of riches; at sunrise, at high noon, and in the waning evening.

I am the laughter and tears of the world, and I shall never die until all things return to the immutable dust.

I am the printing press.

ROBERT H. DAVIS

Preface

The list of authors of the present volume includes men and women who incontestably are or have been in the front rank of their profession; whose work is or has been very conspicuously successful; whose record of service in advertising is long, notable or distinguished and whose claim to be included is self-evident in their contributions. By good fortune, there are included the writings on copy of several outstanding men of acknowledged genius in advertising, who are now dead. One of these, George L. Dyer, has left almost no other written record of his point of view, except in the splendidly successful advertising of his clients. The selection, therefore, the editor believes, is notably representative of American masters of advertising copy.

It is advisable to note here that the authors of the chapters have been permitted to paragraph or sub-head their material in their own way, without attempt at making style uniform. This, the editor believes, is a courtesy inherent in the subject and the plan.

The matter of reproduction of examples of advertisements has, by common consent, been omitted, for the simple reason that, like hats, advertisements go out of style in appearance, and this book is meant to focus attention not on external form, but on the principles of copy.

It may be anticipated that in future editions of this book other contributors will be included, for the problems of advertising are now greater than ever. The editor cherishes the hope that the readers will agree with him that the book is not only practically helpful in the study of copy, but is also historically important, as it collects and conserves the writings of the men who have made history in advertising writing.

THE EDITOR

Introduction: The Story of Advertising Writing

By J. George Frederick

Permit yourself, if you will, to be transported for a swift sight-seeing ride, backward over the dead centuries. The reward will be an adequate perspective on advertising which we moderns tend to regard as rather a present-day invention.

Presto! We are back 25,000 years, among the silent woods and hills of France, in the caves (recently discovered) of stone-age men. Being shades, we enter the rocky hallway unobserved, past the fires around which squat short, hairy men. By the flaring light of these fires we see on the walls many crude carvings, and we move along toward the first advertising workshop. A caveman stands at the wall hammering at the rock, making a bas-relief which will advertise his hunting prowess to his fellow-hunters. He has finished the picture and is cutting the headline of the ad, using some strange symbols—the forerunners, possibly, of language, set in Caslon type!

In another instant, we are at Babylon, 3500 B.C., noting a diligent personage in a high headdress manipulating a kind of stylus upon a little pat of red soft clay. He is working with speed and neatness, making cuneiform letters with an ease and grace startlingly similar to that of the man in a modern department store, lettering a window sign with a lettering pen. Finishing the writing, the Babylonian gently sets his clay tablet into an oven and bakes it. On the morrow he will send a runner with it to some distant points along the Euphrates. It contains a statement of what cattle and feed his employer (I almost said his client) has for sale, and at what prices. He is the first hired advertising man. I have in my possession this very clay tablet or its prototype.

Again we spread wings and let a dozen or two of centuries slip under our feet, and we are in Thebes, Egypt, about 1100 B.C. An austere Egyptian aristocrat is dictating to his *amanuensis a* statement that he will offer a reward for the return of a valuable slave who has run away.

The *amanuensis* is writing this "ad" upon papyrus. It will probably be hung up in public. You can see the original in the British Museum today. Papyrus is the first dim hint of the newsprint and the other members of the paper family upon which millions of "ads" are to be printed 3,000 years later.

Gently we let time glide us forward until we find ourselves in Greece and Rome. Both these great peoples, from whom we have borrowed so much else that has ennobled and enriched our heritage, were very familiar indeed with advertising. There must have been something of a profession of advertising then, for the walls of Pompeii and Herculaneum, which are visible today, were crowded full of announcements painted in black and red. The things advertised were plays, exhibitions, gladiatorial shows, salt- and fresh-water baths. Bills termed *libelli* were the media of news of sales of estates, lost and found articles, absconded debtors, etc. Police regulations were given to the public via such advertisements; and some were permanently cut in stone and terra cotta relief, set in pilasters decorating the front of public buildings.

Even the ancient Greeks had the crier—a most important person indeed, who generally was an officer of the state or municipal government. He went about crying his news like any good advertising man dictating his ads—with this difference: he was accompanied by a musician! The flamboyant advertising adjective was probably born with him, for he is reputed to have used much hyperbole and rhetorical flourish. He must have had good advertising results or he would not have been continued so long.

We now fly over a dark void of many centuries; for with the decay of Roman civilization Europe sank to an illiterate level, to a long period of retrogression. Still, advertising being *a fundamental* human necessity, it did not disappear like other things of civilization; it merely receded to the mode of the ancient Greeks—the crier just described. These public criers of the Middle Ages were actually an organized body of advertising men, functionaries of the state, as in old Greece. They had a peculiar, standardized call, of which one is reminded when one hears even a modern law court called to order with the words: "Oyez, oyez!" When this call—this ad—fell upon the ears of the public, people rushed from out of their homes to hear. The criers had exclusive right to news of auctions and other sales. News of weddings, christenings, funerals, royal decrees, offerings of merchandise fell from their lips. Later individual merchants employed individual criers.

Even in the eighteenth century, the noise of criers in the streets was a fair parallel to our noise of autos and fire engines and Coney *Island.* It was a pandemonium of "Buy, Buy, Buy"; "Rally up, ladies"; "What d'ye lack?"

Later came the English medieval guilds and the huge City Companies who used the equivalent of the modern poster. The Weavers,' the Mercers,' Glovers,' Goldsmiths,' or Haberdashers' Guilds vied with each other to devise elaborate signs, which were suspended from shops, elevated on posts, and even made into archways. An Act of Parliament in 1762 limited the signs, and then more artistry was used. Even such famous artists as Hogarth, Holbein, Correggio and others painted signs. The era of advertising writing and advertising art was begun!

But already that greatest of civilized tools, the printing press, had been acquiring facilities for taking over the raucous job of the criers. William Caxton brought the first printing press to England in 1477. He started to print his signs ("handbills"; from the Latin *si signis,* "if anybody," with which words the handbills usually began). The advertising possibilities of these handbills were quickly evident, and soon taverns, town halls, *walls* and even cathedrals were posted with them; advertising books, plays, boxing shows, merchandise, etc.

Then came newspapers and periodicals, starting with Nathaniel Butter's *Weekly Newes* in London, in 1632. They were mainly what we would today call "house organs" for politicians, parties and persons, but written with delicious venom and spleen. Butter was the first publisher in the world to print an ad, but the first publication to get *paid* for it was *Mist's Weekly Journal.* The first publisher who realized the future of advertising was Sir Robert L'Estrange, who had three publications, one boldly proclaiming itself the especial carrier of ads—the *Mercury, or Advertisements Concerning Trade* (1668).

The London Gazette (1666) carried the following announcement:

> An advertisement being daily prest to the Publication of Books, Medicines and other things not properly the business of a Paper of Intelligence. This is to notifie once for all, that we will not charge the Gazette with advertisements, unless they be matters of State, but that a paper of Advertisements will be forthwith printed apart, and recommended to the Publick by another hand.

It is perfectly evident from the above that disdain was the prevalent attitude to advertisements. This is perhaps reflected in the fact that from 1712 all the way to 1853, the Crown levied a tax on advertisements.

However, with the first daily paper, the *Daily Courant,* London (1762), advertising became a matter-of-fact and important part of daily life in the sense that we know it today.

And with this development came also, naturally, the advertising writer, even the advertising agent. The coffee houses were the haunts of the *literati,* and the habitat of the advertising man in those days—again naturally—was the coffee house. Thus even in those pioneering days, as now, advertising was intertwined with the literary and the artistic life of the people. Dr. Johnson himself did not consider it beneath him to write advertising copy. The coffee houses functioned as the offices of advertising agents, who collected "advertorial copy" and passed it to the periodicals. Such coffee houses as The Star in St. Paul's churchyard, Suttle's Coffee House in Finch Lane and a coffee house in Ave Maria Lane were hangouts for ad men, doing business over the bar, writing ads *on* the bar or on the tables.

What was advertising copy like in those days? Here is an example from the *Publick Advertiser,* May 19, 1657, entitled "The Virtue of Coffee":

> In Bartholomew Lane, on the backside of the Old Exchange, the drink called Coffee, which is a very wholesom and Physical drink, having many excellent vertues, closes the Orifice of the Stomach, fortifies the heat within, helpeth Digestion, quickeneth the Spirits, maketh the heart lightsom, is good against Eye-Sores, Coughs or Colds, Rheums, Consumptions, Headache, Dropsie, Gout, Scurvy, King's Evil, and many others, is to be sold both in the morning and at three of the clock in the afternoon.

Addison's famous *Spectator,* whose literary reputation lingers to this day, carried a typical small ad in 1711:

> Mrs. Attway states that she will sell a quantity of good silk gowns, a parcel of rich brocades, venetian and thread satins, tissues and damasks—great pennyworths bought of people that have failed.

The advertising need and urge have been shown here in historical perspective over the long centuries of humanity's past. This need and instinct have been implicit in human nature and human life, as literature itself testifies. The anecdote of Alcibiades who had determined to become famous will illustrate. He knew he had to make people "talk," so he bought the most famous dog in the community and cut off his tail! Then the public "talked," and Alcibiades was a name known to all! We have also Bob Sawyer in Dickens' *Pickwick Papers,* who, to build his reputation as a doctor, plotted with his boy to call him from church in the middle of the service with all possible commotion, in order to impress the people with his busy practise. We would know these things today as trick press agentry, outside the pale of good advertising.

* * *

The American colonies in the earlier days, being at that period rather an exact duplicate of England, in custom and practise, had much the same advertising history, even to the town criers.

Advertising in America, outside of criers and handbills, was naturally dependent upon periodicals, and it was 1704 before an American weekly was founded *(The Boston News Letter),* which forty years later could boast of having only 300 subscribers! It was 1778 before the first daily newspaper *(The Pennsylvania Packet)* appeared. The first magazine appeared in 1741, in Philadelphia—oddly enough two rivals were born three days apart. Of these one was published by Benjamin Franklin, who claimed that his rival, Bradford, had stolen his idea from the announcement advertisement. But alas, only three numbers of the rival's magazine ever appeared, and only six numbers of Franklin's *General Magazine or Historical Chronicle.* Before the end of the century, however, forty or more magazines were started, and many newspapers.

Advertising in these periodicals modeled itself definitely along English lines, and we now see how perfect a reflex of the life and habits of the people the advertisements of a period can be. The "ads" of that period are like peeps into the windows of the families of the day. The *New York Journal* (which few people realize was published that early) contained in 1766 this ad, rather brutally calling to mind the great distance we have traveled in humanitarian principles:

To be sold, for no fault, a very good wench, 22 years old, with a child 18 months old. Enquire of the printer.

Men wrote their own advertisements in those days; even men like Washington and Jefferson. (It is sometimes overlooked that both these men possessed and operated various business enterprises.)

It is hard, in discussing advertising in America, not to give attention to Benjamin Franklin, for he was an advertising writer by instinct and inclination, and is bound up inseparably with the development of printing, publishing and advertising in America. He began to print in 1728. His *Pennsylvania Gazette* came into existence in 1729. In 1741 he published his *General Magazine* which had a short life, but not too short to print one and only one advertisement, which, it would appear, was *the first American advertisement.* Here it is:

> There is a F E R R Y kept over Potomack (by the Subfcriber) being the Poft Road and much the nigheft way from Annapolis to Williamsburg, where all Gentlemen may depend on a ready Paffage in a good new Boat with able Hands. Richard Brett, Deputy-Poft-Mafter at Potomack.

For a century after this American advertising, as elsewhere, made practically no progress, being confined to classified ads of a local, provincial kind.

The advertising situation at about the Civil War period was the farthest conceivable distance from the present-day status. Not the faintest inkling seems to have penetrated anybody's mind as to what was coming. The establishment of the big dailies (New York *Sun,* 1833; New York *Herald,* 1835; New York *Tribune,* 1841; Philadelphia *Public Ledger,* 1836) did not develop much advertising. Few used the columns of these large city dailies, today carrying millions of lines of display—far much beyond the classified ads of the routine variety.

It was Robert Bonner, who was the Hearst or the Curtis of his day with his New York *Ledger—a* man with the advertising instinct sticking out all over him—who first stirred up the display advertising idea in a really modern sense. He startled people by taking entire page ads to say in large letters: "Fanny Fern writes only for the *Ledger."* He got amazing results, for a significant reason—he had the advertising stage all to himself, and the law of contrast gave him 100% advantage. "I get all the money I can lay my hands on and throw it out to the newspaper," he said, "and before I get back to my office there it all is again, and a lot more with it!" Bonner's instinct for publicity was like Barnum's; he was a great showman. His paper, which Godkin satirically said was filled with "tales of The Demon Cabman, The Maiden's Revenge" and other "low and coarse" material, got Edward Everett to write for it—Everett, ex-president of Harvard, ex-ambassador, exquisite stylist and scholar! It made a sensation.

Now for the paradox: although Bonner used advertising with great success, *nobody else did;* and his *Ledger,* which was the *Cosmopolitan* or the *Saturday Evening Post* of the day, *never carried a single ad!* There were no business houses which considered its space valuable. The magazines of the period were so completely without advertising patronage that George P. Rowell, founder of *Printers' Ink,* once became the owner of the outside cover page of *Our Young Folks* for a year, but even he could not dispose of it, so he used it himself.

The truth is, advertising was looked down upon, not only by the public, but by business men. Not only was it unvalued; it was actually an object of contempt. It is amusing today to note the airs put on by *The Chicago Magazine,* for instance, before the Civil War. It frankly announced that its editorial plans were "to daguerreotype leading citizens in nearby towns" (a little graft game we know how to smile at today); yet it was able to say in the same issue, "we respond to the wish of a contemporary that we might be able to dispense with advertising, but at present the law of necessity must overrule the law of taste." If Chicago felt that way, it may be imagined how Boston and Philadelphia felt.

Scribner's Magazine "broke the ice," about 1870. In 1868 *Harper's Magazine* was still refusing advertisements; in fact, even in the early seventies an offer of $18,000 for the last page of *Harper's* for a year for a Howe Sewing Machine ad was refused. It was not until 1882 that *Harper's* yielded.

Scribner's in 1870 went out after advertising—the first magazine to make the innovation. It was only a year after George P. Rowell had begun—in 1869—to publish the first directory of newspapers and periodicals, and had set himself up as an advertising agent.

It is significant that the average span of life in the U.S. in 1870, when magazines first accepted advertising, was only 45 years, whereas today it is 58. Who could deny that the astounding spread, since 1870, of ideas of sanitation and health, even to the rural districts, has been accomplished very largely through the advertising of sanitary and health-building merchandise, and the ideas printed and widely disseminated in the periodicals made possible by advertising patronage?

The rapidity of growth of advertising is seen in the fact that twelve years after *Harper's* had opened its pages to advertising, it was carrying 144 pages, at a page rate of $250, or $36,000. The six leading monthlies of December, 1894, according to a computation once made by F. W. Ayer, earned $180,000 worth of advertising. Today the December issues of the six leading periodicals carry several millions of dollars worth of business.

* * *

The period of American advertising, such as it was, from the Civil War almost to the end of the last century, was dominated largely by patent medicine advertisers. The only association of advertising men and advertisers was headed by and operated mainly in the interest of the outstanding patent medicines of the day. I well remember a blizzardy day in February, even as late as 1903, when I attended the convention of "national advertisers" at Delmonico's in New York—a hostelry now no more. This convention was the only national group of ad men existing. Scarcely fifty people were present, and if I remember aright, Dr. Pierce presided. Yet even at the moment S. S. McClure was approaching the heyday of his success with *McClure's Magazine,* and the general magazine field was soon to attain its far wider importance in the advertising world. At that pivotal point there was only a handful of manufacturers who advertised consistently. The acceptance of advertising as a matter-of-fact tool of industry was still ten years off. The movement to clean up advertising pages and outlaw the nostrums, which for almost a century had been crippling the prestige of advertising, was only a feeble voice in the wilderness.

Advertising copy in the nineties was a matter of slogans, jingles, pictures, testimonial letters, appeals to fear, and the bare featuring of name and crude trademark. "Use Pear's Soap" as an example of complete copy for an ad was still many firms' idea of good advertising. Dependence by the patent medicine men was upon newspaper advertisements, bought by a sharp bargaining process at very low rates on contract; sign space upon fence and barn signs, and upon almanacs which were calculated to alarm you about your liver while you were looking up a date. I had worked in a newspaper composing room in those days, and some of the old "typos" regularly bought the patent medicine advertised in the copy they set up, so well did the advertiser calculate his copy appeal!

Meantime, for some years, George P. Rowell, owner and editor of *Printer's Ink,* had been serving as a mouthpiece and a focal point for the nascent profession of advertising, his pages carrying articles by the men who were then thinking out the problems of advertising. His policy of wide, free distribution of *Printer's Ink* resulted in planting the advertising idea in many places all over the country, and there began to take shape a body of modernized ideas on advertising writing.

At that time the livest advertising men, from a progressive copy-writing point of view, were the department store advertising managers. Some of these, like Powers of John Wanamaker's, were far-seeing and highly skilful, with a background of high-grade journalism. They wrote about many kinds of merchandise in a manner quite unknown before. They really described, adequately and with imagination, the goods they were selling. Few, if any, manufacturers were doing this in their general advertising, being wedded to economy of space and the idea of very few words and little argument.

Under the impetus of the Powers "school" of retail advertising copy writers, whose ideas and ads were frequently set forth in Rowell's *Printer's Ink,* the enlarged conception of copy's place in good advertising grew apace. The editor of this Volume was one of this group—which included James H. Collins—of early writers in *Printer's Ink,* before Mr. Rowell died. Very soon, the new copy ideas invaded the general advertising field. Charles Austin Bates in New York, N. W. Ayer in Philadelphia and Lord & Thomas in Chicago, were the live advertising agencies applying modern ideas in copy. Bates began to publish a magazine, *Current Advertising,* with Leroy Fairman ridiculing the old-style copy. Lord & Thomas in Chicago published *Judicious Advertising.* Both magazines became propagandists of better copy ideas. A. D. Lasker, then a very young man, was made head of the Lord & Thomas agency, and he soon began a very determined, aggressive campaign to revolutionize ideas in copy in the manufacturing field, by means of a phrase, "reason why" copy. John Kennedy and the editor of this book, as well as several others, were brought to Chicago to be leaders in this campaign, which is acknowledged to have been vital in the history of advertising. This "reason why" idea of copy was an epoch-making rebellion in copy writing from old standards, analogous to Martin Luther's protestant rebellion in religion; it aimed at an appeal to reason and intelligence rather than the time-honored assumption that the public was a mass of dumb, driven sheep, who could be swayed with mere picture-and-catch-word.

This ten-year fight to establish the "reason why" ideas in copy was finally won, because all intelligent men in advertising joined hands with it; though, naturally, at the same time the original extreme position of its promulgators was modified. The editor of this volume well remembers the bitter debates of that period over copy, and remembers also his errors in emphasizing too much sheer reason and logic and over-long copy in advertising. The important accomplishment, aided by wide-awake advertising men everywhere, was the coming of greater flexibility and life into advertising, more sincerity, more information, more fact, more literature. Advertising changed from a museum of inert waxworks into a wonderful stage of living players who gave the public thrills and real values. Words had come into their own; copy was supreme. The manufacturers of standard high-grade merchandise began to use advertising as a vital sales tool—a natural consequence, because advertising brought returns.

The historic fact is, furthermore, that American periodicals from that day forth blossomed also into life and wider usefulness.

The *"McClure's"* and *"Everybody's,"* magazines of important civic services to the country, spawned and grew upon the support of advertising. The live, able newspapers of the country, the splendid trade and general periodicals serving their groups for greater education, took on the hue of health because of the twin service of advertising value which to this day makes it at least a matter of debate whether the advertising pages are not of equal service to subscribers, *purely as reading matter,* as the editorial pages themselves. Certainly the *Dry Goods Economist, The Iron Age, The Engineering News,* etc., would be very definitely less useful without their advertising, which are current technical news bulletins in themselves. Advertising copy became *worth reading,* began to furnish information, to bear a real relation to life, and to affect and stimulate thought, just as editorial pages are supposed to do.

* * *

With the modernization of ideas about advertising copy and the consequent phenomenal increase in advertising came another problem, *that of irresponsible, objectionable advertising.* Sentiment against patent medicine advertising had been forming slowly—Edward Bok of the *Ladies Home Journal* leading the fight—and one by one magazines rejected the nostrums living off the ignorance and fears of the public. The idea gained currency that such advertising was decreasing the pulling power of sound commodity advertising; that public confidence in legitimate concerns was being injured by seeing their advertising side by side with fraudulent, false advertising. The better type of newspapers, such as the New York *Times* and others, set up standards, and soon the entire advertising profession was centering attention on the subject. The advertising clubs movement which had resulted in a national organization (at first a mere junketing group) took up the cry and began a crusade with almost religious fervor. For ten years this fight waged, vigilance committees being organized to take action, and legislative efforts undertaken to secure passage of the *Printer's Ink* model statute against fraudulent and misleading advertising. Today practically all states have adequate laws, and there exists a large and well-organized machine, composed of the Better Business Bureaus, for the work not only of stamping out fraudulent advertising, but of offering constructive guidance in disputed or dubious matters of advertising representation.

Meantime the technique of copy grew in vision and outlook as more and more money was used in application of the advertising method. Advertising became less *a mere* matter of copy and media and more a coordination of practical sales-management and the closer analysis of conditions of distribution and consumption. "Arm chair" copy-writing gave way to market survey-built copy. Intuitive insight into the public mind began to be supplemented by research-backed judgments of consumer-reactions. Particularly so after a period of five or six years of rather unsatisfactory flirting with the science of psychology as a guide to copy. A body of very valuable knowledge was turned up by the interest in psychology as it relates to advertising, especially the contribution of Prof. H. L. Hollingsworth of Columbia University, and Walter Dill Scott, now President of Northwestern University. But the application of psychological knowledge was limited to those who could grasp the subject, and still further to those with minds able to apply its broad generalizations practically and wisely. The need was so much greater for knowledge of practical economic factors in the field that more attention began to be paid to research, a factor now bulking very large and permanently in matters of copy preparation.

But it is true that advertising writing, like any other form of writing, must always, in the main, be instinctive and imaginative; very close to facts at the base, but tempered and planned with use of all the arts and sciences. Literary art, psychological science, sociological insight, biological understanding, philosophical acumen, as well as the unlabeled and unchartered matter of knowledge of life and people—all these enter into copy-writing. An almost gnomic wisdom about the human being—his weaknesses, his perversities, his strengths and his habits—are necessary in the copy writer, *par excellence.* It is, therefore, small wonder that among advertising writers are found men and women whose writing is as acceptable to the public in the form of articles and fiction as in the form of advertising, since writing of every kind must be based on interest, artistic perception and creative capacity.

* * *

Words, printed thoughts, are at the very zenith of power today. Even in ancient civilizations, Greek and Roman, it was chiefly orators, poets and writers who made men act. Oratory has dimmed in power only because of its physical limitations (which radio now has to some degree removed). The printed word, through the genius of the automatic printing press, has now an audience of stupendous size, scope, flexibility and trained attention. It is literally the cement which connects the myriad bricks of humanity together in the structure we call civilization. A blackness comparable to night would settle down upon humanity if its printed word facilities were suddenly to become extinct. It would be a kind of mental death. A taste of it has been experienced by the intellectuals of Russia, who for a while remained almost completely without books, without paper and pencils, without periodicals, without scientific monographs or even mail communication.

The men with the prestige of genius, like Shaw, Wells, Conrad and others; the men who by ownership of periodicals of wide circulation, like Curtis, Hearst, or the late Lord Northcliffe; the men who because of their importance to humanity, like Lloyd George or the late Woodrow Wilson, and men who pay for space to say what they wish, like Campbell, Wrigley, Armour;—all of these are *word masters* on a great scale and affect deeply the lives of millions. To call one a writer and the other an advertiser; one a statesman and the other a seller of merchandise, is, after all, a very faint distinction without a fundamental difference. Each and all of them have aims, some practical, some ideal, which it is their mission to sell to the public; and whether for statesmanship of the highest order or for the business of providing soup and automobiles in large quantities at low prices, *their principal task is the influencing of the minds of people in large numbers.* This is a profession inherently of the highest importance to society. The measure of all public men, as well as of business concerns, is the extent to which they can carry public opinion and responsive action with them for their ideas, and the extent to which these ideas increase the wealth and happiness of society. The advertiser need no more be afraid of this test than the statesman.

* * *

Copy is the soul of advertising. Picture and type may appeal to instincts, to the senses, but copy has no other entry-way into the reader except through his or her intelligence. And yet copy is more potent perhaps than type or picture to reach, if desired, either instincts or senses, for language has power to create an infinitely greater variety of images, symbols and associations than any other medium of communication. *Copy* is, therefore, a supreme consideration.

Thanks to the higher ethical standards which have been evolved among the crafts of advertisers, publishers, newspapers and advertising writers— working as they must, to some degree, in unison—the integrity of the printed word is jealously guarded. There are no higher standards in statesmanship or journalism than those which prevail in advertising; and no profession, not even the medical profession, is so alert and maintains such extensive machinery for the elimination of misleading statements and the prosecution of fraudulent representation in print. The advertising profession is today on a parity, in ethics, with the journalistic profession as a whole; and it may be said with truth that it has actually been a powerful force in elevating the standards of journalism and periodical publishing.

Why? Because of the broadly considered interests of advertisers who have attained their universal distribution, lower price and greater public service through newspapers and magazines. They are intensely concerned about the status with the public of periodicals, the purveyors of the printed word. Reader interest must be at its maximum—the printed word must hold the reader's confidence as well as interest. The advertising word cannot be regarded as separate from the editorial word in its requirement of integrity, restraint and freedom from misrepresentation.

The circulations of periodicals running into the millions are frankly today the result of coalition of interest of advertiser and publisher, but on legitimate grounds of broadening the appeal of the printed word, both quantitatively and qualitatively. The success of this purely commercial coalition, it must not be forgotten, has also had immense public significance. The end mutually sought—that of more power to the printed word—is important to *every* aim of civilization. It was to be expected, therefore, that advertising and publicity men would be of great importance to England and America during the war.

The advertising man, in a very real sense, is a publicist, and as long as it is the aim of the highest statesmanship in a society predominantly economic, to increase the per capita wealth and comfort and happiness of human beings, the advertising writer will be of practical importance. He is a technician in popular education, with the full gamut of type, picture, color and large circulation, local or national, to use toward his ends. He can flash letters of fire forty feet high upon the night in the view of

700,000 people in the "White Light" district of Broadway; he can indeed "sky-write" words upon the very blue of the heavens. He can put an argument for his product in the newspaper at the breakfast tables of most of the comfortable families in all the cities of the country inside of twenty-four hours. He can now even flash across the continent an illustrated ad via radio. He can put a message in a single periodical which reaches practically every village and town in the whole of the United States and Canada—the readers ranging from a cowpuncher in a Montana log cabin to the millionaire at his library table in Tarrytown. He can, through special and technical periodicals, talk to any group or type of people, from hair-dressers and undertakers to motion picture actresses. He can make the very rail fences along the farm roads speak to the passers-by; he can mass the one thousand and one methods of advertising into a concentrated volume of appeal which will make people absorb his thought as though through the air they breathe, and as naturally. He can localize his message as he pleases so that it may strategically develop weak market spots. Yet with all this mammoth technique, no advertiser can hope to prosper for long if he has no fundamental good to offer the public; if he offends taste egregiously, if he cheats and skimps.

* * *

The tool of advertising is a prodigious one—so great that it constantly takes more gold than formerly to occupy the position of the greatest advertiser. Six million dollars annual advertising expenditure buys William Wrigley an advertising predominance in 1924; in 1904 it would have bought a riotous superfluity of advertising, for at that time a million dollars a year was a stupendous, almost unprecedented expenditure. Today it is but a small drop in the $1,200,000,000 annual advertising expenditure in the United States.

It is important to show here, by means of figures, the growth of advertising, as an index to its industrial importance and productivity. In 1880 there probably was not more than $30,000,000 expended in advertising of all kinds. In 1890 I estimate that it rose to $80,000,000; in 1900, to $200,000,000; in 1910, to $600,000,000; in 1920, to $850,000,000, and in 1925 to $1,200,000,000. This represents a rate of growth few, if any, industries could show; and synchronizes perfectly with our general industrial development, except that in the years 1900 to 1910 a particularly phenomenal growth took place; largely, I believe, because our conceptions of advertising copy changed in a revolutionary way during that decade. However, the growth between 1914 and 1924 was also great. In 1914 the volume of magazine advertising was $26,000,000, while in 1924 it had risen to $110,000,000.

Because of this prodigious extent of advertising, one matter is today of great fundamental importance—that of educating the American public to understand the economic function of advertising. Such education is essential not only for the consumers, but also for the retailers, since a research in a western state has disclosed that 75% of retailers are, as yet, unconvinced of the value of advertising. These less progressive retailers—whose information on any subject is limited—are, in many instances, for selfish reasons telling the public that advertised goods cost more, in order that they may persuade customers to buy goods of low quality and irresponsible manufacture, with a high percentage of profit to retailers. The public sees evidences of large advertising expenditure, but is not aware of the rearrangement of selling method which advertising represents, with a resulting lower unit sales cost on an increased volume not possible to secure, except through advertising.

On top of this, we have the propaganda of radicals, malcontents, social theorists and the half-educated, who deliberately argue that advertising is "an economic waste"; that it "plays on human weakness"; that the public should be shielded from the "wiles" of the advertising writer.

Such a thesis deserves to be analyzed, for advertising writers, like any modern professional men, wish to feel certain that they are rendering a public service; that their work is fundamentally sound.

Years ago a brilliant New Yorker, William M. Ivins, aided and abetted by some choice spirits of the time, schemed out a plan "to test human credulity." The famous Madame Blavatsky was the result—a fictitious, invented personality. The public was found to be gullible, all right; but gullible as Barnum had found it gullible; that is, for the things it desired and enjoyed, and fairly quick to discover when it was being "bunked."

In 1924 the new President of the New York Stock Exchange said that "the American investing public was the most gullible in the world." In view of the three to five billion dollars which it squanders annually on fake stocks, or optimistic, highly "chancy" stocks, this is perhaps not an overstatement. This sum represents a good rate of interest on the total national annual income of sixty-five billion dollars; and represents about 10% interest on the total volume of purchases (thirty-five billion dollars) at all retail stores! In the face of such facts, we may reasonably admit as a fact that the American public is *highly responsive;* let us even say that it is "susceptible." Yet in all truth, with all its errors of judgment, now disappearing, it is a princely, fortunate foible, this American "susceptibility!" It has made the country; it has speeded up the wheels of progress, and it is largely responsible for the $3,000 per capita wealth of the people of these United States! Millions more are beating enviously at our gates, longing to robe themselves in this ermine mantle of susceptibility! Some even pay their last dollar to be smuggled across the border into our Elysium of Gullibility!

But, irony aside, it is important to look more closely at the point of view of those who seize upon this admitted fact of American susceptibility as a means of indicting advertising. This point of view pictures the American public as a timid, innocent mouse facing a very complicated, deadly trap. It believes you can really sell lunar green cheese if you hire the right advertising cleverness, write the subtle "ad." You step up and pay your money and lo! the poor public is delivered into your lap. This same school of thought argues also that the advertisers are debauching the public, making bootblacks want Packards, and nursemaids yearn for chaise lounges and pipe organs. The accusation is that advertising is moral ruin to many; and fosters false character standards.

Is it really a crime, or is it a benefit, to stir up a new want in the breast of a human being? If we induce Mary Jane to wear nothing but silk stockings, are we doing her a service or an injury? Beside this question the ancient raging controversies over the question whether woman had a soul or how many saints could dance on the point of a needle are mere nursery squabbles. It is really a lovely and an educative debate. The conclusion— we of common sense know—is obvious; but the considerations you run into on the way toward it are fascinatingly stimulative.

Take the statement of a college professor some time ago that the public is a mere puppet at the end of the advertising writer's string—that it is untrained and, therefore, has no chance in the hands of the trained business people of the country, who systematically, recklessly, insidiously and diabolically labor not only to make people spend all their money, but actually to plunge them into debt.

If endeavoring to sell silk stockings to any woman not possessed of a substantial bank account is a modern way of being a Barbary Coast buccaneer, then we should at least designate a black flag for such buccaneers to fly lest we mistake them for missionaries. If woman's propensity to put her money in stockings is a menace to the country, by all means let us divest her of such pedal sinfulness! But first it is only fair to make quite sure it is sinfulness and not beneficence.

To be strictly logical the holders of the view that advertising is a play on weakness must agree to shield people from the wiles of advertising lest they become extravagant. (You hear occasionally of a man who keeps the Sunday papers from his wife, because if she doesn't see the ads she won't go down town on Monday and "blow in so much!) In other words, the theory is, the less people know the fewer things they want. Advertising weakens character by temptation, is the argument.

The contrary, however, is true: advertising tends, of psychological necessity, to strengthen character. The lumberjack, coming to town after a winter's enforced absence from merchandise (where it might be supposed that he acquired increased power of resistance to it), is notoriously the weakest of all prey to purchasing indiscretion. He rarely has any money left after such a visit. His case is typical of all human beings under like circumstances. Everybody supposes that Mary Jane will spend less money if she does not see so many pretty things. Of course, she will not spend if, like the lumberjack shut up in his camp, she is given no opportunity. But it is pretty certain that she will not be happy—and what is an unhappy Mary Jane worth to anybody? Unless she is compelled to be a hermitess, she will more than make up for lost time when she gets her opportunity. The mail-order catalog is the proof of how isolated people will express themselves through merchandise, no matter at what disadvantage. Every mail-order house can tell of pathetic letters from women without money, who have supped luxuriously at the fount of merchandise through the mail-order catalogs—which are admittedly the greatest aggregations of good advertising copy extant—and who sent along wonderfully selected *imaginary* orders. (Once when short of rations in the wilds, I, too, had great satisfaction making up a menu fit for a king from a dilapidated but well-written grocery catalog.) Any woman anywhere can spend ten thousand imaginary dollars far more glibly than she can earn one hundred real dollars. One-third of the country's annual family purchases, by the way, are now made without seeing the merchandise first.

The cure for weakness of character is certainly not to reduce either the making or showing or talking of merchandise, but is like the cure for inability to swim—put the subject into plenty of water and teach him intelligent self-propulsion in it. The more at home he gets to be in plenty of water, the less he is likely to drown.

The truth is that today there is far more thoughtful buying and far greater familiarity with merchandise, because of greater exposure to advertising and weaker susceptibility of character. There are few Simple

Simons and Docile Doras, because an environment replete with all imaginable merchandise *has compelled a toughening and sophistication of mental and even moral fiber.* Mary Jane can now actually walk past several hundred tempting offers of merchandise, which good judgment indicates she should not buy, to one time that she succumbs to allurement. Think of the miles of marvelous shop windows we have today; brilliantly lighted, gorgeously decorated! Think of the automobile which brings even farm women far more frequently in contact with store windows! Think of the huge quantities of advertising now put before people! There has been a forced development, in consequence, of the faculties of judgment and restraint—also of the use of logic and fitness in making purchases—brought about largely by the ever-presence of advertising and the merchandise-laden environment. On the other hand, this merchandise-laden environment has had another extremely important economic effect—*it has provided quicker recognition and adoption of a valuable piece of merchandise,* even though it revolutionized to a considerable degree habits of living, standards and methods, involving greater efficiency, increased health and other benefits. It is not always recalled that a trademark is just as handy a mark by which to identify and *avoid* certain *unsatisfactory* merchandise, as it is to identify and seek *satisfactory* merchandise.

Merchandise is an indispensable servant of human nature, but a poor master; and the presence of such enormous varieties of goods compels the weakness or the strength of human character to come forth. It is no crime to stimulate wants, *but it is crime to misrepresent their value;* and this crime is being made harder every year. Gullibility is a factor that apparently resides ineradicably in human nature; but at the same time the proof that advertising does not feed on human gullibility lies in the fact that a child can buy Uneeda Biscuits or any of five hundred good standard articles as safely and as cheaply as your most veteran haggler.

* * *

In an age of increased sensitiveness to social responsibility, it is worth while for an advertising writer to ask, *What is an advertising writer?—a* creator, a waster, a parasite, or a constructive economist? He will be a better advertising man, more soundly grounded in his profession if he faces this question clear-mindedly and without buncombe. Particularly so, since advertising has been and still is a selected point of attack on business by many people, including many professedly intelligent classes, writers, a few economists, and a not inconsiderable part of the public itself. Although some circles in advertising feel that such antagonism should be ignored, and aver that "advertising needs no defense," still the truth remains that there is current an astonishing amount of misconception and misinformation about advertising.

In a volume like this, and in an introductory review of the advertising idea such as this constitutes, it would, in the author's opinion, be a mistake not to deal with it, at least in outline.

One of the boldest expressions of the criticism of advertising as a factor in economics is to the effect that the cost of advertising is paid by the public. Those who hold this view argue that advertising should be restricted to minimum by the public need, but even they admit that no sane economist would advocate its complete abolishment. While making an obviously unsuccessful attack on the assertion of advertising men that advertising aids mass production which, in turn, produces lower prices, they must at the same time concede that the cheapest goods are the most widely advertised.

Of course, the public pays the cost of advertising, as it has always paid the cost of all selling. The constantly overlooked fact is that selling expenditure of older days *was unseen;* it represented salesmen's expense and other high cost methods of selling. Sales cost per unit of merchandise was far greater in older days than now. Today the public *sees the sales expenditure,* in the form of publicly displayed, spectacular advertising. Because advertising comprises a considerable grand total in volume and bulks large in public consciousness, it is mistakenly regarded as being an *additional* burden of selling cost, whereas, in truth, it is only an *altered and more visible,* but on the other hand, *lower selling cost.* If what is now spent for advertising were spent for salesmen, circulars to the trade, and old-time sales methods, nobody would be noticing it, or considering anything to be amiss—yet it would bulk to tremendously greater proportions in the attempt to accomplish the same results that advertising produces in the present era.

The real documents in the case are the facts, open for all to see and verify, namely, that, as in the shoe, hosiery or men's clothing industries, for instance, the rate of commission paid to salesmen by *houses which do no advertising* is from 7 to 10 or 12%; whereas the commission paid salesmen *by houses which advertise,* is from 2½ to 7%. With all this difference in commission rates, salesmen prefer to sell, even at the lower rate, the goods of the house which advertises, because they can sell a greater quantity with the same effort.

It is now a standard industrial policy in America for a concern *actually to anticipate* the reduction in cost which can be accomplished by mass production through the use of advertising, and to sell goods at so low a price as to represent a loss for a period of time, in full knowledge that good advertising will in time develop sales to the point of profit. While it is true that there are still some advertisers whose prices are higher than strict business economics call for, such advertisers merely leave unguarded an entry way for competition, and in the end are pushed aside. It has happened many times.

This brings us to what is the *really* vital relation of advertising writing to economics:

Advertising is the only efficient tool available to accomplish the much-needed purpose of raising the buying power and consumption standards of the world to the level of the rapidly mounting capacity for production. Just how serious a problem in world politics as well as in domestic prosperity this is, may be gathered from statements sometimes made that the endeavor to reach and maintain a high standard of living is now and ever has been the principal cause of wars between tribes and nations. Yet the equal truth is that nations and peoples always have, always should and always will struggle to elevate their standards of living. Critics of advertising fail to point out that wars usually result not from peaceful production and consumption efforts, but from predatory efforts at *seizure* of other peoples' goods and wealth. The modern principle is that of *increased productivity and consumption* keeping pace with each other through the use of advertising, so as to make a nation less dependent on predatory struggle with other peoples. The high standards and comparatively peaceful career of the United States is the example *par excellence.*

The famous English economist, John A. Hobson, made a very clear statement of the great need now all over the world for increasing living standards up to the level of production capacity:

There is a universal belief in a limited market, the apparent inability of the business classes to sell at any profitable margin all the goods which can be made by the machinery and labor which they control. In other words, although production only exists to supply the needs of consumers, *the rate of consumption habitually lags behind the rate of possible production,* so that much actual and much more potential producing power is wasted. *Production in the great industries normally tends to outrun consumption.* It is more difficult to sell than to buy. In other words, efficient demand is not quick enough, or full enough, to respond to increased productivity.

This is why the theory of pitting productivity against better distribution, as a remedy for poverty and discontent is fallacious. *Better distribution is essential to higher productivity.* That is why wage cuts, as means of lowering "costs," are bad economy. For only by a more equal and equitable distribution of the product can we get either of two conditions that make higher productivity a feasible policy.

Better distribution alone can insure the regular rise of stable standards of consumption to correspond with and keep pace with every increase of output.

Secretary of State Charles E. Hughes and John Hays Hammond have also in speeches emphasized the need of raising the world's standards of consumption.

The fact is, that by advertising, *and by advertising alone,* can distribution and consumption be increased, its cost lowered, and all levels of the population educated in better standards of living. The remarkably even standards prevailing in the United States—the highest standards in the world and in history—are a natural outcome of the far greater advertising activity here, Great Britain being about 30%, and the rest of the world 80% behind America in advertising expenditures. Altogether few people appreciate the fact that the United States is metropolitanized almost from edge to edge. The farmer's family, near Garden City, Kansas, has living standards astonishingly like those of families in the large cities. They have electricity, radio, ready-made clothes, the same foods; they read the same books, bathe in the same kind of bath-tubs, follow the same fashions, see the same movies, listen to the same jazz music, are obsessed with the same fads (like cross-word puzzles), and buy from the same chain stores almost identically the same merchandise.

Before cynically condemning this as mere "standardization," one has only to contrast the peasants of France with the metropolitan families of Paris. There is an abysmal difference between them, for the peasants still cling to ideas, practices and standards centuries old. Their wants are very few, their consumption of merchandise per family astonishingly low, and their standards distinctly below the modern par necessary for health, sanitation and growth, to say nothing of comfort and enjoyment. America's consumption standards have been shaped and developed by advertising as though with a gigantic tool having an enormous leverage; and it is this tool which must be relied upon for further distribution of goods in the U.S. as well as in foreign countries.

The modern advertising writer is interweaving the story of advertising writing more and more with the story of the era of American industrial coming-of-age, not only in respect to its part in making quantity production possible, but also in respect to humanizing industry and aligning it with public service and public conscience.

Words are the working tools of the advertising craft. They are not things to be picked up and handled by those who have not learned the trade.

Unskilled hands that would shun the surgeon's scalpel or the carver's spoon-gouge sometimes make bold to seize these tools of advertising and ply them with abandon. As a result, advertising is frequently scarred and blemished, when it might have revealed the beauty and symmetry of finished craftsmanship.

T. HARRY THOMPSON

Chapter 1

Advertising Copy and the Writer

By F. Irving Fletcher[1]

Mr. Chairman and Gentlemen: In a Brooklyn paper recently a Turkish Bath featured the following announcement: "Separate Department for Ladies except Saturday and Sunday Nights." And I want to say for myself that I am available for business at almost any hour except 9.45 A.M., the hour assigned for this address. This is midnight for me, for it is my habit to write at night. Moreover, I don't like talking at conventions. The last one I talked at was held in the McAlpin Hotel about three years ago and inside of two days I received three anonymous letters containing varying degrees of vilification. So I cut out speechmaking. I would rather write and be paid for it than talk and be flayed for it. Some people are so inured to the obscurity of a back seat that they resent anybody who aspires to a front pew. Yet it is manifestly unfair to regard any speaker as arrogating to himself the airs of an oracle when as a matter of fact he would rather be relieved of the ordeal than go through with it.

But if a speaker be at a disadvantage, it is nothing to the traditional troubles that have for twenty centuries afflicted those who write for a living. It is still pretty generally accepted that an artist or a writer is without honor in business, and we ourselves are largely responsible for

---

1. *Frank Irving Fletcher* (famous New York writer of retail advertising for leading specialty shops) describes himself characteristically thus: "Born 1883, in Yorkshire, England. Baptized in the Episcopal Church and complete in all his members. Drifted into advertising in 1911 and has regretted it every working minute since. Owes what little progress he has made to the malignity of advertising agencies and the tropic growth of incompetence due to the present system of agency compensation. Has no friends in the advertising business, as he prefers to put his money on the horses."

The chapter presented here is a "speech" before the assembled coterie of advertising experts, evolved by Mr. Fletcher, with typical whimsicality and charm, from an actual address some years ago at the Pennsylvania Hotel, New York City.

it, for, however good we may be at selling other people's wares, we still remain one of the most inefficient professions at selling our own. Now a poet may be an anachronism in a department store, but a good advertising man is at least as important as the shipping clerk. He must, however, be an advertising man and not a poet. Too many of us still wear long hair in our minds and that is something which even the Terminal Barber Shops are incompetent to cure. What I wanted to say is, that we shall have a much more robust and remunerative profession when we learn to sell copy and art and ideas like steel rails, instead of conducting ourselves like supplicants for alms. The medieval idea of procuring a patron still persists among some of us, when all that an advertising writer or an advertising artist needs to sell his wares is to borrow the methods of those he wants to sell them to. It is not necessary for any advertising man to approach an employer in the same fashion that he says his prayers.

But I don't want to be charged with the impropriety of trying to raise wages. I am really not discussing that phase of the matter at all. A division on this issue would suffice to show that many of *you* are getting more than you are worth, while many of us are still underpaid! But after all, money isn't everything in life—only about 98%. What is uppermost in my mind is not our inability to sell ourselves, which is bad enough, but our inability to sell our ideas to those who buy our services. In nearly every instance that has come under my observation in the past five years, the relationship between the advertiser and the advertising man has been wrong. The average advertising job has two phases. First, the advertising man gets the job and then his employer proceeds to take it away from him. I once, and only once, had an experience of this kind myself. He was a remote relative of the head of the house and his ability was also relative and remote. It should be added, in extenuation, that his congenital malignity had recently been aggravated by the hysteria of a belated honeymoon. At any rate, he decided to prepare a Christmas advertisement, for which he stole the sampler idea of a prominent candy concern and then dragged in the Deity to sell Grand Rapids furniture and linoleums. Some people think they want an advertising man when all that they really want is an audience.

There is, of course, a vast difference between being suppliant and being pliant. A tactful man can concede a comma and achieve a page. It is just as foolish and fatal for an advertising man to be overly stubborn as it is for him to surrender his individuality. Some months ago the advertising man for a client of mine sent me a booklet he had written and asked me to go over it. I deleted three paragraphs, but did not add or change a line of the remainder. It is always easy to improve another man's work. But the revision did seem to be desirable. I sent it back and received a very peevish letter objecting to such liberal cutting. So I called him on the telephone and said: "Did you ever see Hamlet?" He said: "Yes, what about it?" I said: "Well, every time they play Hamlet they cut half of it out. And if Shakespeare can stand it, so can you." Still another of our weaknesses is sensitiveness to criticism from those who cannot or do not write themselves. It is absurd to contend that those who cannot produce an advertisement are incompetent to condemn it. You might just as well say that a man has no right to condemn an omelet because he cannot lay eggs. Criticism, if it is at all intelligent, is an invaluable aid in avoiding it! And a wise man really prefers it, for by catering to criticism he secures credit now and may escape censure later.

Now, you are doubtless wondering what all this has to do with Individuality in Advertising. My contention is, that it has everything to do with it. We cannot achieve individuality in advertising until a man first achieves it for himself, that is, assuming that he has any to begin with. Granted that you and I have some ability in our work, two things remain by which that ability can bear fruit. One is that we shall learn both how to create ideas and how to defend them, and the other is, that the only way an employer can develop a good advertising man is to let him alone. There are scores of good advertising men who, through their own pusillanimity, or intolerance higher up, or both, never get a chance to show what they can do. And there are scores of great advertisers continually scanning the horizon for new talent, and overlooking what lies at hand in their own advertising departments. There is an Eastern legend of a man who sold his house to go in search of buried treasure, and the treasure was found in the garden by the man who bought the house.

To come to Individuality in Advertising itself, that is, in the finished product, this is such a large assignment and is susceptible of so many interpretations, depending upon the thing to be advertised, that it is hardly a subject that can be bound by hard and fast rules. But nobody can scan the general run of advertising without feeling that much of it needs fresh air. There is too much talk about space and not enough thought about spaciousness. One cure for this is brevity which I will come to in a minute; and the other is, the need of a little different point of view as to white space. The common conception of white space is that it is a waste of money, whereas it is a genuine investment. It is the first and chief means of giving dignity and character to a layout. That advertisement is quickest to arrest the eye which furnishes a rest for the eye, and there is nothing so restful and inviting, to employ a figure from an old English writer, as a rivulet of prose meandering through a wilderness of margin.

Now, the advertiser says: "That is very pretty, but you are spending my money." The answer is that white space does not involve money, but brevity. There is a French proverb which says: "The surest way to be dull is to say it all." It has also been observed that no souls are saved after fifteen minutes. See how the bubble of length is punctured with a phrase! Take still another example: *Youth is a blunder—manhood a struggle—old age a regret.* There we have a scenario of life in eleven words, embracing the vicissitudes of existence from cradle to crepe, from diapers to death. Brevity really is not expensive to use, though it is expensive to buy because it is difficult to produce. The reformation can come from within, not from without. Everybody sees more of a woman when she is in an evening gown than when she wears a tailored suit. Though the distinction isn't so marked as it used to be. The need is to declaim less and to display more. And the less you say the more you need to say it effectively. And that means that it should be told with originality. People who condemn cleverness in advertising are those incompetent to produce it. Which means that it is often condemned. White space and appropriate art and typography are after all only the clothes of an advertisement which make for individuality in appearance. They are the frills and the furbelows, but the copy is the voice of the institution, which, indeed, if it have clarity, felicity, and strength, will, like Bacon's reference to virtue, look best plain set.

Chapter 2

The Advertising Writer Who Is Bigger
Than His Ad

By George L. Dyer[1]

I asked an attorney the other day why a certain New York lawyer was so uniformly successful.

"I'll tell you," he replied. "It's because he is always bigger than his case."

Copy is a matter of extreme importance. It is so very important that it requires a broad man to prepare it. He should be "bigger than his case."

It is for this breadth of understanding and grasp of business conditions that I contend. An advertising writer should be bigger than his ad. Not, perhaps, to begin with; but he should not be content until he is master of it, till he can walk all around his proposition, go all over it and through it.

To be a good advertising man is to be a good deal more than that term is popularly supposed to imply. However, it is not necessary to go to work in a shoe shop in order to handle shoe advertising successfully.

---

1. *George Lewis Dyer.* Born in Muscatine, Iowa, on October 9, 1869. As a boy was taken to Joliet, Ill., where he was educated in public schools and worked in his father's store. It was there that his native genius laid the foundation for his penetrating knowledge of people and of merchandise. About 1890 moved to Chicago, became Advertising Manager for *The Fair,* later developed an advertising service bureau, and about 1893 joined Hart, Schaffner & Marx as Advertising Manager, where he created the art of modern clothing advertising. Joined Kirschbaum, Philadelphia, about 1902. In 1907 formed the Arnold & Dyer Agency with Clarence K. Arnold. At Arnold's death in 1909, the firm became The George L. Dyer Company, and in 1910 concentrated its staff and work in its New York office. Died June 24, 1921, when his interest in the company was taken over by a group of men who had been associated with him in carrying on the business.

The chapter presented here is the only writing by him which has been discovered. It was rescued from oblivion through the courtesy of John Lee Mahin.

There was a man who tried that once, and by the time he had learned the business he was as little fitted to advertise it as the head of the firm or the intelligent factory foreman. A sure way to lose receptivity and to kill initiative is to become saturated with the technicalities of the trade.

The advertising man must think along broad lines. He must not lose his sense of the relation of his concern to the world. That is something the proprietors and managers themselves can never gauge. He should get out and away from business and mix with people; then come back and see his proposition in a new light.

The advertising department is the human side of a business organization.

When a man makes only a part of a thing, he doesn't exercise the creative faculties. It is no longer a question of mind, but of manual dexterity. He loses his initiative. He depends more and more on others to do his thinking for him.

The so-called advertising "expert" is often a writer of advertising and nothing else. The smaller and narrower he grows the more arrogant he becomes and the busier he is. He is peculiarly subject to the disease George Ade has defined as "Enlargiensis of the Coco."

It is fortunate if he is a general writer. Usually he is still further specialized as a booklet writer, a display writer, a writer of reading notices, etc.

For all their pride of copy, the majority of men who write choppy, disconnected sentences for display announcements are incapable of turning out an interesting or readable article for a newspaper or magazine.

Give such a man as I have described the advertising responsibility of a business enterprise, and he gets into a corner and writes copy. He cannot give any of his time to special representatives or business men who call to see him and who would keep him in touch with the general field and broaden his horizon.

He is too busy making buttonholes to understand the tailoring of the suit.

It would seem that advertising has progressed more in other directions than in the preparation of copy. Advertisers, at least some of them, have learned how to follow up inquiries; how to buy space; how to nurse their investment; how to work special territory; to reorganize their business in conformity with their publicity; to work their sales department in harmony with their advertising. They are beginning to understand the moral effect of advertising on an industry. They are learning that "the best way to improve a business is to write about it."

Looking backward we realize that we have traveled a long way, but, all in all, our advancement is not such as to make us self-satisfied. A man should be judged, not by his achievement alone, but by the relation his achievement bears to his opportunity. The same is true of a business. The old advertiser did not have as hard a competition for the eye of the reader. He was in no danger of being swallowed up by the volume of advertising or obliterated by the strength of the copy next to his. There is everything today to stimulate individuality. The very life of the announcement depends upon it. The price of space has increased enormously. Interest in advertising is widespread and yet we find business men encountering the same old stumbling blocks and pitfalls.

One coming fresh to the advertising problem today must surely benefit by the experience of those who have gone before. But each man is inclined to think his business a peculiar one. It may be suggested that the busy merchant or manufacturer is too close to his work to reason well about it; that he is too much absorbed in himself and the narrow world of his trade to gauge public sentiment or know how to appeal to the mass of his fellows. But whatever the shortcomings of other men and other races, the American business man is prepared to undertake all things with equal success and without previous education or special training. The only reason he does not paint his own pictures, design his own house, conduct his own case in court or treat his own influenza is because his time is valuable, his mind is burdened with weighty things, and the doctor or lawyer, with proper coaching, can carry out his ideas almost as well as he could do it himself.

There is no denying the fact that intelligent advertising is still the exception or that most of the large users of space go at it blindly, trying first one plan and then another until they chance upon a campaign that makes a hit. They have great general faith in publicity as a "good gamble," but evidently little conception of it as an exact science. They do not yet understand it as a force to be directed with economy and precision. Most of them that stay at it long enough flounder into success but at an expense that is quite unnecessary.

It is remarkable what has been done, what is still being done—without brains, without taste—by the sheer force of crude publicity, the brutal paying out of money for space. Better results could often be had for much less money. But some business men and most boards of directors would rather pay for space than for brains; it is more tangible, they understand it better.

It is a step forward, I suppose, that these men have learned to buy space; perhaps some day they will learn how to *fill* it; how to nurse an appropriation and take full advantage of the investment.

Manufacturers of food products are among the largest users of publicity in all its forms: newspapers, magazines, street cars, outdoor display, sample distribution, premium schemes and store demonstrations.

There is no doubt that the food business in recent years has contributed largely to the volume as well as the progress of advertising; but if, without referring to any of the periodicals, we try to set down a list of the various foods and something that has characterized the publicity of each one, we realize from our confused ideas that the work is more notable for its extent than for its individuality.

The general impression is one of a rather high standard of mediocrity with a leaning toward engraving-house illustration and what my friend Beauley of Chicago calls "Steamboat Renaissance."

There is a happy irrelevancy in much of this work; the thought evidently being to separate the picture and the text by as wide a chasm as may be bridged by the reader's imagination.

We are shown waving fields of grain and told how, by a special arrangement with providence, heaven's sunbeams are caught and imprisoned in Mr. Jones' Breakfast Grits.

The chef has been overworked for years. The idea is not bad, as suggesting the preparation of food for the table, but it is usually difficult to tell what is being cooked. He might be frying eggs, for all any one can find to the contrary.

The old Quaker of Quaker Oats is well conceived and, by dint of repetition, has come to be a familiar friend. The recent "smile that won't come off" is too evidently an imitation of the "Sunny Jim" optimism.

I have always questioned the practical selling power of the humorous grotesque in advertising. An appeal to the public's sense of the ridiculous is not the best way to get its money, except on the vaudeville stage.

To make a joke of an advertised article is to cheapen it and at least postpone the serious consideration that must precede a sale. Even those induced to try it lack confidence and ask for it in an apologetic manner.

I believe thoroughly in optimism as a necessary quality in salesmanship; whether over the counter, on the road, or by means of the printing-press. Cheerfulness and buoyancy inspire confidence in the buyer and open the avenues of receptivity. Optimism is one thing and the antics of a clown another.

If the way to man's heart is through his stomach, the food people are neglecting a great opportunity when they do not appeal directly to the reader's eye and appetite by means of good copy.

Some of the best and sanest work has been done for Shredded Wheat Biscuit in their illustrations of dainty and appetizing dishes prepared from their product. This appeals directly to the palate and suggests new recipes to the housewife.

In many ways the strongest and most interesting work ever done for a cereal product is the advertising of the Postum Cereal Company—Grape Nuts and Cereal Coffee. It has an insistent note of personality—the priceless quality in advertising. There is character back of every line of it.

A class of advertisers try to reach their goal by indirection. They assume that any subject is of more interest than the facts about the goods they have to sell.

For instance, a man wishes to advertise shoes. He prints a little romance telling how the heroine wins a husband by the grace of her advertised footwear. Then they go to live with the old folks and save enough money on the family shoes to pay off the mortgage on the farm.

To a man in need of a new derby or the woman who wishes to buy gloves nothing is of such vital moment as the printed facts about the required article. The most interesting news in the world is news of the things we desire to buy. It affects us personally. It reaches our vanity, our taste, our sense of luxury, our desire for happiness, and it touches our pocketbook.

Tell the story of your goods believing that it is the most interesting thing in the world. Then perhaps you can make it so.

Don't try to sneak the facts about your business into the public consciousness by a surreptitious hypodermic injection. Come out with them face to face. Tell the people what you've got, why you can serve them, what it costs and ask for their trade.

Advertising is news.

It will be a great day for advertising when men see it in a large way and stop taking a part of it for the whole. When they understand that the vital parts of advertising are the things that go with it and that advertising is a moral force and not a mechanical toy.

Rule twisting and type sticking and stamp licking and space measuring all have their place and their value. I do not depreciate them when I say that they should not be permitted to obscure the view.

Mechanical details have a great fascination for most minds, especially the mathematical American mind. The average business imagination does not rise much higher than it can travel in a passenger elevator.

An increasing number of men refuse to believe in all but the things they can touch and see, and it is perhaps natural they should dwell upon the material, obvious aspects of the subject and miss the soul in the machine.

Advertisers pay for space, buy cuts and copy, set the wheels in motion and stand by to see them run. If the things desired do not promptly happen it is plainly the fault of the agent or publisher, and they begin to tear things to pieces like a child that wrecks a toy because he lacks the intelligence to make it work.

It may seem that I dwell with tiresome iteration upon this phase of the subject. But there is not a week in the year when some business man does not get me in a corner and pour out his woes—thousands of dollars spent and no adequate results. Best media, good copy perhaps, and replies—but no effect on the business. Selling expenses only increased by the addition of the advertising appropriation. Salesmen squeezing the house and sacrificing everything to their customers. High anticipations, great fun and excitement at first, but the novelty is wearing off.

What shall he do? Discharge his advertising man? Change his agent and quit the publishers? A friend has told him to spend his money in the street cars.

Then follows a long cross-examination as to the general conduct of the business. The man grows reticent and suspicious at deep, researching questions he considers utterly irrelevant. He listens absently and says, "Now to get back to advertising." When he is told that all this is the advertising, he does not comprehend.

A man in an allied line told me the other day that he was conducting a campaign by using all of my literature, worked over for his business. When I said that I considered the best part of my value was in work which he did not see, he was at a loss whether to distrust me or to resent being cheated out of his just dues.

We need less tinkering in advertising and more use of the merchandising brain which builds copy on the well-engineered steel framework of field facts.

Chapter 3

Human Appeals in Copy

By Bruce Barton[1]

My first contact with what might be called "human interest in advertising copy was when I was twelve years old. I read an advertisement headed, "You, too, can become a locomotive engineer." I clipped a coupon. As it promised, I received the literature, and, as was not promised, I received an urbane and persuasive representative who fixed me more than ever in the determination to follow that fascinating walk of life.

My second contact was when I was assistant general sales manager of a large concern selling books. We had been running advertisements on our leader, which was Dr. Eliot's set of books.

The advertising was very well written. It was full pages on the value of owning fine books and on the splendor of having them in your library and the satisfaction of reading them. I used to protest to the people who prepared the advertising. I said, "I realize I am young and underpaid and have not very good ideas about these things. I don't like to criticize, but these advertisements *do not bring coupons.*"

One day I was sitting there in my office, and someone came in and said, "There is a quarter-page vacant in our magazine and you can have it at a low rate to advertise your books if you will get copy to us right away." I leafed the books through and came to a picture of Marie Antoinette. I wrote something like this:

> This is Marie Antoinette riding to her death. Have you ever read her tragic story?

---

1. *Bruce Barton.* Popular writer and advertising agent, New York. Born Tennessee 1886. Editor *Home Herald, Housekeeper* and *Every Week.* Assistant sales-manager P. F. Collier & Son, and now president Barton, Durstine & Osborn. Writer for many well-known magazines. Author of *It's a Good Old World, What Shall It Profit a Man, The Man Nobody Knows,* etc.

In all literature there are only a few great tragedies, great poems and great essays, biographies, etc.

If you know those, you are well read, and if you don't know them, you are not.

Eight Times As Many Coupons From Humanized Copy

It was short and simple. But this is the interesting fact. Marie riding to her death on that quarter of a page pulled eight times as many coupons as we had ever got from one of these fine, full pages on the glory and splendor of owning fine books.

It was my first vivid lesson that a little touch of human interest, a little of the common tragedy or hope or love or success or affection that runs through all our lives will outpull what may be technically a very much better advertisement, but which lacks that human touch which makes the whole world kin.

Writers Must Be Human First

If anybody should ask me how he can get more human touch into his copy or equip himself to become a human interest writer of copy, I don't think I could answer. I might say two rather obvious things: First of all, it has been said, "If you would have friends, you must show yourself friendly," and I might say, "If you would write human interest copy, you have to work quite consistently at the job of being a human being." I mean you have to share the emotions, the experiences, the problems and hopes that are the common lot of the people to whom you write.

I once had to talk before a university class about writing short stories. I was editing a magazine at that time. I said, "If a writer is going to be successful he should share the common experiences of the people for whom he writes. Writers should get married; writers should have children; if they are unfortunate enough to have wealthy parents, they ought to refuse to have any help from their parents; they should pay for a home, take out insurance, have disappointments, struggles, hopes, ambitions, fears, take on the mold and character of the people whom they address, and, living their lives, be able to interpret to them their own thoughts." That is pretty obvious, but it seems to me essential. In our offices, we are somewhat removed from the struggles and experiences of common life, and we must work to keep our contacts keen and fresh. That, I think, is the first thing.

Know Spirits of Other Ages

The second thing, which is equally obvious, is that the little age in which we live is merely a drop in the great river of eternity, and we can very much extend our contacts if we admit to the circle of our friendships the great spirits that have lived in other times.

I got to reading biographies when I was in high school and have continued ever since. For those of us who are writing and seeking to influence human minds, there is a wealth of help in this contact with the great human beings of other ages.

They have a funny story in our office to the effect that when we take a man in to write advertising copy, I give him a copy of the New Testament. That is untrue (factually and by implication)—factually, because I never gave anybody a New Testament, and by implication because it implies that I have a pious soul, which is not true. No man can have a pious soul who has spent his life dealing with printers.

Parables Exemplify Three Principles of Good Copy

I think that three of the best principles of copy writing are exemplified perfectly in the New Testament parables.

FIRST—BREVITY

There is hardly a single wasted word in them. Brevity in our business is a precious jewel.

About sixty years ago two men spoke at Gettysburg; one man spoke for two hours. I suppose there is not any one who could quote a single word of that oration. The other man spoke about three hundred words, and that address has become a part of the school training of almost every child. There have been thousands of prayers in the world, but the only one a great many people ever learned is sixty-seven words long. There have been many poems written, but probably the greatest poem, the one that has impressed the largest number of people, the Twenty-third Psalm, is only one hundred and seventeen words long. So the parables were short and human and that is why they have lived.

SECOND—SIMPLICITY

In the second place, they were simple. Consider their phraseology for a minute. "A certain man had two sons"; "A man built his house upon the sand"; "A certain man went down from Jerusalem to Jericho"; etc. No three-syllable words; practically all one-syllable words. Tom Paine once said that no religion could be true if it had anything in it that would offend the sensibilities of a little child. I think it might be said, no advertisement is great that has anything that can't be understood by a child of intelligence. Certainly all the great things in life are one-syllable things—child, home, wife, fear, faith, love, God. The greater the thought we have to express, the more likely we are to find simple words.

THIRD—SINCERITY

The third thing about the parables—those great human interest advertisements—is, of course, their genuineness. Emerson said, "What you are speaks so loudly that people can't hear what you say." Of course, one of the greatest principles of effective writing is to believe yourself what you are trying to make others believe.

Somebody asked me in that same course I was giving at the University, "What do you think is the first requirement for success in advertising?" I said, "Good health." That is nothing to laugh about. I can't conceive how a dyspeptic could write good mincemeat copy or a man with rheumatism could write about the joy of riding over mountain roads in an automobile. You have to have good human equipment to enjoy the things you are trying to sell or you can't make other people enjoy them. I believe the public has a sixth sense of detecting insincerity, and we run a tremendous risk if we try to make other people believe in something we don't believe in. Somehow our sin will find us out.

Business Is Emphasizing Ideals

I think that in our lifetime we are going to see three very interesting advertising developments in three very great fields of human interest. In the first place, in business. I believe that, without lessening at all the emphasis on products, business is going to give more and more emphasis to its ideals. Here is a very interesting story. Napoleon after he was beaten at Waterloo went to Paris. He was standing in his palace, the windows were open, and a few of his old supporters were around him—a pathetic remnant of those who once hailed him. Outside, the people in the streets cried out his name and called upon him to form them into a new army and march once more against his foes. Napoleon heard them in amazement. He turned to his followers and said, "Why should they cheer me? What have I ever done for them? I found them poor, I leave them poor."

That is the tragic epitaph of almost every demagogue from the days of the Pharaohs down—the epitaph of the self-appointed and self-proclaimed friends of the people, who fill the people with promises and leave them nothing. Contrasted with those noisy and self-proclaimed friends of the people, what is the record of modern business? It does not find the people poor and leave them poor. The General Electric Company and the Western Electric Company find the people in darkness and leave them in light; the American Radiator finds them cold and leaves them warm; International Harvester finds them bending over their sickles the way their grandfathers did and leaves them riding triumphantly over their fields. The automobile companies find a man shackled to his front porch and with no horizon beyond his own door yard and they broaden his horizon and make him in travel the equal of a king.

I say business is the real friend of the people, and the time is coming more and more when big business must in its advertising show its friend-liness. I don't want to enlarge on that. You can do that for yourselves. As that spirit in advertising develops it is going to have an immeasurable influence upon the ideals and practices of business itself. For a man who drinks too much to sign a pledge when he is absolutely alone, is a very different thing from standing up before a room full of people and signing it. The first is a personal and individual matter and may not stick, but the other enlists the whole community as a witness and strengthens by that much the vigor of his own resolve. Similarly it is one thing for a company to say, "We will conduct our affairs the best we can." That is different from a business coming out in full pages and daring to proclaim the ideals and service for which it stands. That has a tremendous effect on the men who pay for it and on the men who work for the men who pay for it.

There is a very big concern for which I am privileged to prepare advertising. One of the officers said, "I think you are going too far. Here you have an advertisement that tells what a wonderful company we are, and one of our dealers just brought it in and showed it to me and said, 'I see you pay $7,500 to tell what a wonderful company you are, and I want to say that has not been my experience with you at all.'" The officer said, "Don't you think we should tone this stuff down?" I said to him, "Don't ask us to tone that down. That advertising ought always to be out in front and not lagging behind. It ought to be something for you to live up to. Don't you ask us to come back and march with you. Go and make that company the kind of company we are telling people it is."

Business the Operation of Divine Purpose

We advertising men understand, and the business men for whom we work are more and more understanding, that the millennium, if it is ever coming, is coming through the larger service of business, because business is nothing more nor less than the machinery Almighty God has set up for feeding, housing and transporting the human race. As that understanding comes into the offices of our great institutions, advertising is going to take on a finer note than it has had before.

The second development which I expect is this: I believe we are going to live to see the doctors, the American medical associations, as national advertisers. I was dining one night in New York with the president of a bank and a prominent physician. It was at a time when they were closing up the "bucket shops." I said to the banker, "You are partly responsible for those bucket shops," and I said to the doctor, "Of course, you are partly responsible for the quacks." They looked rather aggrieved and I continued, "The greatest educational force in modern life is advertising; and any profession or trade that abandons that great force to the use of the charlatans and quacks in its own ranks is absolutely deficient in its sense of public duty."

I had an interesting talk with a country doctor and I wrote a piece that appeared anonymously as coming from a country doctor. I said to this country doctor, "There are five of you doctors in town; how much do you make?" He said, "Two are starving, and the other three are just barely getting along." I said, "Is there any cooperation among you? You are in this noble enterprise of high ideals, ministering to the community. I suppose you work together?"

He said, "Not on your life. I hardly dare to take a vacation, because I am afraid the other doctors will steal my customers." I said, "If you would join together, spend a little money every week in advertising, if you would sell this community on the necessity of having an annual or semi-annual examination, if you would sell the community on the importance of having proper dental care in the schools and having regular health supervision of children in the schools, you would all make more money and the community would be immeasurably in your debt."

I believe that is going to come. We are going to see the medical forces of this country become national and local advertisers, to the financial benefit of themselves and to the health benefit of the whole country.

And finally—this is my third hobby—I think we are going to see the church as a national advertiser. I hope no one will be shocked by that; certainly no one will be who has ever read the New Testament, because Jesus was, of course, the greatest of all advertisers. He spoke in the Synagogue occasionally because that was where the people were, but He did most of His speaking in the market place.

Publications the Modern Market Place

I said that one day to a group of Methodist preachers. They said, "Do you mean we should go out and preach on the streets?" I said, "Not at all." There is no modern market place comparable with the market place of the ancient cities. If a man stood in the market place of Jerusalem he touched all Jerusalem, because everybody went there some time through the day. You could stand at Forty-second Street and Fifth Avenue from now until you die and you would not touch a percentage of the people of New York. The modern market place is the *New York Times,* the *Saturday Evening Post,* the *Cosmopolitan Magazine,* etc. They are the national market where thousands of merchants who have things to sell, meet millions of customers who want to buy, and there is the place where somehow or other the voice of religion ought to make itself heard. It seems perfectly certain to me, as I read the New Testament, that Jesus, who was so exceedingly unorthodox in His own day, if He were here today, would raise His voice amid the thousands of voices proclaiming the merits of shoes, breads, cigarettes and motor cars, and say, "What shall it profit a man if he gain the whole world and lose his own soul?" or "What shall a man give in exchange for his soul?"

Chapter 4

The Underlying Principles of Good Copy

By Theodore F. MacManus, LL.D. [1]

The closest approach to finality of formula that can be attained in the preparation of advertising copy is, in my opinion, the development of a reasonably sound underlying principle.

The application of the principle is, in the very nature of things, bound to vary with the nature of the purpose to be accomplished.

There is always the danger that an able advertising man enamored of the felicity of his own style, will endeavor to erect that style into a philosophy—claiming infallibility of result wherever and whenever it is applied.

To maintain that certain clevernesses of approach, attack, and argument, will inevitably influence all human minds in equal or approximate measure, is, it seems to me, hazarding an undemonstrable assumption.

It is a fact, however, that if advertising copy has attained any degree of definiteness whatever, it has been in those instances in which at least an attempt was made to reduce the process of molding minds in the mass to something approaching a formula.

---

1. *Theodore F. MacManus.* Born in Buffalo, New York. Started as office boy at fifteen. Became city editor of a newspaper at sixteen; managing editor at nineteen. He then became advertising manager of a department store, determined to learn the feared and hated intricacies of business. About to sign a contract a few years later for a large honorarium, he asked to be released, saying he felt sure his usefulness was declining, though it seemed to be at its fullest. Borrowing $500, he opened an office and went into the advertising business. In 1917 was offered retainer in six figures to divide his time between Chicago and Detroit, which he refused. In 1919 offered another six-figure guarantee per year for three years for handling one advertising account. Declined, because it involved giving up account with which he had lived from its inception. Became long ago acknowledged as leader of one of the two schools of American advertising.

Two Types of Advertising Copy

Speaking loosely, there have been and are in America only two types of copy analysis and prospectus which by any stretch of the imagination can be dignified by the name of definite philosophies.

One of these two schools of advertising thought assumes in the mass-mind an almost invariable response to certain adroit and plausible appeals.

The other holds the mass-mind in somewhat higher esteem but assumes a similar responsiveness to appeals of a substantial and more or less virtuous character.

Putting it crudely and bluntly, the first is a clever and semiscientific application of the thesis that all men are fools, while the second maintains that while men may be fools and sinners, they are everlastingly on the search for that which is good.

Needless to say, both formulas have registered great successes because each is at least founded on a half-truth.

The Human Mind the Key to the Copy Angle

The very fact, however, that it is the human mind, in the last essence, which must be subjected to dissection before a formula can be evolved, indicates the hazard involved in any individual attempt to erect a formula even distantly assuming infallibility.

The truth of the matter is, that any such attempt smacks of vanity and, therefore, of narrowness, and in some cases has its origin in a pure spirit of charlatanism.

Nevertheless, definiteness, precision, system and reasonable assurance of results are the great desideratums in advertising, and the pursuit of them should never be abandoned.

It is perfectly true that there are certain definite human impulses, motives and reactions which can reasonably be counted upon either in the individual or in the mass.

It is likewise perfectly true that men and women do respond almost automatically to certain homely assaults upon their sensibilities.

They respond also to the appeals of cupidity and cunning, and they are no doubt influenced by the over-emphasis which is an integral part of the first of the two copy formulas described above.

Truth Is Dramatic and Interesting

My own contention is that the appeal of the ancient verities is the more powerful, and that a business which successfully exerts it is more solidly and substantially built than any other possibly can be.

It is a truism—and yet an important business fact—that we all hate the villain and love the hero, that we prefer virtue to vice and goodness to that which is meretricious.

This, it seems to me, should be the grand central animating thought in any effort to conquer a market.

It is perfectly true that a market can be won for a good product by playing on the other and more ignoble susceptibilities of the human mind and heart. But it has always appeared to me to be a waste of time and effort to offer that which is good by way of the circuitous route of being smart, or sharp, or clever, or adroit, when the other road is so much more direct.

No matter who or what I am, if I can persuade any considerable group that I am honest and that my honesty is practically expressed in my business and in my product, I am in a fair way to build a substantial clientele.

To find ways and means of inducing this tremendous confidence in people's minds is quite another story, but to me at least, it is the one great thing to be achieved in business, beside which all others pale into insignificance.

Better to Suggest Than to Assert

That is why I remarked in the opening paragraph that experience suggested to me that the closest approach possible in advertising to a positive formula is the development of a sound underlying principle.

Surely the principle referred to is sound, since it is based on known facts in human nature; and surely also its corollary—that all men are subject to suggestion—is equally sound.

Working with these two root-thoughts in mind, it is possible to attain a surprising degree of sequence and system in advertising, from which an amazing volume of valuable confidence accrues.

An appeal to the universal desire for goodness—which in business is merely another name for value—a simple and, if you please, apparently artless, way of phrasing that appeal—and if the market be national, a patience and persistence in advertising appearance which does not look to a single announcement to work a miracle—these seem to me, after many years of experience, the safest and soundest of guides in defining and preparing advertising copy.

Naturally, the special circumstances surrounding a case continually tempt one to depart from the root-principle.

Copy More Important Than Size of Space

If the study of sales is not kept continuously thoughtful and sincere, and based upon a knowledge not merely of men's minds but of markets and essential economic facts, there comes the temptation, for instance, to conquer by sheer size and frequency of domination.

It can be done; it has been done repeatedly; and is being done—at a high and heavy cost perhaps, but a cost apparently warranted in some cases by the volume of profit and the scope of the market.

To fly from this extreme to the opposite position of pretending to subject every announcement to the foot-rule of results in tenths-of-one-per cent is almost as vicious as the other.

A Direct Check Not Always Possible

A check on the advertising and the sales of certain sorts of products is easily possible; in other instances almost impossible. Moreover, the more niggardly manner of charting costs and results applied in certain instances might completely ignore a value accruing from advertising infinitely greater than cent-per-cent cost and return.

It was once said of a certain long-continued program of advertising, that it put *something* into a certain motor car which was not built in the factory, and that that something has made the motor car property the most valuable of its class in the world.

That was and is literally true. And yet by the cent-per-cent system of demanding that every advertisement deliver on the spot, that program was altogether deficient and unscientific.

That *something* was reputation. The public knew but little regarding the details of the car and cared less. People did, however, know about the manufacturers. They were convinced of their honesty and sincerity. People bought the car because they trusted the manufacturers. And they trusted the manufacturers because of the suggestive copy in the advertising.

A number of years ago, I had the temerity to say to a great corporation that if a given formula or program was faithfully followed, I was prepared to promise that this great business would pass out of the price class into the quality class.

I named the company which it would oust from first position in the quality class and said that, if we all worked together, the transition would be complete within eighteen months.

It was complete in less than a year—the business did pass out of the price class into the quality class, and the other business was ousted from its preferential position.

In this instance again, public opinion was led and influenced by suggestive copy, which had for its purpose the creation of favorable public opinion. Within a year, the advertiser had the reputation for honesty, quality and sincerity, and naturally the public gave his product the preference.

Copy Should Build Reputation, for Reputation Alone Sells Goods Steadily

I have predicated all my own work on the basic truth that people *are* susceptible to suggestion. We live, move and have our being in a swirl of suggestion, from morning till night, and from the age of reason to the edge of the grave.

One suggestion accepted by one person becomes his or her personal opinion.

This personal opinion, accepted by a group of people, becomes the thing known as public opinion.

A favorable public opinion concerning a man or a manufactured product becomes the thing known as reputation.

Good reputation, in turn, is a thing that sells goods.

I maintain that it is no more difficult to convey a suggestion to a multiplicity of minds than it is to one mind.

If that much is granted, or if I can prove that it has been accomplished, we have established a very simple premise which carries in its train very astonishing results.

If it is true that by printed propaganda, a favorable and friendly opinion can be generated in a multiplicity of minds, then it is equally true that we have found a hothouse in which a good reputation can be generated, as it were, over night.

In other words, the thing for which men in the past have been willing to slave and toil for a lifetime, they can now set out to achieve with semi-scientific accuracy and assurance of success, in periods of months instead of years.

The Real Copy Problem

The most difficult of all requirements is a simplicity and artlessness of expression which will render it reasonably certain that the suggestion when received will be accepted without resistance or resentment.

The real suggestion to convey is that the man manufacturing the product is an honest man, and that the product is an honest product, *to be preferred above all others.*

Skill of Expression Needed

Just as it is exceedingly difficult for a man to choose words which will convince a group of strangers of his honesty, so does it require an exceptional degree of skill in expression to convey the same suggestion in regard to a manufacturer and his product.

No matter how difficult it may be, however, if it is possible of achievement, even by the expenditure of an infinite amount of effort and skill, it is, as I have said, a result almost priceless in value.

It is priceless because the thing that really determines the life or death of such products as we have in mind—in the long run—is public opinion.

If a multiplicity of people can, by suggestion, be induced to approach the purchase of a product with a conviction of its honesty and goodness, they approach it with a preference and a predisposition in its favor.

No state of mind which personal salesmanship can arouse in them is comparable—in its effect on the decision—with this *self-induced opinion,* formed as the result of the suggestions contained in the advertising copy.

First Necessary to Determine What Thought Is to Be Floated

The first necessity is that the advertising writer and the manufacturer should know and agree upon the thought that it is desired to generate in the public mind.

The second is that those thoughts should be true thoughts, and reasonable thoughts, which constitute in themselves a reason why the product should be preferred.

The big point of all this is that the root-idea or principle as expressed in the advertising not only influence and guide the public, but actually become the all-controlling policy of the advertiser and his organization.

It comes, in time, to regulate their manufacturing and selling conduct.

It influences and establishes their policies; regulates their correspondence; determines the degree of profit and the rate of discount; and affects the quality of their manufacturing.

For it must be remembered that the manufacturer himself reads the advertising and tries to live up to it by making his product and his service worthy of the thoughts the advertising expresses.

How Advertising Copy Influences Salesmanship

Its object is to make sales quickly, of course, but not to sacrifice the institution for the sake of the immediate sale.

Always the copy writer of this type must have in mind the idea that he must win confidence, establish good-will of a permanent character.

Confidence in an institution is, after all, the only basis for buying the product.

It is the only basis for permanent success.

If it is built up rightly and soundly by the advertising writer, it will even tide the institution over a depression.

It will lead the public even to forgive a temporarily poor product.

It will do this because the copy is human—because it won friendships.

It inspires loyalty. Establishes confidence. Wins friendship. And all of us make allowances for friends, so long as we are convinced of their sincerity.

Over-emphasis, a too-obvious striving for effect, is dangerous. These are used, of course. You see them in copy every day. But their success is more apparent than real.

In fact, the very success carries the germ of failure in it, because every sale made on such a basis leaves a bad taste and alienates the purchaser's good-will.

We can all of us point to some glittering advertising successes, which shortly become business failures, as the result of wrong advertising copy.

Sound Copy the Basis of Permanent Success

I do not know of a single instance in which, when intelligently used, advertising copy has not made it possible for the advertiser to "cash in" a higher price, and a greater profit, than would have been possible without it.

The man who heads a business for which constructive advertising copy has built a public friendship is master of his public, though it is his public which has made him.

They are subject to his product and his prices, because they are subject to their own conviction concerning the goodness of that product.

The head of such a business, again, is master of his selling process, because the strength and dignity of his position makes his product desired, and the right to sell it a highly valued and most valuable franchise.

He is at least partly safeguarded against one of the great wastes of modern merchandising—the mediocrity and inertia which mark the greater proportion of most salesmanship.

For the customer, predisposed in favor of a product by his own mental processes, *helps make a sale to himself* and fills up the gaps and flaws in the salesman's technique from his own thoughts.

Thus you see advertising copy of this type tries not to move a job-lot of goods, but to foster a friendship, a confidence and desire which lead the purchaser to *buy* the product.

Therefore, it controls the market for that product, because it controls the thoughts which impel people to give the product the preference.

Advertising Should Formulate Opinion

The first duty of advertising, of course, is to get itself read.

And, when read, it must leave something with the reader—must help him formulate a predetermined opinion as to the goodness of the product.

So all advertising that is worthy of the name must be prepared with the definite idea of producing a definite state of mind in millions of people, in a definite period of time.

If you do that, you won't have to strain after sales—for the public will buy. And because people buy as the result of their own convictions, they will continue to buy so long as the manufacturer continues to foster that goodwill.

Many companies have applied these fundamentals. Many have not.

The volume of good-will controlled by the first group is in proportion to the thoroughness with which the principle has been applied.

Have you ever figured why it is that some companies which were successful a comparatively few years ago, or some products which were sold everywhere, are now no longer heard of?

The answer always is, "They lost their public."

And they can come back only by winning their public again.

How to Write Advertising Copy

Think of your copy in terms of one individual. Think of one man or one woman.

Think of a man sitting on the bank of a creek fishing for bullheads.

Think of the woman knitting or rocking, or busily bustling about a store.

Think of that man's thoughts. Think of that woman's thoughts.

Think of the remembrance of the product you are writing about flashing through their minds.

Think of that momentary flash followed by a warm feeling of approval. It comes—it goes—but it has registered.

That friendly thought is stored away in the brain cells. It will rise to the surface when occasion arises.

There is a predisposition there in favor of the product—a preference which may even amount to a prejudice.

When you have gotten thus far, set your own mind at work.

Ask yourself if it is possible to create such a state of mind in the individual.

The answer is unmistakably and emphatically—yes, it is. How is it done?

By suggestion.

By endless and interesting iteration. Because people are human beings.

Because they live, move and have their being under the influence of suggestion.

Seldom are those suggestions systematic or scientific.

The copy writer's job is to determine the basic thought that he wishes to implant, and then to ring the charges on that thought until he literally creates a state of public conviction.

What to write depends on the product, the institution, economic conditions, markets.

The copy must be true and human and sincere. It must be reasonable, suggestive and interesting. The people will read it and accept it.

They will even quote words and phrases from the advertising while telling you they do not read advertising.

And they are sincere when they say it because suggestive advertising implants thoughts not by force but by infiltration.

Its sole aim is to make a buyer think a predetermined thought, because what a man thinks he will do.

That attitude of mind finally settles down into that priceless thing called reputation.

And, while reputation may be intangible, it is real—solid, concrete, definite and worth millions of real money.

To create reputation is finally the only aim of advertising copy. Sales will then grow steadily as more people buy.

Chapter 5

Emotion and Style in Advertising Copy

By James Wallen[1]

It was a little-known philosopher, Roannez, who stated a great truth in tabloid, "Reasons come afterward, but at first a thing pleases or shocks me without my knowing the reason."

A few years ago I listened to possibly the first presentation by Charles W. Mears, of the argument that advertising copy should be composed primarily of emotion and not logic. This was during the era of "reason why" copy, and, therefore, Mr. Mears did a very daring, though useful, thing. He contended that emotion has a more universal appeal than sheer logic. In this Mr. Mears is supported by one of the world's greatest novelists. Bulwer Lytton wrote: "Emotion, whether of ridicule, anger or sorrow, whether raised at a puppet show, a funeral or battle, is your grandest of levelers."

A brilliant but anonymous writer in the *Atlantic Monthly* likens the advertising writer to the poet and makes out his case. But to my mind, the advertising writer of the future will partake of the qualities of the novelist. Few advertising writers may attain the grace of Richard Le

---

1. *James Wallen.* Born in Green Bay, Wisconsin, January 8, 1885. Essays in *Green Bay Gazette,* correspondence for *Milwaukee Sentinel,* cream puffs for theatrical offerings were the first writings for which James Wallen was paid fees. From Wisconsin, Mr. Wallen journeyed to Philadelphia to join Percival K. Frowert Advertising Agency; later became closely associated with Elbert Hubbard in the capacity of secretary and advertising manager of *The Philistine* and *The Fra.* Mr. Wallen's study is now in Fieldston, New York City. His chief interest is narrative advertising, that is, copy which has theme and sequence. Author: *Cleveland's Golden Story* for Win. Taylor Sons & Co. of Cleveland; *Things that Live Forever* for The Art Metal Construction Company of Jamestown; *On the Fair Fingers of All Time* for H. W. Beattie & Sons of Cleveland and a biography of Harry T. Ramsdell of Buffalo, *The Hilltops of Fifty Years.*

Gallienne, prose poet, but many will be able to approximate the style of, say, Rex Beach.

In this discussion, I am not going to treat of the obviously essential emotion in the advertising of fire extinguishers, skid chains, revolvers and disinfectants, but of the feeling and sentiment in every-day wearing apparel, furniture and food.

Promise is the essence of advertising. To my mind, the greatest advertisement ever written is the 23rd Psalm of David. My first claim is that it is the most satisfying. My second consists of the fact that with this psalm you convince yourself, and to sell one-self is a great deal more difficult than to convince the other fellow. I take it that you know the 23rd Psalm:

> The Lord is my Shepherd; I shall not want.
>
> He maketh me to lie down in green pastures: He leadeth me beside the still waters.
>
> He restoreth my soul: He leadeth me in the paths of righteousness for His name's sake.
>
> Yea, though I walk through the valley of the shadow of death, I will fear no evil: for Thou art with me; Thy rod and Thy staff they comfort me.
>
> Thou preparest a table before me in the presence of mine enemies: Thou anointest my head with oil; my cup runneth over.
>
> Surely, goodness and mercy shall follow me all the days of my life; and I will dwell in the house of the Lord for ever.

This psalm is all promise. It is undiluted emotion. It gives no reasons why, and yet, as Henry Beecher said, "it has charmed more griefs to rest than all of the philosophy of the world." Most of the great consolations of the human heart do not particularize.

Let us remember that man does not live by the bread of reason alone. He lives partly by the inspirational word. We speak of pictures as a power. They are not nearly as potent as a few words of consolation that have gone down the ages. "Surely goodness and mercy shall follow me all the days of my life." The mere affirmation couched in the language of faith without a shred of explanation suffices all of the needs of the average heart and mind. Now, here is the great secret of emotional writing. There is reason back of it, but the machinery is not revealed. The author finds that his thought is logical—that it analyzes, so he presents it. It is not necessary to print the formula on the glass of wine nor count the molecules in the pearl. I am conscious of reasoning about emotion now and, in so doing, I open myself more to debate than if I wrote a song instead of a lecture.

In advertising copy, we went through several stages from the card style to "reason why," from "reason why" to more or less exact description. Now the emotional appeal seems to be in high favor. It seems to me that it will remain, for, as Victor Hugo said, "emotion is always new." There will be no need of changing, for we have struck the well of human feeling which never runs dry.

Our fascinating but unknown friend of the *Atlantic Monthly* says: "In selling tea, we are not concerned with ugly, shriveled leaves which color hot water a yellowish brown, but with a cozy fire, the silver tea set, the memory of a lovely woman, a thousand rich and beautiful experiences, haunting pictures of Japanese hillsides and sunshine." Remember that emotion is not ever violent. It does not always pulse with passion nor burn with fervor. It has the haunting quality of romance and may be induced by a mere word, the master of English may intensify the feeling that underlies an entire sentence.

I would refer you for example and guidance to the writers of novels rather than of advertising of the present for examples as to what advertising will be in the future. If you are called upon to prepare copy for a hotel, read Arnold Bennett's praise of the American hotel.

The great American hotel is a wondrous haven for the European who in Europe has only tasted comfort in his dreams. The calm orderliness of the bed-room floors, the adequacy of wardrobes and lamps, the reckless profusion of clean linen, that charming notice which one finds under one's door in the morning, 'You were called at seven-thirty, and answered,' the fundamental principle that a bedroom without a bath-room is not a bed-room, the magic laundry which returns your effects duly starched in eight hours, the bells which are answered immediately, the thickness of the walls, the radiator in the elevator-shaft, the celestial invention of the floor-clerk—I could catalogue the civilizing features of the American hotel for pages. But the great American hotel is a classic, and to praise it may seem inept.

Now, what are the words that make this passage alluring? "Haven," "reckless profusion," "magic laundry," "celestial invention," "classic" are words charged more with emotion than logic. Ask any hotel proprietor, for instance, if he does allow a "reckless profusion of clean linen."

Read John Galsworthy's description of a pair of boots in his story, "Quality."

> Besides, they were too beautiful—the pair of pumps, so inexpressibly slim, the patent leathers with cloth tops, making water come into one's mouth, the tall brown riding boots with marvelous sooty glow, as if, though new, they had been worn a hundred years. Those pairs could only have been made by one who saw before him the Soul of the boots—so truly were they prototypes incarnating the very spirit of all foot-gear.

Here again some rather illogical groupings of words give vitality to the description—"inexpressibly slim," "marvelous sooty glow."

No writer on interior decoration listing facts, measurements and details could so comprehensibly describe a room as Frank Swinnerton, with a few simple but eloquent phrases, has done with the dining salon of a yacht in his novel, *Nocturne.*

> It seemed, partly because the ceiling was low, to be very spacious; the walls and ceiling were of a kind of dusky amber hue; a golden brown was everywhere the prevailing tint. The tiny curtains, the long settees into which one sank, the chairs, the shades of the mellow lights—all were of some variety of this delicate golden brown. In the middle of the cabin stood a square table; and on the table, arrayed on an exquisitely white tablecloth, was laid a wondrous meal. The table was laid for two; candles with amber shades made silver shine and glasses glitter. Upon a fruit stand were peaches and nectarines; upon a tray she saw decanters; little dishes crowding the table bore mysterious things to eat such as Jenny had never before seen. Upon a side table stood other dishes, a tray bearing coffee cups and ingredients for the provision of coffee, curious silver boxes. Everywhere she saw flowers similar to those which had been in the motor car. Under her feet was a carpet so thick that she felt her shoes must be hidden in its pile. And over all was this air of quiet expectancy which suggested that everything awaited her coming.

This passage emphasizes one of the truest elements in advertising appeal. One does not sell an upholstered chair but really the depression made by the body as you settle into the chair. It is the effect, not the medium, we are selling. The contributor to the *Atlantic Monthly* says that you do not sell a man the tea, but the magic spell which is brewed nowhere else but in a tea-pot.

What do you buy when you go to an antique dealer and acquire a decrepit old chair? Not the sensation of comfort which you secure with the upholstered chair, but an even less material element—that of tradition, of bygone association and historical legend.

Personally, I have found the appeals to sentiment, ambition, a sense of luxury, more compelling than reams of logic and pointed argument. The most effective advertisement in inquiries and interest in a series which I wrote for Berkey and Gay ran as follows:

> Mary Lamb wrote to her friend Barbara Betham, saying that her famous brother Charles could not write in a room not properly furnished. So with loving care she plenished a little study to his liking. This is but one of the historic examples of the influence of furnishings on mind and soul.
>
> It is the mission of Berkey and Gay to make beautiful, restful and gently inspirational furniture accessible to the many.
>
> Once you become the proud possessor of a piece bearing the shop-mark of Berkey and Gay, you will understand the abiding sentiment and truth in the phrase—"furniture for your children's heirlooms."

In the skilled advertising writer there is much of the historian, a good bit of the biographer, some of the scientist, an alloy of the philosopher, and more than an atom of the economist. In short, he is an editorial writer crossed by a tendency to produce a wholesome story.

The skilled advertising writer, even though he is keen on readability, consorts on good terms with truth. On this point I quote you Clayton Hamilton with regard to where the novelist stands in relation to truth.

> It is only in the vocabulary of very careless thinkers that the words "truth" and "fiction" are regarded as antithetic. A genuine antithesis subsists between the words "fact" and "fiction," but fact and truth are not synonymous.
>
> The novelist forsakes the realm of fact in order that he may better tell the truth, and lures the reader away from actualities in order to present him with realities.

I think I can illustrate Mr. Hamilton's point graphically: A mattress is a very definite piece of furniture to the average mind. The makers of the Sealy call their mattress, "a pillow for the body." It requires a lift of the mind from actuality to visualize what this mattress really is.

For popular interest and affection, I will stake soft, winsome Mary Pickford against all of the Dr. Mary Walkers in the world, useful as these women may be. Mary Pickford represents emotion intelligently directed. Mary Walker was intellect without the graces or arts.

Even as Mr. Mears has proved, motor cars, things of steel, rubber, leather and other unyielding materials, may be sold through the sense of luxury and refinement. When it is necessary to show in an advertising illustration the interior of a foundry, an artist like Everett Shinn puts the wonderful miracle of industry into the picture rather than the hardships of labor as George Bellows might do. Persuasion is born of pleasant association.

An advertisement should affect the reader with some of the glowing zest that the works of Fabre, the naturalist, brought to Maurice Maeterlinck. If we inject just a trifle of this intense interest into our copy, the trite question of whether copy shall be brief or lengthy will not be raised.

> We take up at random one of these bulky volumes and naturally expect to find first of all the very learned and rather dry lists of names, the very fastidious and exceedingly quaint specifications of those huge, dusty graveyards of which all the entomological treatises that we have read so far seem almost wholly to consist. We, therefore, open the book without zest and without unreasonable expectations; and forthwith, from between the open leaves, there rises and unfolds itself, without hesitation, without interruption and almost without remission to the end of the four thousand pages, the most extraordinary or tragic fairy plays that it is possible for the imagination, not to create or conceive, but to admit and to acclimatize within itself.

And by the way, the most effective passage in Maeterlinck's "Chrysanthemums" is that in which he makes their blooming coincide with a human movement.

> They are, indeed, the most universal, the most diverse of flowers; but their diversity and surprises are, so to speak, concerted, like those of fashion, in I know not what arbitrary Edens. At the same

moment, even as with silks, laces, jewels, and curls, a mysterious voice gives the password in time and space; and docile as the most beautiful women, simultaneously, in every country, in every latitude, the flowers obey the sacred decree.

Now just a word of warning on humanizing copy. Next to being half-baked, the most serious thing that can happen to a roast is to be over-done. Someone has warned, "Don't get humaner than life," like some of the underwear advertisements which exhibit all of the members of a family in the drawing room in negligee. Or the ads of a certain silverware in which language is used that only two people could possibly understand, the secret code of a single pair of lovers. Do not partake of the qualities of Joe Mitchell Chapple's "Heart Throbs," for while mellow may mean ripe, it may also imply a further stage in the life of the choicest verbal pippin.

Do not strain too far for effect. George H. Daniels, the famous General Passenger Agent of the New York Central Railroad, used to employ the simile, "Like the dreams of fair women or the cars on the Twentieth Century Limited." I suppose that Mr. Daniels' only aim was to provoke a smile.

There is a certain type of merriment which is fatal to your advertise-ment. There was a girl who pleaded in the divorce court that she had taught the complainant in the case "not to use bay rum." This reform was her major argument for consideration. Doubtless she had rendered a great service, but she could not alter the judge's decision for she had made him laugh right heartily. There are products and media which lend themselves to humor, but they are few, and caution is wisdom.

Let me quote you a practical rule laid down by Sir Arthur Quiller-Couch to the students of Cambridge University:

> Whenever you feel an impulse to perpetrate a piece of excep-tionally fine writing, obey it—wholeheartedly—and delete it before sending your manuscript to press. Murder your Darlings.

There are just five points that I desire to urge:

First: That emotion or feeling is a most vital feature in advertising copy.

Second: That to secure it use the methods of the novelist; study the ways of the fictioneer.

Third: Reserve is the guardian of true emotion. As Elbert Hubbard has said: "Pack your pauses with emotion." Pauses are simply a leaving out. In being emotional also be reasonable. For common-sense is the mentor of sentiment.

Fourth: Base your romance on facts. Know everything the shop, the store and the books can tell you about your wares. Create an atmosphere of authenticity. Surround your products with the aura of greatness.

Fifth: Memorize the 23rd Psalm for the good of your art as well as your heart.

The Copy Style

And now as regards copy style.

The perfect symbol of the epigram is the dewdrop. It has clarity, compression and isolation; it is transient, yet permanent; it is repeated a thousand times, thus proving its essential truth. And in such a verbal dewdrop, John Galsworthy has defined style: "What is style, in its true and purest sense, save fidelity to idea and mood and perfect balance in the clothing of them?" This definition applies with exactitude to advertising copy. The advertisement must be faithful to its central idea and be without flaw in the dressing and presentation of its theme. Whether the advertisement be in the minor chord or in the grand manner, it is needful that it hold to its *motif* from initial letter to the last period.

This, then, is the first requirement of style in an advertisement, but style implies some other meanings, as well. In fact, J. Middleton Murry draws three distinct definitions of the word style as applied to writing: "Style as a personal peculiarity; style as technique of expression; style as the highest achievement of literature." The difficulty attending these definitions is that they melt one into the other.

When we speak of a certain writer's style, we likely mean his peculiar characteristics. John Corbin once reminded an actress who imitated Mrs. Fiske that the gyrations of the sibyl are not the secret of the sibyl's inspiration. I think that these personal qualities are almost wholly a matter of inborn genius and should not concern one who is endeavoring to help others attain style in writing. One seems to have personal style or not. Originality is the rarest gem and cannot be simulated.

Artistically, I am sure, there is no such thing as imitation. There is only parody. When writing advertising literature, profit by the example of others, but do not copy their peculiarities of style and construction. If you are a writer, a craftsman with words, you will have a style of your own.

The imitations which make Cecilia Loftus famous are other characters seen through the camera of Miss Loftus. When the clever Cecilia imitates Mrs. Patrick Campbell, it is her interpretation of the other actress just as definitely as a photograph of a subject by Alfred Stieglitz represents his own ideas of the model which will differ radically from those of Pine MacDonald. Take, for example, Louis Untermeyer's "Parodies of Poets." They are neither imitations nor burlesque, as he himself has said.

During the years in which I was advertising manager for Elbert Hubbard's publications I never attempted to follow the style of *The Fra,* though there were many copy writers under my direction, who did consciously and laboriously try to imitate the Sage of East Aurora. They succeeded in being imitations only, unconvincing and as full of poses as a Greenwich Village model. Everyone who has tried to put on the mantle of *The Fra,* as a writer, has succeeded only in getting lost in its folds.

There are words and arrangements of words which are native to one individual and foreign to another. In the discussion and vivisection of words, let us carry in mind this very vital fact. There are elements of the expression of thought for which you have an affinity and others with which you have only a speaking acquaintance.

Sir Arthur Quiller-Couch says that all literature is personal and, therefore, various. One must learn all that he can of the best writers. Saturate yourself with their manners, then escape from them, go into the open and write out of your own heart and mind.

Most people express themselves today in ready-to-use phrases. The writer must, of all people, avoid this fault. He must be a maker, rather than a mere retailer of phrases. The best way to test originality in a writer is to study his comments on a subject with which you are familiar and see if the author engages your interest. Then, in the same fashion, read the work of another writer on the same subject. This will give you a scale by which you can judge what you might possibly do with the same subject, influenced, perhaps, by other writers but still at variance with them as your own personality invests the topic.

Originality is as elusive as a wood fawn; to endeavor to chart this phase of style is like trying to measure a certain bird's song. There are, however, a few points about style as technique and style as manner, which deserve discussion from an academic point of view. And even here Sir Arthur Quiller-Couch imagines that his pupils say about his lectures that "at the final doorway to the secret he turned his back and left us. Accuracy, propriety, perspicuity—these we may achieve. But where has he helped us to write with beauty, charm and distinction; where has he given us rules for what is called style, having attained which an author may count himself set up in business?" And Sir Arthur's answer to his own question is, that style, for example, is not, cannot be extraneous ornament, and he quotes Cardinal Newman who says that "style is a thinking out into language." We are to conclude that when one has expressed fully that which is in his mind he has achieved style.

Most people are truly inarticulate; the very thing that they cannot do is to put into language what they have in their minds. It was Cardinal Newman who told how the Oriental lover engages a professional writer to express his emotions for him. "The man of words duly instructed, dips his pen of desire in the ink of devotedness and proceeds to spread it over the page of desolation." This is exactly the position in which the advertising writer finds himself. He is speaking for someone other than himself. He is playing the Cyrano de Bergerac to the business Christian, with the public in the character of Roxane. If he were speaking for himself, the task might be easier. Having taken on the character of someone else, it is doubly difficult to achieve style.

Sir Arthur Quiller-Couch seems almost willing to leave style in writing on the plane of good manners. While I think that good manners are important in writing advertising, I feel that we should have something finer than good manners. We should have an impressive manner. We are even urged to write advertising as we talk. To my mind this would be most unfortunate—a most humiliating concession. If most men would write as they talk, their letters would not be admissible to the United States mails. I contend that there is a conversational manner, a telephone manner, a platform manner and certainly a writing manner.

I recall four advertisements from which I received a sense of style and fitness—"fidelity to the idea and mood and perfect balance in the clothing of them." These advertisements were: "Time and Chance," by Elbert Hubbard, an exhortation for the Equitable Life; that famed "I Am the Printing Press," written by Robert H. Davis; Frank Irving Fletcher's "On the Wings of Morning" for Harrod's of London; Bruce Barton's "The Years That the Locusts Have Eaten," for the Alexander Hamilton Institute. These advertisements had the fervor of oratory, and it is a peculiar coincidence that they all savored of Biblical literature as if the writers had dipped their pens in the incense of the great Hebrew poets. No one can, however, deny that the Bible has commanded some influence in this world.

If I had, however, to lay claim to having evolved a major advertisement, I would be willing to rest my laurels on the double page entitled "The Black Pearl of Furs, Being the Saga of the Silver Fox," which appeared in Hearst's *International.* I have evidence that this form of advertisement, in addition to making good reading, does produce returns.

The advertising writer is a special pleader, and some of the quality of exhortation must be in his work. I am sure that style comes more spontaneously when one is filled to overflowing with his subject. The reason that Bourke Cochrane was persuasive as an orator was because he had more of his subject in him that he could hold. When the mind is surcharged with a subject, it becomes electric. When Daniel Webster made his deathless reply to Hayne, the accumulation of the knowledge of the years came to his assistance. 'Webster said of his oration: "The air around me seemed to be full of arguments; I had only to reach out and pull down a thunderbolt and hurl it at him." Robert Louis Stevenson stated with clarity the only scheme by which a man may write without effort:

> When truth flows from a man, fittingly clothed in style and with-out conscious effort, it is because the effort has been made and the work practically completed before he sat down to write. It is only out of fullness of thinking that expression drops perfect like a ripe fruit; and when Thoreau wrote so nonchalantly at his desk, it was because he had been vigorously active during his walk. For neither clearness, compression, nor beauty of language, come to any living creature till after a busy and a prolonged acquaintance with the subject on hand. Easy writers are those who, like Walter Scott, choose to remain contented with a less degree of perfection than is legitimately within the compass of their powers.

The French formula for writing love letters—"Begin without knowing what you are going to say, and end without knowing what you have said"—cannot be applied to the writing of advertising.

John P. Altgeld, the Illinois statesman who was one of America's most moving orators, once spoke of the requirement of accuracy in all artistic effort: "Art does not admit of random touches. It demands entire accuracy. In music the singer is not permitted to be guided by his feelings in dropping or adding notes; the laws of harmony must be followed, and like fidelity is demanded in speech."

The threatening danger in the lack of preparation is the committing of the sin of formlessness. Unless you have a plan, you are apt to wander all over your subject, like a colt in a meadow, without direction. Your accumulation of data may prove your undoing unless you methodically arrange the stuff according to its sequence and importance.

One of the most helpful of teachers is the Abbe Bautain, VicarGeneral of the Sorbonne, who has written earnestly of the necessity for method in writing and speaking:

> The preparation of the plan of a discourse implies, before anything else, a knowledge of the things which you have to speak; but a general knowledge is not enough; you may have a great quantity of materials, of documents and of information in your memory, and not be aware how to bring them to bear. It sometimes even happens that those who know most, or have most matter in their heads, are incapable of rightly conveying it. The overabundance of acquisition and words crushes the mind, and stifles it, just as the head is paralyzed by a too great determination of blood, or a lamp is extinguished by an excess of oil.

You will note that the Abbe Bautain treats of this "overabundance of acquisition." He tells you exactly why it is too heavy a load to carry. It is just knowledge badly distributed.

When material is properly arranged, it becomes pliable rather than unwieldy. It becomes better clay. It admits of higher craftsmanship. Lord Tennyson contended that "an artist should get his workmanship as good as he can, and make his work as perfect as possible.

A small vessel, built on fine lines, is likely to float further down the stream of time than a big craft."

I cannot emphasize too earnestly that when one has a poverty of ideas on a subject he cannot attain a great style. If one has a wealth of information he is free to take what he needs at the time of writing to express his idea and to leave the rest for another day. Because you have found a mine of data, there is no reason why you should garnish your copy with all of its gold. Restraint and reserve are the writer's means of thrift.

Eden Phillpotts has observed, "Nothing without a skeleton can endure. Some art is alive; some art is fossil; but everything that has lasted, was built on a skeleton of form and modeled with the steel of stern selective power." Because you are called upon to write short copy is no reason why you should not have a heavy van-load of information. This enables you to select the best for your brief presentation.

The talk of an idle hour about being too near a subject to write about it, receives no sympathy from me. The speaker in such a case has merely neglected to formulate his understanding into usable shape. He needs what Professor Shaw calls "a cream separator for the brain." The successful attitude toward a business or a product implies about the same qualities that make a happy marriage—a familiarity that breeds not contempt but romance. Not everything you hear, see or read is grist for your copy mill—there is a lot of chaff. The result depends entirely upon the miller.

The study of words is an important aid in the accomplishment of an authentic style. However, the ownership of a copious vocabulary does not mean a writing style. You might empty before me a cask of gems and I would not be able to arrange even a few of them into an artistic pendant. Which words are slow and which are fast in conveying ideas; words which humanize; those which form the North Pole and those which form the South Pole of your picture must be recognized on the instant of writing.

I remember an announcement by Selznick Pictures which described Norma Talmadge as "the lady of tremendous contrasts." "Buttercups and orchids; spring water and champagne; tropical midnight and mountain sunrise; thrushes and peacocks; storm clouds and sunshine." This is skilful juggling, displaying the child of the field and the flower of an exotic civilization in chromatic compositions of words. It is not high art, but it is loftier than the flights of most advertising writers.

Copy style implies that one can determine the style of copy to be utilized in a certain advertisement at will. There are a great many things that set the style of an advertisement. The first, of course, is the character of the product to be advertised; the environment in which the product is to be used; the media in which it is to be advertised. The copy then must be faithful to these three elements. What Galsworthy defines in such exquisite English is known in advertising circles by a brassier expression—
"slant." To bring Galsworthy down to the terms which we use every day, an advertisement must be loyal to its slant.

Mr. Murry has said that all style is artificial in the sense that all good style is achieved by artisans. We should all endeavor to become good artisans. The outstanding virtue is consistency—keeping to the Galsworthy formula. It was Galvin McNabb, a San Francisco attorney, who in a famous case warned the opposing counsel against "carrying a valentine into a cathedral." I am not willing to grant that all advertisements are mere valentines. 'We advertising writers are privileged to compose a new chapter of civilization. It is a great responsibility to mold the daily lives of millions of our fellow men, and I am persuaded that we are second only to statesmen and editors in power for good.

Chapter 6

Some Lessons I Have Learned in Advertising

By Claude C. Hopkins[1]

My first lesson in advertising was learned as a boy of twelve. Mother was left a widow so we had to join in supporting the family. One thing we did was to make a silver polish. We made it in cakes, wrapped it up nicely, and I went out to sell it after school.

I found that when I met the housewife at the door and talked the polish to her I sold hardly to one home in ten. But when I got into the pantry and cleaned some of the silver I sold nine times in ten.

That taught me to let products sell themselves. Since then I have probably given away more samples and free packages than any other man. I would no more think of starting an advertising campaign without samples than I would think of selling goods on the road without samples. Or as a house-to-house canvasser.

But I later learned that giving unrequested samples often does more harm than good. It cheapens the product, brings it into disrespect. So I never give samples except on request. I give them only to those who read my story and are interested enough to write.

I often offer a full-size package, but never in a way to cheapen my product. I buy the package from the dealer and pay his price and profit. There is a vast difference in the psychology. People find it hard to pay for

1. *Claude C. Hopkins* started with Bissell Carpet Sweeper Co., Grand Rapids, Mich., and there first learned how to sell goods by letter. Went from there to become first advertising manager of Swift & Company, packers, Chicago. There, for several years, handled very large appropriation for that time. After various other adventures in advertising, joined Lord & Thomas. Was there for seventeen years and was President of Lord & Thomas for seven years. When Mr. Lasker returned from Washington and took his place as head of his agency, Mr. Hopkins started his own. Author of *Scientific Advertising,* which has been translated into numerous languages.

a product which once was free. But buying the product and paying the price in order that one may try it impresses the recipient. The product must be excellent, else you never would do that.

My next lesson in advertising was learned at the age of twenty. I was writing ads for numerous retail dealers. Aluminum ware was just coming into vogue. I specialized on it because I felt that every home should have it, and few homes were supplied.

I found that ads inviting women to an aluminum display brought few responses and the cost was high. But when I offered a souvenir on a certain day I got quick action, and the saving in cost per visitor paid for the souvenir some twenty times over. I supplied that plan to aluminum dealers everywhere and thus made my first success in advertising. Then I applied it to other lines, and developed in that way a large retail clientele.

I have used that idea in countless lines since then. Instead of saying to women "Come any time," I set a certain hour or day or week. I print in the ad a reminder for the woman to cut out. That is so she won't forget. To insure inspection of my product I offer some gift or inducement. That reduces my cost per visitor. Thus I get prompt action and decision at minimum expense.

Later I found that I could quadruple results by not telling what the souvenir was. Curiosity is a greater pulling factor than a gift.

About the same time I learned another great lesson. That is, not to talk mechanics to a woman. I was selling carpet sweepers, but not selling very many. Under pressure from the management I was talking broom action, cyco bearings, patent dumping devices, etc.

Then I went out on the road with a sample sweeper and a bag of bran. I went into stores and showed women customers how the sweeper swept up bran. I taught dealers and their clerks to make like demonstrations, then went back to my office and taught them by mail. Then carpet sweepers began to sell.

I enlarged on the plan by offering special exhibits. I had the sweepers built in peculiar or rare woods. Or I had them built twelve woods to the dozen to make a forestry exhibit. I furnished circulars for dealers to put in their packages, inviting women to see an exhibit which would never appear again. Sales multiplied over and over. My methods brought me reputation, and I received numerous offers to enter wider fields.

Since then I have never discussed mechanics with women. I have used very little logic. I have brought them to see what my product would do in some interesting manner.

My next lesson was learned in the advertising of a vegetable shortening. I made very slow progress in merely talking that shortening against lard. I saw in a few weeks that I would lose my job before I won a profit. So I built in a department store in Chicago the largest cake in the world. It was made with this shortening. I advertised it like a circus and brought one hundred thousand women in one week to see it. I served them samples. Then I offered premiums to those who would buy that day.

The plan was a tremendous success. The shortening was placed on a profit-paying basis in one week. Then I built a like cake in the leading stores of a hundred cities and made the product a nationwide success.

That saved my job, gave me added reputation, and taught me to dramatize my subjects when I could.

My text lessons were learned in mail-order advertising. I did this on numerous lines at night. There I looked cost and result in the face, as all mail-order advertisers do. I found that any wasted space increased my cost. 'When I used a useless picture to attract attention, and that picture occupied one-third my space, it increased my cost fifty per cent. When I used a type twice larger than necessary it doubled my cost per reply.

That taught me economy of space. I found that people would read ads set in small type just as readily as in large type. They read about everything they care to read in 8-point type or smaller. Larger type brought no additional readers. Nor did any meaningless picture or display. People read ads, like everything else, because the subject is interesting to them. They judge by the headline, on news items or on ads. I have saved advertisers millions of dollars through that well-proved principle of economizing space.

Mail-order advertising also taught me that headlines differ immensely in their pulling power. A certain ad with one headline will pull ten times better than the same ad with another headline. That taught me to learn in every line what appeals pay best. It taught me to key all advertising, to compare one ad with another, just as mail-order advertisers do. And never to use an ad in wide circulation until I have tried it out.

In the twenty-five years since then I have put thousands of ads to the test. I found on one line that a certain appeal cost $14.20 per reply. Another appeal on that same line cost 42 cents per reply. One ad on one line cost me $17 to get a coupon for a sample. Another ad on that same line, telling almost an identical story, cost 35 cents per reply. In almost every line I have found certain lines of approach which would have made profit impossible. And those were often the ads which everybody favored.

There lies the main reason for the success I have gained. I have never spent much money on a gamble or a guess. I have compared dozens of ads, sometimes hundreds of ads, before going into large circulation. The best-paying ads were selected. Then I constantly tested other ads in a small way to find something better still. On one line I tried out 56 series of ads, and after five years I found a way to bring results at one-fourth the cost of the best way I had found before.

I am convinced that nobody, save by some rare accident, can do effective advertising without those comparisons, based on known returns. Certainly others must make the same mistakes that I made. They must get the wrong viewpoints about as often as I did. Decades ago I would have wrecked myself and wrecked my clients had I not known my results.

My next lesson was learned in starting numerous products. I was gaining reputation. Countless people came to me with what they considered good advertising projects. I made several great mistakes by relying on my judgment and on theirs. The products were not as salable as we thought.

So I decided to attempt nothing until I had tested the project in a limited way. I set the limit on a test campaign at $5,000, but most such campaigns cost less. Thus I found out in a few towns the cost of winning one thousand customers. Then I waited to see what those thousand would buy. Before branching out I always knew the cost per customer and the sale per customer. I let the thousands decide what the millions would do. When I did branch out I operated on a certainty.

That is why I have remained in advertising thirty-six years so far. That is why I have been trusted with the expenditure of $60,000,000. I limited losses. The mistakes I made cost little. The successes made fortunes without risk.

With advertising ventures and advertising men the fatalities are enormous. Nearly all the stars of advertising have perished before their prime. I believe that all of my early contemporaries are out of the field today. Many were brilliant men, but they made the mistake of working in the dark. They had no compass, so they landed on the rocks.

Another lesson I learned was the value of information. It first was taught me in a pork-and-bean campaign. It had not been very successful, but the maker of the product still believed in advertising. He was willing to venture another $400,000 on a logical plan.

I sent investigators from house to house to measure the situation. When their reports came in we found that ninety-four per cent of the housewives were baking their own beans. Only six per cent were buying any canned beans. Yet several makers were spending large sums to win that six per cent.

I went after the home bakers, the ninety-four per cent. I cited the sixteen hours of soaking, boiling and baking required on a dish of beans. I pictured the beans in glass dishes, crisped on the top, mushy in the middle, all under-baked, all hard to digest.

Then I told them how we baked—in steam ovens, at a temperature of 245 degrees. How we baked without crisping, without breaking the beans. They came out nut-like, mealy and whole, fitted for easy digestion. I won on that line a place and a career in a great advertising agency—a career which continued for seventeen years, which brought me both fortune and fame. All because I learned the situation and multiplied the power of my appeal.

Another lesson I learned was in the days of beer advertising. All advertising brewers were then talking pure beer. They displayed the word "Pure" in big type. Finally one brewer used two pages, putting PU on one page and RE on the other, to make the "Pure" more emphatic. But it was all like dropping water on a duck.

One brewer who held fifth place asked me to take up his advertising. I went to a brewing school. Then I went through his brewery. I saw a plate-glass room where beer was cooled in filtered air. I saw the beer filtered through white pulp wood. Bottles were washed four times by machinery. Every pump and pipe was cleaned after every operation. The brewery was on the shore of Lake Michigan, but they bored down 4,500 feet to get still purer water.

I went to the laboratory and saw a mother yeast cell kept in glass. They told me that yeast had resulted from 1,200 experiments to get an ideal flavor. And that all the yeast used in that brewery was produced from that mother cell.

I was astounded. "Why," I asked, "have you never told this story?" They told me that their methods formed common brewery practice. Any rival could claim whatever they claimed about them.

But I pictured that plate glass room and told of those filters and processes. In two years that brewery jumped from fifth place to first place. Largely because I gave convincing reasons for purity and flavor.

In the early days of automobile advertising there existed a general impression that profits were too high. In a line I was advertising our chief opportunity seemed to lie in combating that impression.

Others were claiming low prices and low profits. I came out with a headline, "Our Profit is 9 Per Cent." I told the exact cost of engine, chassis, wheels, tires, etc. I cited exact costs of $762 on a $1,500 car, without mentioning body, top or upholstery—the things most conspicuous in a car.

The success of that campaign taught me to be exact. When we claim the best or the cheapest, people smile. That is advertising license. But when we state figures, they are either true or untrue, and people do not expect a reputable concern to lie. They accept the figures at par. Ever since then, whenever possible, I have stated my facts in figures.

In other ways I learned the fearful cost of changing people's habits. One was in a campaign on oatmeal, another on a dentifrice. I tried to induce more people to eat oats, and I found that the cost of winning new users was vastly beyond any possible returns. I tried to convert new users to the tooth brush habit. As nearly as I could figure, the cost was $25 per convert. If all converts used our tooth paste all their lives we could scarcely get the money back.

So I quit that. I am letting others convert people to new habits. I simply try to get them, when they are converted, to use my type of product. Since I learned that lesson, I have spent millions of dollars in advertising oatmeal and tooth pastes. But I have never used one line, one word, to win people to a habit they have not as yet adopted.

I learned another lesson in connection with oatmeal. We knew that countless people failed to serve oatmeal because of the time required for cooking. So we put out a ready-cooked oatmeal called Two-Minute Oats. It was so flavory, so enticing, so easy to prepare that we wanted to jump into national advertising without the usual limited test. But we made the test, and we quickly found that people did not like Two-Minute Oats. It was a delightful product, but it did not taste like the oatmeals people knew. We were appealing to oatmeal users, and they all had certain educated tastes. They refused our innovation.

Later came another idea for quick-cooking oats. This method did not change the flavor. The advertiser did not think the idea worth a trial. They cited the fact that we had already failed on a quick-cooking oatmeal. But I argued the difference and urged them to submit the question to two thousand women. We did that at a cost of about $1,000—by buying a package of the new product for them. We stated the facts, told them that here was a product with a flavor like the oatmeals they knew. But it cooked in three minutes. We wanted their verdict on it. To the two thousand women who asked for a package we sent a letter stating the facts again. We said that it made no difference to us which type they preferred. We simply wanted to learn their choice. We enclosed a stamped envelope for their reply. Ninety-one per cent of those women voted for the new type, and the concern which makes it has gained a new hold on that field.

Good advertising is a matter of experience and experiment. All of us make at least ten mistakes to every success we create. Any of us, acting on judgment alone, would meet with quick disaster. This is truer now than ever. Advertising is more costly than it used to be. The competition is many times as severe. We cannot win out on a guess. We cannot hope to succeed unless we carefully test our ideas.

We cannot know enough people to measure up public opinion. We cannot anticipate the wants, the prejudices or the idiosyncrasies which confront any new undertaking. We can learn only by experience. We must feel our way, else the best man among us will soon find a precipice which may forever destroy men's confidence in him.

Chapter 7

Copy—Good, Bad, and indifferent

By Richard A. Foley[1]

Not only the beginner in advertising work, but the old hand, may find it worth while to consider the plain fundamentals of advertising copy and to get as far as possible away from the altruisms and "untrueisms" so plentifully besprinkling the pages of magazines and books which seek to make plain the proper and profitable ways of advertising.

There is a deal of misinformation vouchsafed beginners, and to the old practitioner—much that passes for inspiration is silly nonsense.

Perhaps with what I have in mind, the chapter might well be headed: "Common Sense in Advertising," for although this kind of sense is supposed to be the heritage of all, it is indeed most uncommon, having become varnished over and decorated with all sorts of fantastic, grotesque and whimsical interpretations and outgivings.

If it were convenient or necessary to put into one phrase the secret of advertising copy that really attains the full measure of its purpose, that message would read:

Be Natural and Sincere.

Now to be *natural* and *sincere* is by no means easy of accomplishment.

The real artist is one who conveys to the auditors the meaning of the melody which he plays, or the soul that animates the character he delineates in the play.

---

1. *Richard A. Foley.* Died in 1923. Was head of Richard A. Foley & Company, advertising agents, Philadelphia, and had a national reputation as a writer of advertising copy. He was a newspaper man for a number of years, and also a forceful speaker.

The great painter is not photographic, but suggestional—he makes us see not merely the visible things, but the significances which the wonderful eye of his mind has focalized.

Great literature must necessarily be sincere. The more natural its technique, the more livable and lovable it is.

True art, therefore, in advertising, consists in making the reader see for himself that which the advertiser is eager to have him see, and doing it without the appearance of eagerness.

Few Fixed Principles

Advertising is such an enormous force and so widely used—and its economic history is of such recent scope—that we have few fixed principles by which to judge the value or comparative worthwhileness of any particular type of advertising. Hence, many prophets rush into print claiming wonders each for his favorite method, when, upon close analysis, it would be revealed that too often it merely represents the meretricious, the easily clever, the varnish laid thick and glossy upon a poor foundation.

Three forms of advertising seem most to call forth praise from the unthinking—the Slogan, the Versified Advertisement, and the "Stunt." Under the latter head may be rated all sorts of bizarre presentations of more or less bright subjects, such, for example, as—"I am the Anvil," followed by a long series of "I-am's," telling what an otherwise uninteresting anvil really is and does. This "I am" method in various guises has been applied to all sorts of merchandise.

Then there is the "Say Jones' Spuds to the Grocer" idea—the repetition of a phrase or a picture, in magazines, newspapers, billboards, street cars, to the saturation point with the expectation of *forcing* the merchandise on the community.

The slogan is probably the most overrated form of advertising cleverness. The mere smoothness of phraseology—the "aptness" of the thing—marks it as merely the work of an advertising phrase-maker. It is representative not at all of the sincere effort of the manufacturer or the actual character of his product. In a world of slogans, a plain statement of honest fact, marked by sincerity, carries great weight.

It is as though a listener were in the midst of a company of stimulated, bright men, making epigrams, regardless. His ear would soon tire, and his brain fail to respond to the artificial stimulus. The sincere, worthwhile statements of a man of character, carrying with them the conviction that back of these statements were truth and honesty, would clear the atmosphere for the auditor and make a lasting impression.

Here and there during the last twenty years a slogan has been developed which, because of its sincerity and the thoroughness of its description, has carried weight and value.

But I am not afraid to go on record as saying that ninety-five per cent of the slogans are useless, and, if anything, harmful and are merely a habit of the advertiser or the urge of an over-wrought advertising man.

Why Jingles Are Artificial

As most of us in this work-a-day world are in the habit of expressing ourselves, as did Moliere's character, in prose, even though we don't know it, the artificiality of the jingle soon becomes apparent, and, concurrently, loses force. Now and then there is a reason for putting over "atmosphere" in versified form. As in the case of "Velvet Joe" in the tobacco advertising, the character was evolved for the purpose of surrounding the article with a romance, a philosophy, a kindliness that constitutes probably the chief reason for the use of pipe and tobacco. And to get this across, occasionally verse was necessary. But here it was not permitted to dominate. Verse in dialect form or copy in dialect is usually a great handicap, and the character of Velvet Joe was put across with a modicum of dialect, although the impression was given that the verses were really full of the *patois*. If the copy were to be examined, it would be found that very little real dialect entered into it.

Dialect is a dangerous thing—so is verse and so are slogans, for they nearly always fall short of being *sincere* and *natural*.

Now it may be said that people who are sincere and natural too often are dull and that advertising copy based on these premises would be uninteresting and flat. However, the dull man being natural and sincere is more likely to be impressive than were he to attempt cleverness. In the latter case, he adds insincerity to dullness. But if he were to tell his story in his own simple, sincere way, it would at least have the weight of truth and earnestness.

There are a number of advertising writers who endeavor to put on surface cleverness without the solid backing of thoroughness. The biggest task any director of advertising energy has today is to insist that the men having the trick of writing, acquire likewise the stability of sincerity and thoroughness.

In my advertising agency experience, I have employed many writers who, while possessed of cleverness, lacked thoroughness. It has been my observation that a man who will not dig for all the details that should be remembered in writing advertising, is not likely to be perfectly sure of himself on any of them. If there are ten possible points of copy, and a man is uncertain about points 1, 7, and 9, he is likely to be wrong about any of the ten. In advertising writing, *it is necessary to know everything in order to convey anything.*

A vast amount of advertising printed today is purely surface stuff, and results are largely achieved by the brute force of the space, the constant reiteration of the firm name and product, and that rather intangible aroma of success which hangs about an "advertising campaign."

Advantages of Being Natural

But when a manufacturer enjoys the privilege of reaching millions of people in one printing of his announcement, it is his duty to see that the statements which appear above his name are both natural and sincere. If he has an advertising agent or writer who possesses his confidence and has the ability to carry out his work properly, then his sincerity and naturalness can be made all the more convincing and interesting.

The stories of Robert Louis Stevenson—Treasure *Island* and *Kidnapped,* for example—are natural and sincere. Yet they lose none of their beauty because they are. Rather do they grow more wonderful with the reading and more fixed as gems of literature with each succeeding generation. On the other hand, the "best sellers" which pick out some little freak of existence or some peculiar sex or social entanglement and build a fearsome or a daring story around this vortex, supply the fireworks of literature, seen and forgotten quickly. The work of the real writer burns torch-like—steadily and constantly for those who would follow the right path.

Advertising involves the expenditure of so many millions of dollars and upon its true direction depends the growth of so large a number of splendid business enterprises, that its wrong use, its careless use, is unpardonable.

It must not be supposed that advertising men are alone responsible for this. The fault is quite frequently with the advertisers themselves, and this makes the task of the average advertising man, from the very beginning, the more difficult, and is quite likely to lead him into wrong conclusions that will later affect his worth.

It is too commonly believed that success is a faculty in itself rather than the possible product of some one or two faculties quite individual and distinct. A man may be a great organizer, and through this develop a fine business, reach a high position, and achieve a high situation. In this particular place, he may have the direction of the expenditure of large sums of money for advertising. But is he qualified?

The genius for organization characterized both Washington and Napoleon. They had, of course, additional great abilities. Some men have one ability; others two; and some, many. Washington and Napoleon both believed in relying upon their generals. They picked out the best men they could find and then entrusted important movements to them, exercising their own ingenuity and time for further combinations and for judgment when it was most needed.

Such a man, too, was General Grant. In the planning of his campaign, he employed the forces at his command with full reliance upon their strength and availability.

On the other hand, some of the princes and generals opposed to Napoleon trusted none but themselves, and, as a result, they were most of the time in confusion. One of the great failures of the American Revolution was General Gates who trusted no one, not even Washington.

Now there are advertising managers and advertisers who cannot trust the best generals they employ, and hence their plans of campaign oft go astray and work out poorly. There are men—and it has been my privilege to work with some of them—who have several qualities of success besides leadership—in some instances, being possessed of a thorough knowledge of human nature in the main, as well as in the individual. These men have generally very good reasons for their criticisms of advertising and their constructive suggestions. But a great many advertisers, on the other hand, assume that because they have been successful in business, they are also first-class judges of advertising and advertising phraseology and method. Being in power, they give orders, regardless, overwhelm all suggestion and carry things with a high hand. Sometimes this wins out, because of its very sincerity. But too often, we can read in expensive pages of advertising "snap judgment."

How to Attain Sincerity

How, then, is the sincere and natural to be attained?

First of all, by the avoidance of the rubber-stamp phraseology of advertising. No man looks well in the clothes of another. No advertisement sounds well clothed in the cant or professional phraseology picked from the advertising pages.

Descriptive phrases, adjectival draperies and the "Sunday-go-to-meeting" garb prepared for one product, do not very well fit another. Any one who cares to go through the magazines and newspapers will find not scores—but hundreds—of phrases, combinations of words, so called "ideas," applied without regard either to originality or sincerity, lending to advertising a smooth, unimpressive sameness which sometimes makes the thoughtful wonder at the success of the great economic force itself.

Let us take one phrase, for example:

> Discriminating men have unanimously declared in favor of Blank's safety razor. You are not doing justice to yourself unless you examine into its marvelous comfort, usefulness, etc., etc.

It seems from the advertiser's point of view, that practically all men are discriminating men, and that their article has been entirely or *unanimously* in favor with the said discriminating multitude. In advertising we learn that practically everything is the "best"; or "unequaled"; or "most"; or "the favorite." Nothing by chance is ever second in line—very few things stand upon their own merits, but must achieve by comparison, invidious or otherwise.

Too Much Over-Claiming in Advertising

Every advertiser "takes his pen in hand" with the determination of setting forth the fact that he is the prime manufacturer in everything relating to quality. There is an unblushing conceitedness and egotism about a great deal of advertising which absolutely removes it from the class of the sincere and natural.

To this sometimes is added effrontery. It need not be necessary to go into detail, because any thoughtful reader can select for himself an advertisement which affronts and displeases by its tone, sometimes approaching vulgarity.

Now a vulgar person may imagine himself to be very forceful and dominating, but his exit is usually followed by a shrug of the shoulders and a deprecating smile. They do not carry conviction. And the same with advertisements of this kind. To avoid this seems like a very simple matter, indeed, but this simplicity is what makes it difficult of achievement, because it hardly seems worthwhile being natural and sincere, when so much stress and importance are placed upon the "brilliant," and the unusual—the bizarre in advertising.

Now, if the reader agrees with this premise, let us go along a little further into deduction.

First of all, let us induce in the advertiser, if we can, a sensible, frank, thoughtful mood. He has a story to tell about his product. He believes in it. If he thinks it is somewhat better than another, or than the general run, there must be a reason for this beyond the mere idea that "the wish is father to the thought."

A lot of us wish that we were brilliant, and wonderful, and leaders of men, and that, being manufacturers, our products were unequaled in their character and value, of great use to the world and something to be proud of. But there must be something more than wishing. There must be reasons—real ones.

This is not a plea for "reason why" copy in advertising. By "reason why" copy we mean the argumentative, explanatory style of advertising which begins at the beginning and after a considerable period, winds up at the end.

There is a time and a place for the "reason why" of advertising. The public will not stand a whole lot of it, as a rule, because they have their "ups and downs" and their own affairs, and they are not to be intrigued by a long dissertation written from the standpoint of the manufacturer.

When an article is of sufficient importance and its *differentness* is easily understood or explained, "reason why" occasionally is good.

But *reason why in the product itself* is really necessary to success.

Now, having obtained, if possible, the frank, unbiased opinion and explanation of the manufacturer, we endeavor to see wherein lie the points of contact between his ideas, his product, and the public's needs, inclinations and prejudices.

Dig Out "The Story"

Years ago, I had experience as City Editor of a large newspaper. One of the questions we usually asked the reporter who brought in an account of any happening was: "What's story?" This meant—what was the highlight of the thing—the dominating feature of it—the most unusual or interesting thing about it? Which section or part of the story had the most interesting points of contact with the public?

If there was a fire in a three-story house—and $500 loss, this was worth three or four lines, but if a woman threw a feather bed out of the third-story window and then carefully lowered her little children out onto the bed, saving their lives, this exhibition of maternal thought and height to which the mother spirit could rise, would be worth half a column. In this case, the fire was not the story—it was the mother's action.

Back of the career of almost every manufacturer there is a warm, vital story of achievement which, while not always of interest to the public, still colors and vitalizes his work.

To find these highlights—"to get out the story"—is the biggest thing that an advertising copy writer can do—and then to present it in a sincere, natural way, making it interesting, giving it variety of presentation, if possible, without abandoning the main theme, and avoiding all the insincerities.

In other words, cutting the cloth to the proper measure and having a pattern suited to the subject, with thorough care in every detail.

Under "detail" we must consider art in advertising—that is, the picturizing of the product, its use, its application to the individual or the family, or the sense of satisfaction that comes from its use. A pipe and a tin of tobacco on a brass plate mean very little, but there are a hundred ways of vitalizing this subject, as will be seen at a glance in any magazine or newspaper.

See how the hosiery advertisers have conveyed the thought of lasting quality of hose, good fit, fine appearance, social correctness, high value, and other qualities, by the use of pictures.

On the other hand, pictures are frequently carried to the extreme. There is a mad riot of color in some of the magazines, and certain advertisers seem to have entered into a kind of vaudeville competition for the entertainment of readers, in which more or less eccentric art work plays a large part, to a great extent dimming the luster of the product and the convincingness of the advertising itself. We often hear that these things are successful, and yet the greater successes are achieved in other ways.

The advertising beginner, or even the old hand, must not be misled by stories which find currency in advertising circles, relative to the success of this or that company or product. The bank balance, the dividend record, the price (if listed) on the New York Stock Exchange, frequently tell more than fantastic stories of success achieved by circusing or methods somewhat akin.

The Merchandising Tie-Up

Of course, in all this, what is known as merchandising, the tying up of the effort of the advertiser, his salesman, the jobber, and the retailer, in one unbroken line—to reach and influence the public—plays a large part. Advertising cast like bread upon the waters may return, but along with advertising today should really go the motive power of good selling methods. Advertising is used not only to influence the consumer but to influence the "trade," beginning with the advertiser's own organization.

There are various ways of doing this, and too many of them have fallen into the rubber-stamp class.

What will be proper and right and helpful for one manufacturer might fall far short with another.

It is dangerous to assume that all house organs, and all "follow ups," all circularizing matter, all sales conventions, all direct-mail efforts, will get results of equal value. Some of them reap a harvest of money, and others over-emphasize one side or the other in a way which is likely to "rock the boat."

Here, too, being sincere and natural with one's own salesmen, organization, and retailers, is wise. Don't try to hand "bunk" to the salesman. That's the way they put it. An ounce of horse sense will get more genuine enthusiasm out of a salesman than any quantity of theoretical "hot air."

Is Advertising "Salesmanship in Print"?

In a chapter of this kind, it is not possible to touch properly upon the relationship of selling-effort to advertising-effort, but right here I should like to nail one glaring misconception and that is that "advertising is salesmanship in print."

To be sure, the object of advertising is to sell goods, but it cannot replace the salesmanship which must take place in the shop or in the meeting of the salesman with the jobber or the retailer.

It is not salesmanship in this sense, at all. It is more education, enlightenment and—above all things—suggestion.

The chief reason that advertising cannot be "salesmanship in print" is that a salesman or a retailer can sense quickly the unresponsiveness or prejudices of a potential customer. He can answer questions, avoid issues or close them. He can be extremely specific. As an advertisement must be all things to all men, it must be suggestional rather than argumentative, more often than not. It cannot attempt to answer questions, because it would become interminably involved.

The "salesmanship in print" kind of advertising pretty often is the sort that will pass muster among an advertiser's employees who are invited to judge of its merits. Written with an eye to the home office viewpoint, this sort of copy usually gets by a jury, but the fact remains, none the less, that the real jury in the case is the consumer.

Another reason why it is sometimes a doubtful expedient to call upon employees for judgment on an advertisement, is that immediately upon being asked for advice or criticism, the average man or woman becomes *unnatural or insincere*. If it were decided to obtain, *before printing* a thing, real substantial expression of the *reaction* of the advertisement on the average run of individuals, it might be excellent. But spontaneity immediately dies when criticism is called into conscious functioning.

Some members of the impromptu jury are bound to endeavor to find out what the predilection of the "boss" may be, and in more or less hit-or-miss fashion try to approximate this.

Others become unnatural, seeking out all sorts of details which would in no wise affect them as advertisers, or readers, or possibly purchasers of this or that similar line of goods.

Therefore, the advertising writer or counselor, either in the beginning or well along in his or her career, cannot afford to be swayed too much by the judgment of those called into council, who are not equipped by advertising experience and knowledge of advertising and the proper judgment.

This advertising judgment is built up likewise by long experience, observations; by study, investigation, practice. It becomes a sixth sense and cannot be achieved quickly by textbooks, by amateur incursions into advertising, or by the re-hashing of second-hand opinions.

When business men become imbued with the knowledge that advertising is a serious matter because it is a factor of such tremendous strength, they will give it the right attention; and then advertising counselors will receive the same measure of respect and confidence which (as far as they personally deserve it) is bestowed upon physicians, lawyers and others who specialize by study and practice in any definite form of service.

Something about "Style in Advertising"

Style in advertising is a much discussed subject. I have tried to point out that style should be natural and sincere.

There are two great divisions of advertising in which two distinctive styles are necessary—retail advertisements which are largely the announcements of stores and which, to some extent, depend upon the bargain inducement; and general advertising, which aims to develop new habits of living—personal and household—on the part of the readers.

This sort of advertising has exerted a tremendous influence upon life in America, even more than it has in other countries. The modern home today largely owes its development to advertising, which has instilled into homekeepers the desire for mechanical, electrical and other improvements in the home, and has raised the standards until all, irrespective of social class, live on a better plane than the very best families lived thirty or forty years ago.

Any advertising writer who forgets this big fact is overlooking the chief reason for the success of modern advertising.

The people of this country desire to live better and they put their *wish* into *work*, in order that they may earn more, which again means that they may spend more, and so the ascending spiral goes.

Any suggestion looking to the cutting down of comfort, even of certain luxuries, would be a backward step in American development.

Here, then, is another point worth remembering—in writing advertising copy, have in mind an audience that lives better than it did five years ago and is likely to live still better five years hence; that is learning every day; and is, consequently, not to be patronized, but, rather, informed.

On the question of style, further, it must be remembered that advertising written for an exclusively feminine audience must have quite a different tone from that which reaches men, or even the general family. Certain phrases are characteristic of the description of women's garments, women's articles of luxury, of the toilet, and the impedimenta dear to the feminine heart.

The only way this phraseology can be attained properly is by a study of similar advertising, or, better still, by frequent interviews with those properly equipped to explain the ins and outs and to talk in the current language of the women's shops or departments. It is not necessary that women writers should handle this, because there are men who know exactly the way to phrase a story or to follow it up in order to obtain the right results.

But the right style appeals to women, and fashion and vogue have much greater sway over them than substantiality and long wear.

The "Urge" in Advertising

In all discussions of advertising style, the so-called "urge" must be considered.

There are two ways of expressing urge—one is to argue strongly with the reader—"tell it to the dealer"; another finds expression in the last few lines of the advertisements, wherein the advisability of doing this, that, or the other thing *today is* magnified.

Read the average magazine or newspaper—especially the former—and see for yourself how much time you would have left for other things, if you did everything "today," "now," "immediately," "before you forget it"—which you are urged to do by the impatient advertiser. It is advertising treason, almost, to leave off the "urge." Yet in a world of urges, one is apt to take one's time and pay no attention to the clarion calls.

As to these urges on the dealer, suppose you try one of them yourself on the dealer, providing you are not a man of family and have no care for what is likely to happen to you. Just imagine yourself going to a dealer and saying: "Mr. Dealer, I want Blank's (here insert jam, sugar, hammers, chocolates, oatmeal, griddlecake flour, patent fasteners, or any of the thousand and one things you see advertised). I will not be satisfied with a substitute. I want the only, genuine Blank's. All I need do is to say—'Blank's'—and you will see that I am a discriminating man or woman. You are not doing justice to yourself or me if you do not keep this article in stock. I insist upon it," etc., etc.

Before you follow the advice in some of the advertisements, however, practice this speech, or parts of it, that are urged upon you, on your own family. If this proceeding does call into question your sanity, then try it on the dealer, if you will.

Here, indeed, is the acme of the insincere and unnatural in advertising, and so far as style goes, the less of it used, the better.

Where to Put the Advertising Urge

Good advertising will put the urge into the prospective buyer's mind rather than merely give it utterance in the language of the advertiser. The best style technique is the telling of a true story attractively and in terms of the reader's understanding and sympathy, and in being sincere rather than smart; consistent rather than clever.

Furthermore, the use of more verbs in advertising and of fewer adjectives and nouns would be a blessing. Let advertising represent action from the reader's viewpoint rather than adulation from the advertiser's.

Remember that generalities are cheap and can be picked up with no effort. It is the specific that calls for digging and is hardest to obtain.

Remember that no advertisement can be properly written unless the man who writes it has a real interest in writing it—the pride of creation, the pride of service, or the pride of knowledge.

He should be inclined towards advertising work, or he will never be successful; he should be glad to render service which is helpful not only to the advertiser, but to the purchaser of the article. Advertising based on selling insecure securities, harmful patent medicines, or other things that would establish loss or bad habits, cannot properly inspire any man.

Service, therefore, upon which the progress of life really depends, should be the expression of the advertising writer's inspiration.

Then comes knowledge—knowledge of the product, knowledge of the men back of it, knowledge of the object of the campaign, knowledge of all the factors that enter into production and distribution; knowledge of the article in its various forms of use and its effect on the public welfare.

If it be an article that renders service, inspiration, helps to make life better—all the better, for it makes for clearer and more inspired advertising. Then there must be knowledge of the people as a whole—of the great public mind wherein rests the final verdict of success or failure for any advertising campaign.

Knowledge, too, of the tools of the worker—the language, the type, the pictures, if they be used. Upon these fundamentals depends what the advertising may achieve.

The Individual Requirements

Having begun work with some knowledge and understanding of the things to forget and the things to remember, the success of the individual advertisement writer will depend upon his own power of understanding and assimilation. Some are more gifted than others, and so with even the same details for a working basis, they will achieve better results.

The advertisement writer who for inspiration confines himself largely to the perusal of works on advertising, or of advertising journals, will fall short. Advertising today competes with the best writing—not the most fanciful but the *best* writing.

Given naturalness and sincerity, a wide acquaintance with the various methods of presenting facts or conclusions is a necessary corollary.

The broadening of vocabulary is an excellent thing, not because this means that the advertisement writer should use big words, but that he should use the *right* words. An advertisement should be a mosaic of properly fitted pieces, not a thrown-together thing filled in by the plaster of phraseology.

Broad reading is necessary to the accomplishment of right phraseology. Advertising plays an important part in life, and a knowledge of life, of character, of the various reactions of events upon character and peoples, is of great value.

Giving Advertising Copy a Pleasant "Tone"

Pleasant, cheerful, sympathetic advertising can be sincere and natural, and yet too many writers mistake harshness for sincerity.

A man can be a gentleman and still be honest; and an advertisement can be kindly, friendly, and still sincere and truthful.

Through inexperience, ill-equipped writers too often mistake blatancy for force.

Refinement in writing and expression can be appreciated and understood by the uneducated as well as by holders of college degrees. The time is coming when advertising must meet a higher standard—when brag and bluster in the presentation of professional claims will be discounted as they should be.

A doctor is not a better doctor because he publishes broadcast his cures. It takes years of effort to build up his reputation. There are quack doctors in advertising as well as in medicine—sometimes individuals, sometimes organizations. As business men acquire knowledge of the potentialities of advertising and its effect on the public, there will be a more determined effort to obtain worth-while advertising truly representative of the co-partnership between the various classes in the making of American life.

Miss Flora Klickman—editor of one of the largest and most successful women's publications in England—says in her recent book—The *Lure of the Pen:*

The sounds produced by people are invariably a direct indication of the degree of their refinement—the greater the blare and clamor attendant upon their doings, and the more harsh and uncultivated their speaking voices, the less their innate refinements. . . . Unfortunately, the twentieth century, so far, has been primarily concerned with the making of noise rather than music.

Advertising Is a Reflex of Life

There is much "jazz" in advertising today. Some of it screams forth raucously. Advertising that gets away from this and presents its ideas and claims in a pleasing, interesting, and, if possible, sympathetic way, will most quickly achieve. The copy writer should endeavor to get this spirit into the idea back of the advertising—the soul of it, so to speak—as well as into the words that clothe it.

Remember, too, that in advertising, as in literature, and, in fact, in life itself, there must be a beginning, a development and a climax.

Some things, therefore, to avoid in advertising, are—putting too much force and "buying urge" into the opening paragraphs, too little information in the development, and little, if any, conclusive inspiration at the end. Advertisements, indeed, should be assembled as well as written. They should be gathered together in their component parts, and all the arguments, reasons and appeals weighed and considered; then the best for the space and purpose carefully coordinated and set forth.

In the words of a well-known critic: "Hard writing makes easy reading."

Chapter 8

The Research Basis of Copy

By J. George Frederick[1]

From the very first modernization of advertising copy—in the work, for instance, of Mr. Powers at John Wanamaker's in the nineties— information was the keynote. The reputation of Wanamaker advertising, made conspicuous by its proved selling power, was a reputation for telling people the facts. The Wanamaker advertising was a rich education in the lore of merchandise, and the people liked it, because of Mr. Powers' journalistic genius. For it was actual journalistic genius; the genius of re- porting, of a "nose for news" and of making facts interesting. Mr. Powers was not an advertising genius in the sense of being a brilliant salesman or merchandiser, *per se*. He was an advertising genius in the sense that he demonstrated the selling power of information, as against mere clever plays upon words; and it is no distortion of history to say that Mr. Powers was probably the first modern advertising man. His work created the American department store era, and indirectly he inaugurated also a new era of advertising copy in all lines of business.

---

1. *J. George Frederick.* Born 1882; was reporter on a newspaper, became department store advertising man and wrote articles on advertising for *Printers' Ink.* Went west to become a member of the Lord & Thomas staff during "reason why" propaganda, and edited magazine *Judicious Advertising.* Came to New York, joined Ben Hampton Agency and later was copy chief for Ward & Gow, subway advertising.

He then became managing editor of *Printers' Ink,* when George P. Rowell sold the magazine and the new owners began to develop it. In 1910 he resigned to form the Business Bourse, International, a commercial research organization, of which he is still the head. For several years, he was editor in chief of *Advertising and Selling Magazine.* He is author of five business books, and many articles in *Saturday Evening Post, Review of Reviews,* etc.; and is prominent in the New York Sales-managers' Club, New York Advertising Club, Commercial Standards Council, etc.

This new conception of copy had probably its severest test and most monumental triumph when it was applied to the mail-order field, for Richard Sears, founder of Sears, Roebuck & Co., carried Mr. Powers' idea to its logical conclusion and built a great institution, which many others have successfully emulated. None of these has ever departed, nor likely will, from the principle that mail-order buyers tend strongly to "sell themselves" if you give them a logically complete battery of information. A good mail-order catalog is a veritable encyclopedia of facts about the goods it advertises. The more information, apparently, the better the returns from mail-order copy.

The building of advertising copy on information advanced into new developments as years went on and as the advertising men gave more and more conscientious attention to all the circumstances and conditions upon which the success of advertising depends. Newspaper, magazine, street-car, poster advertising, to stimulate sales through dealers, had to contend with all the loose links which occur in the chain from manufacturer to consumer; had to contend with distribution and sales organization conditions, questions of package, of prices, competition, sectional differences, dealer states of mind, consumer conditions. These matters require research for finer fractional adjustment to the market and sure success.

The writer of advertising copy has, therefore, gone through a cycle of development in relation to his data requirements before dipping his pen in ink. Once he sought merely to devise adjectives describing the goods, or concoct catch phrases. Then he sought to individualize the goods by specific differences; and later again he sought to attach to it the atmosphere of quality, and used subtle, indirect methods.

Finally an entirely new phase arrived—a merchandising phase—forced upon the attention of advertising men by the failures of many purely general publicity campaigns, or by the brilliant successes of more practical, skilful merchandisers who wrote their copy from a completely new angle—the selling plan. These merchandisers focused the advertising on a coupon; they turned periodical advertising into a mail-order and distribution-making tool; they stressed a new sampling or trial plan, a new sales plan for eliminating sales resistance in the reader's mind. They made a working tandem of the sales force and the advertising; in short, they virtually made advertising a sales management, field operation, instead of the rather cloistered semi-literary performance it had been.

Once more, therefore, the advertising man changed character—he had to become more of a merchandising man, with sales-management vision and genius. It took ten years to shake out of the advertising field the predominance of mere "word-slingers," the men without business capacity. Advertising men of today are better business men, because the merchandising development in advertising compelled it. More advertising men are in consequence graduating to positions of sales-manager and higher up.

To advertise an article in a terrifically competitive field, in a complicated distribution situation, such as generally exists today, is no task for mere literary facility. The copy must be the apex of a solid base of merchandising plan, and it must be consciously written to aid that plan. It must be tailored to fit the campaign. It is for this reason that criticism of advertisements is conceded to be almost impossible without full knowledge of all the facts regarding the campaign and its aims and strategies. Like the iceberg, the visible part of the advertisement is but a small part of the real thing, and the visible part may look very unbalanced to the superficial critic until he sees the whole iceberg— the trade condition, the competitive, the consumer and the strategic situations. It is an absolutely naive point of view to judge advertising as one would judge a story or a poem.

Conceding, then, the modern need and use of research, before writing advertising, what are the angles of research used, the type of data which a fully modern advertising writer uses?

Data Questions for Advertisers

The need for copy data starts with the first contact with the advertiser and is best exemplified in this preliminary stage by a system of questions for the advertiser to answer. The following series of questions represents perhaps a more elaborate set of data than may be needed in the average case, but it has the merit of being inclusive. It is, of course, for general advertisers, and is most useful for advertising agencies, who can keep it on file systematically to enable different copy writers to have ready access to it.

Nature of business.
Proposition you wish to push (give details as fully as possible).
Description (if some specific article, describe fully).
How long has article been on the market?

How, when and where did the marketing of this product start? How put up?

Do you sell the wholesaler? When does he buy?

In what quantity?

Prices and discounts to wholesalers.

Do you sell retailers direct? In what quantity? When does retailer buy?

Prices and discounts to retailer.

Do you sell consumer direct? In what quantity? When does consumer buy?

Prices and discounts to consumer?

Do you sell through canvassers?

How do you secure them?

When does canvasser buy?

In what quantity?

Prices and discounts to canvassers?

Do you grant exclusive territory? (If so, give details.)

Do you cooperate in pushing the sale of your goods? (Describe in detail just what you do for wholesaler, retailer, or canvasser.)

Do you employ traveling salesmen? How many? On whom do your salesmen call? Give territory goods sell in? Give sources from which inquiries emanate? How many inquiries do you receive a year? What percentage order your goods? What season is best for your business? After you get an inquiry, how do you handle it?

Have you ever put out a systematic Direct Advertising Campaign?

How was it handled and of what did it consist? (Give complete details— nature of pieces and the returns in inquiries and orders.)

Do you issue a catalog?

How many times do you follow up an inquiry by mail?

How many letters do you send a prospect? How many circulars?

What postage, one or two cent stamp?

Is article to be advertised Trade Marked? (If so, attach print of Trade Mark.)

How is Trade Mark shown on article? Is Trade Mark registered?

Are any special inducements or concessions made to wholesaler, retailer, consumer or canvasser? If any, describe them.

Do you give free trial to consumer? What are conditions of free trial? Do you offer samples? If so, how are they distributed?

What competition have you?

Give total annual sales during the past five years.

How much may present sales be increased without interfering with your present manufacturing facilities?

What goods do you manufacture besides those to be directly advertised?

Are they marketed through the same channel as those about to be advertised?

What other lines can be added to advantage?

By what method do you keep record of inquiries, sales, etc., resulting from your advertising?

What mailing lists have you on hand now? How new are they?

How are they obtained?

How many names do they contain, and what classifications?

What facilities have you for handling the detail work of an advertising campaign, such as office devices, help, etc.?

What advertising literature have you on hand at present? About what amount would you appropriate for a campaign?

What previous advertising has been done, and average cost per year?

What class of media were used?

What has been the average cost per inquiry? What has been the average cost per sale? What is the amount of your average sale? What is your margin of profit?

What has been the sales history of the product?

(a) with regard to selling plan;

(b) with regard to road men;

(c) with regard to direct selling;

(d) with regard to retail outlets and dealer and jobber policy;

(e) with regard to schemes and special plans;

(f) with regard to analysis of market, class of people, profit, etc.;

(g) with regard to territorial work.

What has been the advertising history of the product?

(a) with regard to the appropriation spent;

(b) with regard to media used;

(c) with regard to agency service;

(d) with regard to copy: type of appeal;

(e) with regard to cooperation with sales department;

(f) with regard to follow-up work;

(g) with regard to direct-mail work;

(h) with regard to local advertising by dealers;

(i) with regard to sampling;

(j) with regard to the trade mark and the package.

Just what is the present situation with respect to the above outlined facts?

What are the main factors which limit your market?

In what direction is your product of your organization weak?

Where and under what conditions—

Have you found it easiest to sell?

What class of people are the quickest buyers?

What excuse do dealers give for not stocking up?

What is your policy in respect to—

(a) price maintenance;

(b) quantity discounts;

(c) dealers' and jobbers' profits;

(d) guarantee;

and (e) mail-order selling?

Competitors—

(a) how strong; volume and activity;

(b) names and brief history of competitors and of class of goods in general;

(c) price in comparison with competitors.

What is the volume of business done and margin of profit?

What are the manufacturing conditions?

(a) capacity of production;

(b) season variations;

(c) by-products;

(d) ratio of costs to increased volume.

How fully stocked are dealers at present?

What grade men are on the sales force?

What is the exact present status of distribution; how many dealers and where located?

What follow-up literature do you now send out?

After a full line of information about the advertiser is available, the advertising man is ready to raise the following questions about the proposition and answer them, or set about answering them by further research:

(1) What kinds and types of people purchase goods?

(2) What individual influences them or has joint authority or activity in making the purchase?

(3) What are the habits of mind and general conditions surrounding the purchaser?

(4) What is the exact need which the consumer feels, how does it arise, and what instinct, needs, desires and feelings does the article satisfy?

(5) What preconceived ideas, prejudices and notions does the consumer bring to the purchase of the articles?

(6) What are typical past experiences of consumers in endeavoring to purchase such articles?

(7) What are the shopping or purchasing habits or modes of procedure of the average consumer?

(8) What impression, reputation and general standing of brands prevail in the buyer's mind?

(9) What standards in the matter of price and quality and service prevail in the mind of the consumer?

(10) Analysis of consumer preferences for sizes, marking, types and models, etc.

(11) Statistical study of consumer, from a quantitative basis, giving facts as to number, distribution, location and concentration of consumers.

(12) Inquiry into possible manner and means of developing applications or uses of article.

Ten Tests of an Advertisement

Both before and after completing advertisements, it is a most valuable thing to apply critical estimates. I am setting down herewith a suggested series of tests to be applied to copy as a means of checking back whether it squares with the very high modern standard. These tests are by no means complete or inclusive, but as very few others have been compiled, these will stand for my own conception of such a test:

(1) What was the advertisement planned to accomplish? What were the results?

(2) Has the copy man thoroughly grasped the editorial character, the limitations and opportunities, both from the standpoint of the publication readers and also the typography, space, position, etc., of the periodical in which the advertisement in question is to appear?

(3) Has the copy man thoroughly visualized the general mass mind to which he is appealing, and has he figured out what the mass reaction will be toward the article in question, the distributive situation which

stands between the advertisement and the reader, the particular hold which the publication has upon that reader, the mood it finds him in, and the temper and tone and language of the advertisement?

(4) Has the general level of literacy of the mass of readers, in relation to the copy, the illustration and the typography been carefully planned to fit the kind of people whom the advertiser desires most of all to reach?

(5) Has the copy writer studied and balanced and rotated suitably the fundamental consumer appeals inherent in the particular article in hand?

(6) Have the advertisements been laid out with the right tone and atmosphere for the article?

(7) Has the series of advertisements been carefully coordinated one with the other, in relation to the proper importance to be given to all considerations?

(8) Has the relative display position of the headline and outstanding features been calculated so that the large percentage of readers who merely glance through a magazine may catch something as they run which will be of value and may lead to either arrest of attention or the fixation of a name or an idea?

(9) Does the close of the advertisement give all the necessary facts and stimulate thought to get the reader to do what you finally wish him to do upon finishing the ad?

(10) Has each single advertisement been constructed upon the basis of *unity of effect,* both typographically and from the point of view of content—its ideas and logic? Has the copy the right "ring"? Is the English used checked over for double meanings, confusion, error, etc.?

Finally, has the copy been checked by the proper authorities, O.K.'d by them, and have all necessary corrections and instructions been provided for it?

Shaping the Product for Good Copy

There's a considerable difference between merely a "product" and a thoroughly *merchandisable* product. Millions of dollars are sunk annually on this rock, and it is well to hang a red lantern on it. Many articles now on the market—even fairly successful ones—are suffering handicaps through package, price, size, or other purely manufacturing errors. There are hundreds of thousands of patents, of course, in the archives at Washington representing "products" of one kind and another which will never be known outside of these archives. They are unmerchandisable; they are not commercially adapted to the market. Some could readily be thus adapted; others could never be.

It is the relation a product bears to a present or possible market that fixes its value; and as a sales product is a thing that is usually alterable and flexible in some degree, there is a great deal of profitable thinking and planning to be done on products either new or already on the market. This is often to a large degree an advertising man's task quite as much as a sales manager's. There are many instances of products which have had high sales resistance, but when changes in the product were made, based on copy and market analysis, the resistance greatly lessened.

Let us take first the case of an entirely new product. It comes often fresh as a new-born babe from someone's hands. It should be viewed chiefly as raw material and a starting point for development. People often wonder why it is axiomatic that the inventor or originator rarely makes a success of his project. Someone else so often makes the thing a success after taking it over. The explanation is simple: the inventor or originator nearly always has an emotional faith and pride in the exact rightness, *"as is,"* of his article, whereas the subsequent purchaser cares nothing if the reshaped product bears almost no resemblance to the original, so long as it *does lit the market and sell.* The inventor or originator does not perform a complete job—he originates only a material thing, whereas the *complete* creation of a merchandisable product must be material or mechanical and must possess the following:

(1) average adaptability,
(2) wide marketability,
(3) compactness, neatness, attractiveness,
(4) psychological appeal,
(5) popular or fitting price,
and (6) individuality.

It will, therefore, be seen that the advertising man of the modern type examines the article to be advertised, from the above points of view. Live advertisers apply inventive and market research quite as serious and important as the first work of the inventor. In fact, the modern idea—one of great significance in business teamwork—is combination research and technical work on a product, so that there will not be the frequent and wasteful lack of completeness in an article, from a marketing point of view. So much time is often lost by false starts, when this is neglected.

Such preliminary analysis, whether or not done by or through the advertising man, may very well be watched and studied by the modern copy man, who is, after all, the central genius in the work of successful advertising, if he functions on all four cylinders.

The research of the product should gather facts and reach conclusions on such factors as—

(1) Adaptability in cost, nature, operation and use, and general commercial availability.

(2) The usefulness, volume of possible sale, technical excellence or defects under average conditions of use and abuse.

(3) The devising of new models or materials to fit certain market conditions or opportunities.

(4) The reshaping and planning of an article or device to fit the commercial necessities and advisabilities, from the point of view of price, profit, class of users, public psychology, etc.

(5) The selection and study of a new article of manufacture desired, which will meet with equal success the suggestions of technical economy and feasibility as well as maximum sales and profit possibilities.

(6) A technical examination of all competitive goods and an analysis of competitive claims, and the working out in figures of the exact comparative standing of various brands or types of goods.

One of the practical methods of analyzing a product from the market side is to make a consumer investigation which will produce a cross-section of consumer attitude to the line of goods, and develop any defects, suggestions or opportunities. As an illustration, the "corset-buying history" of some thousands of women was taken in one investigation in order to learn why the women changed from one brand to another. The details of five separate corset purchases by each individual were recorded. When all the returns were in it was possible to see on what point each brand of corset had "fallen down" or "stood up," under consuming conditions.

Rating the "Appeals"

A similar plan was successfully used in a watch investigation to determine how the different makes of cheap watches fared in the hands and minds of purchasers. Such data revealed the weak points of all the articles in the market—a most important matter to be informed about in planning *the copy appeal;* that is, the effective arguments. A product, to a sales and advertising manager, is simply an aggregation of appeals, some strong, some less strong. The problem is to build up a product which has a maximum of powerful appeal for the particular field desired, *and to know the relative strength of each appeal the article has.* The average firm knows only in a rough way the relative strength of its appeals; why not analyze them accurately and fully?

The combinations following: usual range of appeals for a product is made up of

in various degrees of strength of about the

(1) Price;
(2) Utility;
(3) Convenience;
(4) Appearance;
(5) Service;
(6) Reliability;
(7) Recommendation;
(8) Taste;
(9) Economy of use;
(10) Prompt availability;
(11) Reputation and familiarity
(12) Advertising.

It has been proven over and over again that salesmen will select their own ideas of the strongest appeals, or insist that the appeal varies in strength according to the prospect he is talking to. They are often encouraged to do this; but it is also proven that there is always one fundamentally *strongest* appeal which is wisest to stress to practically all prospects, and through all salesmen and advertising. In other words, an analysis for any given product will show that certain appeals are supreme; that for a certain article appearance may be 60%; reliability 20% and recommendation 20%, and for another product the appeal may bear some other ratio.

It is, therefore, not theoretical, but highly practical to make a searching analysis of the appeals for a product, so that they can be rated accurately. It makes the sales manual more definite and valuable; it is of immense value and importance to the advertising manager and agent, and it permits the writing of copy that strikes far closer to the bull's eye in results.

The analysis should, of course, also be extended to the wrapping of an article—to the shape, size, color and general appearance of the article as it will look in the store. In many articles, notably toilet articles, this factor rates astonishingly high in sales value. It rates more than is suspected in almost all articles. The eye and the sense of touch are the mechanisms of the brain that must be affected, and if an adverse current of feeling is started by a product's appearance, even strong logic has little chance. A few years ago consumer research work was done on a talcum, disclosing the heretofore unsuspected truth that *odor* has by far the strongest appeal to women in any talc article. New advertising copy based on this appeal quickly expanded sales. Yet contrary opinions had been held by all who had anything to do with the article.

It is typical of most articles that a dozen broad claims are made for it, and that constant debate goes on between salesmen, executives and dealers as to which one has the most weight. The good copy analyst easily sees that this problem of the relative strength of these appeals is vital to his copy campaign, and that facts must be developed as to their precise strength, not in the client's mind, but in the consumer's mind. If sanitation, let us say, is 60% of the entire appeal in strength and power, he can intelligently plan his advertisement so that this strong appeal shall never be absent, but shall be related and associated to all the other appeals in such a balanced manner as will give them all their proper weight, as will cripple no single expensive advertisement by merely minor appeals, and as will provide a wise rotation of the appeals.

The particularly painstaking copy analyst will also make a further test, if his client will permit it. He will prepare a varied line of copy, and then with sets of proofs conduct a carefully guarded test upon consumers (so planned that their unconscious judgment and not their conscious judgment would be obtained). The truly best series of ads can thus be decided upon from such analysis. The judgment from a competent test of this kind will get 10 to 20% closer to actual fact than even the best judgment made purely on opinion.

It is generally supposed that the public is dormant and incapable of indicating its mind; but this is a poor conception both of the public and our modern measuring instruments. No other profession dealing with the human being is without its means of measuring reaction, and it is absurd in this day of highly developed laboratory psychology methods that reliable tests should not be obtained in advance of large expenditures of money for advertising, since without such tests the relative efficiency of an ad is a mere matter of opinion. There are a great many advertising campaigns which fail by reason of wrong copy; and there is not the slightest reason why preanalysis of this copy cannot to a large extent avert the mistakes before the expenditure is made. Nowadays space costs far too much money to experiment with and hold mere *"post mortems."* The results must be at least 70 or 80% sure in advance if we are to retain the name of being practical advertising men, and if the advertising profession is to rest upon very permanent bases. An engineer, building a longer bridge than was ever built before over a tremendously difficult river, is able to calculate within a reasonable percentage what will happen. All advertising, as well as all sales effort, is to a certain extent guessing, it may readily be admitted. Construction engineers admit the same thing. The thing to do is to reduce the ratio of guesswork to the total by every known means of obtaining exactness.

Analyzing Media

No advertising copy should be written without visualizing the medium in which it will appear. To fail in this is to talk sporting-page language to an audience of nursing mothers. Especially is this true today, when periodicals have particularly distinct personalities of their own and special followings.

The plan of campaign in which the medium plays a part is the first thing to be studied. This goes back to the very core of the campaign object and goal, which, as every good advertising man knows, is often a psycho-logic or strategic goal. This is illustrated in the tremendous volume of advertising which a certain well-known weekly carries, mainly because it has become a commonplace thing to use this medium "for dealer effect" and similar strategic reasons.

In spite of fulmination about "waste circulation," "duplication," etc., as used by some advertisers, many such purchases are undoubtedly justifiable and profitable, from a strategic point of view. The broader a campaign policy is, the more sure it is to mean a three-, five- or ten-year policy consistently adhered to, in which media are considered coolly and fundamentally and copy planned an adequate time in advance.

There is a very considerable temptation in purchasing advertising to be an opportunist rather than to operate on principle. There are so many enticing ideas sprung, so many space bargains peddled, and so many last minute offers of exceptional position; there is such a welter of ups and downs in business and changes of personnel and policy, that advertising plans are buffeted about far too frequently for sound economy. The objective changes too often; the appropriation is inflated and deflated too frequently, and there is no clear picture of the advertising plan as a whole. Advertising—it cannot be too often and too insistently repeated—suffers when it is handled by opportunists. Advertising is a deeply submerged principle operating upon the unconscious of the public, slow-moving but powerful as the tides. You cannot successfully toy or juggle with so deep-seated a principle.

The strategy of the effective use of media, coordinating with a strategy of sales over a long period, must calculate upon long-continued, educational and reiterative steps and a desire to build solidly and safely. Like everything else that is orderly, it must have a logical beginning, middle and end. A program of advertising should have its try-out, preliminary and long-pull stages; it is sound to use media in a preliminary period for certain strategic elements of purpose; to use other media in the middle of the long, full campaign for the hard constant labor of education, and to use other media or new media at the close of the campaign for the logical last wallop and special drive. It is logical, in absolute necessity, to trim sails with an eye to the strategy of a breathing spell in expenditure; using certain media to create a greater impression of activity than the facts warrant.

The temptation to be a mere bell-wether is very strong in the use of advertising media. Because one sees competitors and others using a certain list of media is far from assurance that such a list is best. It is appalling how much advertising is written because competitors and others are "doing the same." Many of the best successes in advertising have been made by men whose attitude toward media was courageous and based on far-seeing policies and clear analysis. Their idea of media was individual and correlated to their own thinking. Wrigley, of Spearmint fame: Post, of Postum Cereal and others built on this principle. The advertiser who "follows along" is the good medium's worst enemy, because he cannot be appealed to; he is operating upon an imitative instinct which is beyond the reach of reason and he cannot be shaken loose. Only when he begins to think does he become different, and the many excellent media which are not getting from advertisers the attention they deserve could not hope for anything more blessed than a greater realization of this fundamental principle in medium selection. We would then see some of the super-inflated media lose their large and often not wholly deserved mass of advertising, and we would witness a more logical distribution based upon clear analysis of media.

It is wearisome—very especially so to a man who has been in the advertising business a long time, as I have—to hear over and over again each year the same old debates as to the relative merits of different types and classes of media. It is all the question of a merchandising situation, the strategy of the campaign and the type of article, state of distribution, etc. To one thoroughly versed in merchandising tactics it is not alone wearisome, but more or less dishonest to glorify or over-emphasize one type of media over another, because it indicates a woeful lack of study and analysis of the advertiser's problems.

The president of one of the most brilliant companies in the United States, a man who has raced up his sales in half a dozen years from half a million to fifteen million dollars annually, has as fixed and definite a policy regarding media as an engineer has measurements and rules of orientation. He made his success by working out a broad policy, selecting type of media adaptable to his strategic policy, and these media made his proposition successful. Many of his aping competitors do not today know anything about the general policy behind the campaign. The president of this company is a theorist on his subject—that of newspaper advertising on a zone basis—and his analysis and his method of linking up his advertising to his sales work have made him successful in his plans. He therefore dogmatizes about his plan. Yet still another large advertiser is equally dogmatic about his success, which was won entirely on magazine advertising. Both are in the same field with virtually the same problems. It must thus be seen that advertisers do not sit down to "analyze media"— they sit down to make policies work and to make their sales campaigns a success. The medium is only a tool in the general kit of tools, and they use the medium because it fits the job as they lay it out.

Imagine a broad executive working out his campaign in consultation with an advertising man. What might be said to be the line of questions that would come out? They might be somewhat as follows:

(1) What publication or group of publications have as their audience the most interested readers, in the largest numbers, at the cheapest rate per line or per page per thousand, of the kind of people on whom I am trying to produce an effect?

(2) What publication or group of publications, by means of the type or size or frequency of the copy I intend to use and of the proposition I have to make, will exert the most influence upon my distributive and sales organization?

(3) What publication or group of publications, or kinds of media, might I use to achieve the necessary auxiliary campaign effects or side pressure or flank movement with which to fortify my general campaign and complete it?

(4) What publication or group of publications or media can provide me with the highest ratio of reader-value, based upon the peculiar strength, scope and nature of the editorial appeal?

(5) What media, publication or group of publications should I use, and for what period, to perform the preliminary, or psychological, or specialized part which I desire them to play?

(6) How may I be sure of getting my money's worth from them, and how shall I check up their claims?

(7) How may I so coordinate the work of my sales organization and my distributive organization with my use of such media so that the largest percentage of the readers of my ad may find my representatives, my jobbers and dealers on their toes and ready at the moment consumers' interest is highest?

And Finally, Strategy

Considered as the practical sales tool, advertising copy is the very heart and center of the particular sales strategy which is being operated by any concern. Advertising copy strategy is, therefore, sales strategy as well; often the chief expression of sale strategy by reason of its flexibility and wide application.

I cannot here give full details of advertising copy strategy, but would refer to my books "Modern Sales-management" and "Business Research and Statistics,"[2] wherein are discussed in full detail the matters of merchandising strategy and the research data on which they are erected.

There are a dozen or more principal lines of sales strategy, and these can be listed as follows:

---

2. *Modern Salesmanagement,* by J. George Frederick, D. Appleton & Co., New York, Chapter XIX. Also, *Business Research and Statistics,* by J. George Frederick, D. Appleton & Co.

(1) Strong direct action: a frontal attack, so to speak; a smashing use of space and forceful language; a direct grappling with the obstacles, a use of sheer power and punch. Useful when analysis shows that sheer force can do the job; costly and hurtful when the obstacles are not of the kind which will yield to force.

(2) Indirect effort: when opposing forces are too powerful or deep-lying for frontal attack, the situation requires attack "on the flanks"; it requires the line of copy or the appeal which will be an intermediate step to the desired goal.

(3) Secret action: this is merely a term for the kind of copy wherein one's real purpose is not evident; where the sales plan and purpose must be not alone indirect but unobserved; the real purpose being to secure an unconscious action.

(4) Complicated logical series: this is only a more intricate line of reasoning for indirect effort; a logical, planned series of "moves," as in chess, which will inevitably and necessarily lead to desired results.

(5) Confusing or "feint" moves: this is a rarer type of strategy which in a legitimate way aims to divert attention from weaker points while remedying them; or to shift the emphasis, or to hide from competitors situations which might be taken advantage of.

(6) Wedge action: this is a method of applying force to get results—a method comparable to the lever and the fulcrum, or well-known football formations. Concentration on Uneeda Biscuit advertising put over the entire "N B C" line, when it was not likely that equally distributed advertising could do so.

(7) Defensive action: copy aimed to build up strength to resist attack; to ward off competitive criticism or unfavorable events or trends.

(8) Educational strategy: a long pull or short pull effort to implant information; to alter a state of mind or change habits.

(9) Time annihilation strategy: a special and delicate technique of copy which aims to accomplish very rapidly what ordinarily requires considerable time.

(10) Distribution strategy: copy preparation with the main objective of influencing dealers, securing distribution or otherwise using it as a tool in achieving desirable ends in distribution problems.

(11) Good-will strategy: "institutional copy" is a name sometimes applied; but the varieties vary. The purpose is always the same—primarily to make the name, the house and the article better known.

(12) Domination strategy: this is often sound strategy in advertising— to *"maintain* the lead" either by weight of volume of advertising; by size

of advertisements, by new developments featured, or by sheer superiority of quality in advertising copy.

(13) "Caveat" strategy: a significant plan of advertising early a new article or invention, especially when competition on an equal basis is likely or possible; thus "filing a caveat with the public" on the theory that the public gives credit to the originator and first advertiser.

(14) Quality strategy: the specific all-pervading aim being to imbue the public with the feeling and instinctive impression of the high quality of the merchandise. This is subtle copy preparation, calling for the full range of the arts of copy preparation and advertising layout.

(15) Inquiry strategy: focusing all the power of the ad upon the matter of securing a reply. This may be as much the aim of the advertiser selling through jobbers and dealers, as that of a mail-order house, the "pull" being possible by various means such as coupon, booklet, sample, prize scheme, etc.

(16) Economy strategy: it is sometimes necessary or advisable to appear to be maintaining a previous volume of advertising when the previous appropriation is not available; or a new advertiser with small appropriation may need strategic handling of space afforded, so as to give the impression of larger space.

For all of these strategic purposes, and for others not mentioned here, the use of research is valuable, for strategy is a thing which turns upon hairs, being, as the dictionary says, a use of finesse.

Chapter 9

Axioms of Advertising

By Joseph H. Appel[1]

Advertising is the "speech" of business. Advertising is to business what language is to man—its mode of self-expression.

A business that will not advertise is both deaf and dumb; and as heavily handicapped in the world's progress as a deaf and dumb man.

Back of speech is thought. Back of thought is mind. Back of mind is spirit. Back of business speech is the spirit of the business—its individuality. To express this individuality fairly and completely is the province of advertising.

Simple, direct, plain speech is most easily understood by the greatest number of people. Simple, direct, plain language makes the best advertising speech.

People talk mainly of two things; of themselves, of other people. Advertising that is saturated with human interest is bound to be most widely read.

The word "news," as reflected in our American newspapers, has come to mean "human interest." Newspapers tell the news of a community. Stores, being a community, must tell their own news in a human interest way.

To present the news of a community, newspapers send out reporters to gather the news first hand. To present the news of a store, the advertising bureau must send

---

1. *Joseph Herbert Appel.* Author and merchant. Born Lancaster, Pa., July 19, 1873; A.B., Franklin and Marshall College, 1892. Admitted to Lancaster County Bar, 1895; Philadelphia Bar, 1892. With Editorial Department *Philadelphia Times,* 1896–9; with John Wanamaker since 1899; director advertising and publicity Philadelphia Store until 1912; New York store since 1912; also general assistant to Rodman Wanamaker. Author: *My Own Story,* 1913; *Seeing America,* 1916; *Living the Creative Life,* 1918; *The Making of a Man,* 1921.

out its reporters to gather the store news first hand. First hand means at the source. The source of store news is the merchandise and the merchandise chief who buys it. Efficient advertising requires the writer's personal examination of the merchandise and the hearing of the "story" of its purchase directly from the lips of the buyer who secured the merchandise in the wholesale market. Every purchase has its story—tell that story.

Merchandise is dumb—until seen; then it speaks louder than words. To bring people into the store to see the merchandise—to speak for the merchandise until it can speak for itself—is the first step in advertising.

Advertising must be fair to the merchandise as well as to the people it invites into the store. Advertising must "square up" with the merchandise and with the store.

To "square up" with the merchandise and with the store, advertising must be accurate. To be accurate, advertising must be truthful.

Advertising is as honest as the man who signs his name to it. A store is as honest as its advertising.

Efficiency in advertising is impossible without honesty. But honesty is possible without efficiency. Waste in advertising is the natural result of dishonesty.

Honesty in business usually means life; dishonesty surely means death.

Honesty in advertising is not a question of comparative prices or comparative values. Honesty is never comparative nor relative. Honesty is absolute—it means telling and living the truth, the whole truth and nothing but the truth.

In advertising, as in everything else, the people are the Court of Last Resort. The people soon begin to discount the statements of a store that habitually exaggerates in its advertising.

Advertising cannot be made honest by means of law, any more than people can be made honest by law. Education only can make advertising and people honest. The most that laws can do is to safeguard people against fraudulent advertising.

Stores—and their advertising—reflect the morals, manners, customs, habits and desires of the community and of the age in which they live. The brazen, big-type, blatant, extravagant advertising is evidence that we are still in the pioneer stage of civilization. Lying advertising exists because people of this nature still exist in the world. Fawning advertising, anemic advertising exist because people of this nature still exist.

But the successful advertising of the present—and what will be the real advertising of the future—is the red-blooded, truthful, plain, simple, dignified, cultured, courteous, common-sense "human" advertising—because people with these attributes rule the world and make it progress.

Advertising is the creative force in business—the electric dynamo that keeps it going—it literally creates demand for the things of life that raise the standard of living, elevate the taste, changing luxuries into necessities.

Advertising is not to sell goods; it is to enable people intelligently and economically to buy goods.

Efficient advertising must take the customer's viewpoint. The advertiser is counselor for the public.

The only economic reason for advertising is to make more efficient the distribution of merchandise, reducing its cost, standardizing qualities and products and stabilizing prices.

Distribution—the distribution of wealth, of natural and manufactured products, of people, of property, of education—is the problem of the world today.

Advertising is the greatest aid to distribution yet discovered by man.

Advertising becomes a tax upon the people unless it aids distribution and lowers the cost of commodities.

Advertising, when efficient, does aid distribution and lowers the cost of commodities, because it becomes the million-tongue salesman making possible the multiple merchant, who reaches a million people with less cost and effort than the peddler or the cross-roads store—the father of the modern department store (so-called)—could reach one or a dozen people.

Advertising is, therefore, an investment because it is a service—service to the people.

In its final analysis, advertising is to serve the public; to give information that will help to satisfactory buying; to present the true character and personality of the store; to represent the store as it is—its merchandise, its service. In doing this, advertising becomes what the store is itself—a distinct economic aid to those who will use its service, an inspiration to those who will study its spirit, an education to those who will understand its message; a pioneer in art, in science, in merchandising, in civilization—a leader in human service.

The retailer is the natural advertiser. Direct to him come the people. Of him they ask questions. Of him they buy. Of him they demand a guaranty of satisfaction. The retailer is the only other party to the deal, and the people hold him responsible.

Retail advertising is born of the people, is for the people, and is used by the people more than any other advertising. Retail advertising is the people's guide in their every-day living. It reflects their daily needs and desires and supplies them. It is the people's market reports—to women, especially, it is what the stock market is to men.

The newspaper is the natural medium for advertising. Distribution of merchandise is most efficient when concentrated and cooperative, under freedom of competition, with just rewards to the most capable. Distribution is greatest where the three elements of a sale are densest— merchandise, people and money. Newspapers circulate in the densest centers of population, where are also congregated the largest stores with the greatest column of merchandise; they are, therefore, the most efficient media for all advertising.

The newspapers that are best for advertising are those that will sell merchandise; that are clean, reliable and fair; that have the largest circulation and the readers' interest developed; that are creative—constructive and not destructive; cheerful, not "knockers"; not blindly partisan; not overrun with advertisements; that stick to their jobs; that have a fair rate.

The prosperity of a community depends upon its retail business. Manufacturers can make, and farmers can grow, only as the merchant sells. And merchants can sell only as the people buy. When the people buy and the merchants sell—when money and merchandise are kept in motion— then the whole world is prosperous.

In the last analysis, all advertisers are merchants; all branches of advertising are merchants. Publishers of all kinds; advertising solicitors; advertising agents; organizers of big business; copy writers—all are merchants; they must sell the goods they advertise, and they must distribute them more economically than they could be distributed without advertising, or they are building on the shifting sands and their houses will go down in ruins.

If we ever reach the point of "diminishing returns" in advertising, then advertising will go to the junk pile. Advertising must be an asset to business, not an expense. Advertising must produce and not consume wealth.

Chapter 10

Copy First

By Kenneth M. Goode[1]

Imagine all the telephone wires you ever saw strung together along one giant set of poles. Picture these poles full of men solemnly burnishing those telephone wires, rubbing with pungent aromatic oils, polishing with chamois and sandpaper, chittering with joy when their highlights flash tiny glints of fire.

If you would still become a copy man—climb one of the poles and join us!

For there is nothing so absolutely unimportant as copy for copy's sake. Copy is only the telephone wire that carries the message: if only it carry the message clearly, swiftly, accurately, powerfully, the wire itself may be as rusty and bent as an old nail.

And so, I say, when you find yourself tempted to dash off a tricky string of winged words for publication at somebody's expense, or, what is worse, tempted to lecture somebody else on how to do it, just grab your manicure tools and join us among the telephone wires.

Not that copy isn't important! On the contrary, copy is the only thing that counts in advertising. Research develops facts that may help sell goods; but a hundred men in a hundred Fords, filling out questionnaires all day long, wouldn't of themselves sell enough goods to pay for their gasoline. Wise choosing of places to put advertising copy unquestionably enables that copy to sell more goods; but you could sit and choose media

---

1. *Kenneth M. Goode.* Advertising writer and editor. Formerly associate editor of *Saturday Evening Post* and of Hearst's *International.* Later advertising agency experience with firm of Goode & Berrien. Now with P. F. Collier & Sons, New York book-trade and mail-sales division. Has had the unusual experience of having been on both sides of the writing field—editing for large mass circulation and advertising to it.

until you were black in the face, and never move a boy's express wagon full of toy balloons. Mechanical departments help copy find favorable expression; but the most meticulously symmetrical piece of typography that ever lulled a roving eye will never turn a nickel, unless it eases home a message some real copy writer has cut and hammered until it means something very vital to every man who reads it.

Copy, in one form or other, is the heart and soul of advertising. Except as an aid to the preparation of copy, or to the extension of copy after it has been prepared, everything else is more or less meaningless. Much of the unnecessary complication in modern advertising thought is due to straying away from that one simple fundamental. If copy is good enough, it can succeed without a dollar spent on anything except white space to print it in; if copy is bad enough, the most elaborate merchandising and marketing plans will only pile up the possibilities of failure.

This blunt truth will, I fear, run athwart many able men whose generous conceptions of "advertising" have grown to embrace everything— from finding an architect for the factory to placing fair-haired boys behind the merchant's sales counters.

You may remember an old story of the man who proposed to trade his cow for his neighbor's bicycle: "I'd look fine, wouldn't I, trying to ride a cow?" was the ungracious answer. "Yes," returned the proposer, "but think how I would look trying to milk a bicycle."

Respectfully I commend this primitive form of reasoning to any who feel I unduly overestimate the importance of copy. On a pinch, you can easily imagine an advertising campaign—mail order, for example— simplified down to nothing but copy. But try to think of an advertising campaign without copy!

Or try, for instance, to imagine this week's issue of the *Saturday Evening Post* without any advertising copy, with all its great advertising pages, one after the other, showing blank white space.

Yet, with a pair of scissors in hand, I turned yesterday to the latest issue of the *Post,* and out of one advertisement, without touching a printed letter, cut in one piece $3,700 worth of blank space! I got $2,500 worth out of another, $2,000 out of another; and I could have filled a small waste-basket with solid unbroken strips of virgin white that different advertisers had bought at $1,000 or more apiece.

Then I turned back to Mr. Lorimer's able editorial page, and searched in vain for $100 worth of wasted space.

Entranced with the eagerness with which advertisers paid for white space they didn't use, I began counting words to find out, if I might, what the average advertiser paid per word of copy in the space he did decide to utilize. Try it for yourself. In the meantime, I may give you this much of a hint: If advertisers could hire famous writers at the regular rate they receive from editors, you might easily engage Booth Tarkington, George Ade, and Irvin S. Cobb—all three—to write your copy at a cost per word less than most advertisers pay per word to have it printed in a single advertisement.

If the advertiser paid for his copy by length, and the editor didn't, this economy in the use of words might be more easily understood. But it's just the other way round. Why, then, does the advertiser—who pays for his space and not his words—turn his space back into white paper, while the editor—who pays for his words and not his space—jams his space chuck-full of words and pictures?

Is it possible that the advertiser is not quite sure of the importance of his message?

Does he mistrust the strength and attractiveness of his copy?

Is he so uncertain of real *interest* that he must mince words and sugarcoat his story with thousands of dollars worth of white space?

Or, is it that advertisers, generally unaware of the vital importance of good selling copy, and, perhaps, even less aware of what constitutes good selling copy, allow their message to be determined by the way they want the advertisement to *look?*

At any rate, as every advertising agency man knows, copy, in an astonishing number of cases, is written more or less to fit a preconceived layout. The layout, of course, is determined by the space. The space is determined by the schedule. And the schedule, by the size of the appropriation. And so, in what we advertising men are fond of calling the "last analysis," the expression of the advertising message, if not the actual message itself, is far too often determined in advance by the approximate sum of money available for advertising.

Suppose—to take an extreme example—a man decided to send a telegram. His reasons for sending a telegram may be various; he may have heard that telegrams are good for business, he may have read so many telegrams that he wants to send one himself, all his competitors may be sending telegrams, the Western Union may have an able solicitor selling telegraphic service—or what not. However be it, our man decides he can afford to spend, say, $4.63 for telegrams.

This $4.63 he finds will pay for a night letter to Los Angeles.

Obviously, all he has left to do is to sit down and think out what he might like to telegraph to Los Angeles!

And anything he writes will be just about as important as the copy of an advertiser who buys his space before he knows exactly what he wants to say in it.

There are a few of us who think no advertiser has a moral right to spend money on white space before he has a pretty clear vision of what he intends to accomplish with it.

To accomplish anything at all with it, he must first get rid altogether of the idea that anybody in the world is interested in his goods or what he has to say about them, except as they translate what they read into something of purely selfish interest.

If any advertiser doubts this, let him make a test:

When he starts looking through next month's magazines for his new advertisement, let him stop long enough to recollect that every one of the other advertisements he skips over so lightly is equally the pride of some other advertiser; and that each of this multitude of other advertisers is, at the same moment, skipping just as lightly all the other advertisements in the same enthusiastic search for his own.

The only difference between this group of self-seeking advertisers and the ordinary public reading this same magazine is that they are looking for something, while the public is looking for nothing. But, passively, each person who looks through the advertising pages is just as self-centered—just as keen for his own interests—as any of those advertisers.

The next step, therefore, for our successful advertiser is to project himself out of the place of the proud father of an advertisement and into the place of the average man—that casual reader who, if he is kept interested, idles away half an hour on a magazine that would take three or four hours to read through hastily.

Let the advertiser then try to imagine what, if anything, he can say to this average man interesting enough—to *the man*—to hold his attention against all other advertising and editorial attractions long enough to give that single proposition thought enough to repay *his* share of the money that advertiser spent to reach him.

Here, for example, are fair samples of copy for which somebody paid $7,000. They are picked practically at random, not from one poor inexperienced amateurish effort in some country newspaper, but from five different high-class advertisements—tremendously expensive words of great national advertisers!

Those motorists whose appraisal of a car is influenced by its fitness to reflect their standing in the community agree in according custom built closed bodies their unqualified approval.

Far beyond any previous high mark, the new extends and amplifies those superiorities of performance which seem to belong peculiarly to ——.

It is rare indeed that the best things in life can be purchased on a purely bulk value basis. Genuine quality is seldom to be gauged by the inch, the ounce, or by a strict price measure.

Everybody now knows of the tendency of experienced owners to step up from the class of ordinary cars to the proud possession of a good looking, economical, balanced, lightweight, distinctive car of the highest resale value.

These impressions of interior comfort are further emphasized when the car gets under way, and you experience the admirable balance and buoyancy of the new spring suspension.

Memorize a dozen or so of these lines and try them on your wife, your partner, the man next you on the train, or even your office boy.

Just repeat them in a quiet conversational tone.

See if you can detect any quick glint of interest in your listener's eye, an attentive flash of the ear, an exclamation, "By Jove, that's true! I'm certainly glad you reminded me of it."

Why does any one spend thousands of dollars printing for distribution among millions of miscellaneous people a bunch of words that he can, in five minutes, prove definitely won't hold the interest of the first three men he meets on the street?

The answer is, of course, the words interest *him!*

He is fascinated with his own advertisement. As he views his clean white proof gleaming before him in solitary splendor and pronounces it "O. K.," he is honestly—unconsciously perhaps, but none the less honestly—of the opinion that this advertisement is going to look to a vast number of people the same as it does to him.

Just as a beginner in polo is so conscious of the fact he is on a horse that he gives little thought to the ball, so this average business man adjusts with infinite care to his own taste an advertisement intended for an absolutely different type of reader.

Thus, men without the slightest real training in theory or practice of writing copy, men wise enough to heed explicit direction from their lawyers and expert accountants, will, nevertheless, with calmest assurance dictate to experts just how an advertisement must read and look.

This subjective element—this very natural idea that other people are interested in the things of most interest to oneself—costs the business men of the United States far more money annually than the nation's standing army.

Nothing but years of professional training in the practical psychology of advertising enables a man to regard copy and layouts before him simply as a sort of photographic negative, and so to disregard pretty completely what he wants to say for the sake of what he wants his readers to *do*.

Nobody will deny that the man who pays the bill has a perfect right to have his advertisement read anyway he likes. Or, like the little girl in the Metropolitan Museum, he may simply proclaim, "I don't know anything about Art, but I know what makes me sick!"

Such a frank recognition of the fact that he is putting out an advertisement to please himself—to get a little kick out of seeing his own words in print—would immediately put things on quite another basis. There is, in fact, no reason why a successful business man shouldn't find legitimate self-expression in this sort of advertising just as enjoyably as in yachts, owning professional baseball teams or offering peace prizes.

But to regard these mandatory messages as "copy," and then to add insult to injury by calling that copy successful because the company that pays for the advertising is successful, is to fall into error as frequent as it is dangerously misleading. Weight of circulation is one thing; effective copy, quite another. Yet the two are constantly confused.

Wilbur Wright used to say that he could fly on a kitchen table if he could get a powerful enough engine. So, regardless of how bad the copy may be, you can make some sort of a success of any advertising campaign *if you spend enough money*. So, too, any South Sea Islander might thrash a golf ball completely and successfully around the golf course with a croquet mallet. But the youngest caddy would know better than to call it "golf"

Successful copy, on the other hand, is like good golf.

It isn't a matter of brute force. Nor of luck. Your trained copy writer knows exactly what he intends doing with every word and sentence. He knows his average man and just how he is affected by various uses of printed words. He knows the few basic motives that govern all human action. With certain carefully calculated appeal he makes a definite play upon these motives to make large numbers of people perform some simple act he himself has clearly and definitely in mind.

All "general publicity" and "institutional" advertising to the contrary notwithstanding, it follows inevitably that any advertiser who hasn't in his own mind a pretty clear picture of the definite *action* he aims to bring about in the minds of his readers may expect to waste a very large percentage of the money he spends on advertising.

For, reverting to the golf metaphor, your really good copy man makes always an attempt to hole out. He is not content just to shoot in the general direction of the green in the hope that the hole itself will somehow contribute something that he didn't! And when golf holes do begin to meet your puts half-way, readers will begin doing, on account of your advertisement, things you fail definitely to ask them to do in words they cannot fail to understand.

Chapter 11

Making Advertisements Read

By F. R. Feland[1]

For years I have been annoyed to hear advertising men say when some feature of the readability of an advertisement was being discussed—"That is a matter of opinion and one man's opinion is as good as another's."

In the first place, one man's opinion is not as good as another's, for the one may be an expert and the other a dunce. An opinion is as important as the general responsibility of the man who utters it. There are some points about the readability and probable effectiveness of advertising that are not matters of opinion, no matter who says they are. They are matters of fact, and it is into these facts that the following inquiry will be directed.

The few conclusions I have to offer as a means to making advertisements read are the result partially of a logic which I consider incontrovertible, and partially are drawn from careful observations extending over a period of years. Since none of us is infallible—not even the youngest advertising man in the business—I will ask you to remember that advertising is still a science almost as inexact as medicine or law.

Let us first inquire into the questions:

Why do people read at all? What is it they read?

What are the general attributes of the things they will not read?

Now for the first question, "Why do people read at all?"

---

1. *F. R. Feland.* Born in Kentucky in 1887, educated at common schools and State University of Kentucky, served as printer's devil, compositor, reporter, etc., on a country newspaper and later worked as compositor at The Roycroft Shop, East Aurora, New York, under Elbert Hubbard; then entered Hubbard's advertising department where he remained for about two years. He then went to New York and took a position in the copy department of George Batten Company in 1910. Served fifteen years with George Batten Company, practically altogether on service work. Now Director and Vice-President of the Company.

At the risk of being almost childlike in my simplicity, I am going to say that they read because they have been taught to read. Just as soon as the child's mind has developed to a point where he can identify all the letters on his building blocks, we teach him to combine those letters into words and to be able to identify as words combinations which others have made. We send the child to school and he is taught to read—all that the child may be better able to exercise his instinct of self-preservation. We read because it is self-preservation to read.

Next, what is it that people read?

You can put it down as a definite rule that people read only those things which interest them. You will read only that which interests you, and even if I force or pay you to read something that does not interest you, your lack of interest will create an inhibition that will prevent your remembering or being affected by what you have read.

Since you will read only the thing that interests you, the question arises, "What is the thing that interests you?" Let me assure you that no pun is intended when I say that the thing that interests you is the thing it is to your interest to know.

The word "interest" is derived from an old word "interess" which seems to come from the Latin "inter" and "esse," literally "to be between." Idiomatically it means "concerned with." Basically, the word "interest" means "concerned for private advantage," "biased by personal considerations." We do not need to consider it in the sense of premium for the use of money, although this meaning is akin to the conception of a private advantage.

The verb "to interest" is a curiously formed word, but nevertheless traceable to the same derivation, and means "to concern," "to invite participation in," and to "engage," "entertain," or "occupy." In other words, I am not forcing an association of meanings when I say that the thing which interests you is the thing that holds your attention, because it contains matter which you are conscious it is to your advantage to know.

Now, you may have an interest in a subject or a thing for a number of reasons, but practically all of them trace back to the elemental law of self-preservation.

The basis of interest is in self-preservation. Few of us hope that we can avoid our taxes any more than we can avoid death, so we accept taxation stoically and can scarcely be persuaded to read an article on taxation or an editorial on the National Budget. Family affairs come closer to us—we want to get along with our wives and husbands; we don't want to get caught if we stray from the paths which they would have us tread, and it is instinct of self-preservation, after all, that accounts for the story of a divorce case being on the first page of your newspaper and Senator Watson's remarks to the Ways and Means Committee on the inside sheets.

If we examine the general attributes of the things which only a minority of people read, we see that they are things far removed from their problem of self-preservation. For it is not self-preservation to attempt to read everything. That cannot be done. It has been said of the Vatican Library that it contains so many different volumes that a child could begin reading these books as they come on the shelves and read from daylight to darkness every day for a normal span of life and never get out of the first alcove.

There *must* be a discrimination; hence there must be a basis for discrimination and I submit that we automatically only read those things which minister to our self-preservation through our need for—

Information
Beauty
Entertainment

Information. —We constantly seek information as to saving time, avoiding dangers that others have encountered (hence the popularity of sensational news), personal safety (feeding our hunger for adventure by the vicarious process of reading in news and fiction of the exploits of others), saving labor, making money. We thirst for more information about all the devices that minister to our greed, our vanity, our fears, our desire for luxury. We seek more information about such social, political, philosophical and religious ideas as our impressions and experiences have awakened in us.

Beauty.—We may admit that the love of beauty is more or less inherent, and if we admire a picture we will read its title. If the picture tells a story we are inclined to read a little of the story. Then, too, about one person in twenty has a word sense and will read beautiful poetry and prose out of sheer delight in the elegance of composition. This is not recommended for advertising text, however, and just here I want to say that while rhetoric is a great study, a rhetoric for advertising copy writers has never been written. For rhetoric as taught in the schools and colleges treats fine writing as an end in itself. To the advertising copy writer, good writing is not an end, but a means to an end, and that end is the sale of an article, an idea or a service. Advertising writing is a means to effect a sale of something. In the advertising rhetoric that I hope some day to write there will be no force but clearness; no emphasis but clearness; no elegance but clearness—there will be no god but clearness, and clarity will be its prophet.

Entertainment.—This we must have or we become morbid. Even a comic strip which has no purpose but to amuse is interesting because it is founded upon the difficulties which human beings encounter and the futility and incompetence of their attempts to cope with situations in which they find themselves. The basic fun in Mr. Charles Chaplin's pantomime is his utter incompetence to meet any situation and his complete inability to cope with conditions either natural or unexpected.

I do not admit that it is the function of an advertisement, however, to entertain, because I do not believe that advertisements are approached by readers seeking mere diversion of spirits save for the limerick and jingle styles of advertising (dangerous tools in the hands of the neophyte). The use of entertainment in the reading matter of advertising should be handled with extreme care.

The things that people read may be again classified in the order of proved interest. People read news more than any single thing. Next comes fiction. As basic factors of interest, these two may even be included under one head, as News and Fiction.

When news and fiction are combined, they so far outweigh the popularity of articles on history, travel, science, criticism, music, religion and philosophy that no compilation of actual relationship is necessary.

Indeed, the majority of people receive most of their history, travel, scientific and philosophical information when it is sugarcoated in the form of fiction, as in the historical novel, the scientific detective story or in such books as *Main Street,* which is a fictionalized, sex-seasoned study in social ethics.

Now, having analyzed the reading taste of a mass public, we are at the point of applying the results of this analysis to advertising construction.

Take these precepts in your memory: When you start to write an advertisement, assume absolute indifference on the part of your reader. The word "indifference" says it. He is not interested; he is not predisposed; he is not hostile; he is not friendly to what you have to say. He is 100% indifferent.

In the past, when I have made this statement, I have had it challenged, largely on the basis that it was not entirely clear to the challenger just what was meant by the statement that a reader's attitude toward any given advertisement was at the outset absolutely indifferent. I will take the trouble here to attempt to make perfectly clear what I mean.

As a unit in the general public, you never search through a magazine or a newspaper to find any particular advertisement. A few women may do this, with department store advertising; in this case they are not looking to see what the advertiser has to say but are looking to see if he is saying something about what they want to buy tomorrow. The actual message that an advertiser has for you means nothing until you have begun reading it. In looking through a national magazine, you are not in the least concerned as you turn page 33 with what may be on pages 34 and 35.

Again, assume that you are a manufacturer of baking powder, let us say, and that you have decided to do a lot of national advertising. Tell any friend not interested in advertising or in your business, that you are about to begin national advertising of your baking powder, and his natural rejoinder will be "Zat so? I expect it will cost you a lot of money. What are they getting now for a page in the *Saturday Evening Post?*" He may even ask how much money it will cost and express a hope that it will pay you, but he will never turn bright, expectant eyes and inquire what it is you are going to say in your copy. He will not for an instant think of your "going out to buck Royal" or advise with you as to the lessons that may be learned from what Ryzon did and did not do.

The only people who will be in the least interested in what your copy is to be or in the media you are going to use will be advertising agencies and men who have space to sell, and they will be interested for reasons that touch precisely upon the definition of interest given in foregoing paragraphs. I will repeat the statement that the public is entirely indifferent to what any advertiser is *going to say* next week, next month or next year.

Your attention device catches the reader's eye. This device may be size, shape, picture or what not; now you want him to *read* and to continue reading.

You must work entirely from his needs, his likes or his dislikes. There is no drama, there is no interest in advertising that does not have its roots in the need of some person for something, or in the fact that the person likes or dislikes a certain thing or certain ways of doing things.

The simple retail store copy says—

"Fashionable strap pumps in gray suede $8.00—all sizes"

—and that is enough because they are addressing the woman who needs shoes, who needs fashionable shoes, who likes gray suede shoes she has seen, and whose foot may be large, small or medium. It ignores the woman who hasn't $8.00. They will get her next week when they reduce them to $5.95.

National advertising is different. It says:

> "The makers of the finest blankets in America tell you how to wash them."

There is news about your needs and all it has to do is to tell you what it promises to tell you and so long as it is doing this a woman with blankets to wash will read until her credulity is strained.

I noticed an advertisement today headed "A Smiling Baby." That headline was founded on one rule of human likes and dislikes I referred to. We like smiling babies: we don't like crying babies. For that reason I call it good.

The next precept to remember is—People are not interested in a one-sided pleading. They are willing to take sides; they are willing to take your side if you raise an issue, but do not, in the guise of argument, offer a contention against which there is no resistance.

> "The oldest muslin mill in America"

means very little.

"Does 80 years' experience making muslins mean anything?" raises an issue.

If it is possible to get news value into your story, do it. It is possible more often than you think. The reporter writes as though the thing were taking place as he wrote it. Have you noticed that? Their headlines say:

> "German Empress Dies in Exile"
> "Giants Win"
> "Train Hits Auto"

Always the present tense. Use it wherever you can and, above all, write the thing you write as though nothing of the sort had ever been written before. Keep in your own mind the illusion that you are saying the thing for the first time. That will almost add news value to the statement that the Eastman Kodak Company makes camera films.

Keep constantly in mind your reader's needs, his likes and dislikes. Write about these things or not, as the situation may require, but never let any other point dominate your conception of the thing you are writing about.

Think of your goods as things which the reader needs, never as something you want to sell.

Just here it will be helpful to consider that all merchandise from a copy point of view comes into one of these classes:

Goods that people don't want to buy
Goods that people want to buy
Goods that are in a state of transition from class one to class two.

People don't want to buy anything that is a part of something else. They don't want to buy blank paper, filing cabinets, shoe strings, underwear.

They want to buy phonographs, automobiles, candy, jewelry. When they dream of being rich, they dream of spending money for such things. That is a good test. Is the longing to be rich due in part to the desire to be able to buy plenty of the things you have to sell? Young women do not marry rich old men in order to buy ice boxes. They think of theater tickets, furs and Newport villas.

There are goods in the transition stage, such as linoleum, cord tires, fine house-heating equipment, etc., that advertising is changing from a dull necessary purchase to a luxurious and attractive possession. Copy must be governed accordingly as to length and the intensity of the interest appeal. Long copy can be made interesting about any new thing— anything which the race is using for the first time. It is hard to make long copy interesting about something which humans have bought for many generations and for identically the same reasons. You can safely risk long copy on a vacuum cleaner, whereas long copy on a hat or a lock would be tiresome.

The ideal advertisement from the hired writer's point of view is not written and probably never will be written.

For the ideal advertisement must inform and so please the reader that he enjoys airing this information to others in word of mouth advertising. In addition, it must make him feel an impulse to buy something.

Also, this advertisement must please the advertiser, and this it is unlikely to do because the things about pins that interest the maker of pins are usually things that the casual reader would rather he told someone else about.

Such facts as I have mentioned here may be helpful to the man who is writing copy on a salary for some other man who is paying the bill. The man who is having copy written for him feels, not unnaturally, that he wants it written to please him and he is not going to be shaken from that view by anything but facts. If you get into a discussion of opinions you are going to lose in nine cases out of ten, because his opinion has more weight than yours. You must be able to show that your writing is fitting his goods to human needs—related to established human likes and dislikes, and for those reasons only can be expected to interest folks in his goods.

Chapter 12

Copy Don'ts

By J. K. Fraser[1]

Don't start to write until you have the facts.

Don't start to use the facts until you separate the important from the unimportant.

Don't fix your own opinion of the value of a fact until you have tried it out on average people.

Don't try to gather all your copy ideas inside the four walls of your office. Get out. Mix with the trade and with the public. You will save time.

Don't assume that all your useful copy facts are bound up in merchandise. Some of the most successful advertising campaigns talk mainly about the service behind the product.

Don't miss taking in an occasional sales convention. It will stir up your thoughts.

Don't overlook the problems of the advertiser's sales force. They may furnish the vital clue to your advertising.

Don't expect an engineer to be lucid. Keep patiently at him. In time you will discover what he is driving at.

Don't assume that your reader is sitting before you in a buying frame of mind. He may be half asleep. He may be worrying about his own troubles. In either case, you will have to hook him hard with some quick point of interest.

---

1. *J. K. Fraser* went into advertising immediately after leaving college. His first job was with Ward & Gow, street-car advertising in New York; next Assistant Advertising Manager of the National Biscuit Company, next with the Mahin Advertising Agency at Chicago; next with the Street Railways Advertising Company of New York. He left them to join The Blackman Company, fourteen years ago. He is now President of The Blackman Company. He originated the famous "Spotless Town" jingle years ago.

Don't fail to make a special study of headlines. The headline makes or breaks many an advertisement.

Don't imagine that a short text solves the problem of getting a reading.

Don't forget that the public is chiefly interested in its own troubles.

Don't talk about your product as if it were in the factory. The public won't go there to see it.

Don't talk about your product as if it were in the retail store. So long as it is the dealer's property, it won't give the public much service.

Don't forget that the product's real advantages come out in use. Talk about your product *in use.*

Don't fail to bring out the virtues of your product in meeting some trouble common to your possible buyers.

Don't leave your product to prove its own case in use. In many lines only an expert can tell the good from the bad. Explain the merits which are not obvious.

Don't expect your public to read successive advertisements, unless each in turn contains some fresh bit of interesting information.

Don't expect "delicious" to sell candy. Almost any candy is delicious.

Don't expect "nourishing" to sell food. Most foods are nourishing.

Don't expect "warm" to sell overcoats. Almost any overcoat is warm.

Don't expect "becoming" to sell hats—half your readers will know it is hopeless.

Don't talk too much about what your product is. What it *does is* more important.

Don't imagine that your reader has never heard good claims about articles similar to yours. Choose a line of thought which will reawaken his tired interest.

Don't address your message to the thin air. Talk to real people.

Don't let familiarity with your subject lead you into technical terms which the green reader doesn't understand.

Don't get discouraged when the ideas fail to flow. Keep on trying. The happy thought may wake you up in the middle of the night.

Don't exaggerate—unless you are willing to plant mistrust.

Don't expect to get a fair-minded hearing, if you employ unfair claims and phraseology.

Don't whine. State the facts and trust to the reader's sound judgment.

Don't figure that any product of itself makes a tame subject for advertising copy. A good writer can put a thrill into the nebular hypothesis.

Don't assume that people won't read long advertisements. Rather admit to yourself "I don't know how to be interesting."

Don't imagine that any combination of words will take the place of a real thought.

Don't look down on Rhetoric textbooks. They hold many valuable practical pointers on force, clearness and precision.

Don't fall back on the word "best." It's a sign you are slipping.

Don't consider your job finished when you have brought out the merits of the product. Make your reader like the company which offers it.

Don't convince your reader and leave him guessing at where he can buy.

Don't lay too much stress on the value of a trade-mark figure. By the time it gets established, it is liable to give a chestnut flavor to the whole advertisement.

Don't work too hard over a trade-mark style of lettering for your display line. The trade-mark style will never make or break a campaign.

Don't waste too much time over slogans. Most of the notable advertising slogans cropped up as happy phrases in copy. Few have sprung out of cold-blooded thinking.

Don't agonize over a distinctive type for your text matter. If it is too distinctive, it will hinder reading. If it is quickly legible, its individuality will be scarcely noticed.

Don't quarrel with the artist. If you reason with him, he will come around—or perhaps he is right.

Don't take too seriously the criticisms of the star salesman. If you want to see what he really knows, ask him to write an advertisement for you.

Don't put the advertiser in a position where he sits in cold judgment on your copy. Make sure you are mentally together before he looks at the words.

Don't be fooled by dumb advertising which has succeeded. Look behind the scenes for expensive sampling, clever sales work, an extraordinary product or some other important factor which turned the trick.

Don't figure that you have rounded out your experience till you try copy dictation. It saves time. It stimulates a flow of thought. It runs out too long, but cuts down easily.

Don't become hide-bound by rules—even these.

Chapter 13

Wanted—by the Dear Public

By Charles Addison Parker[1]

Gay commands . . . delightful invitations . . . wonderful bits of information . . . confidential messages (otherwise called Advertisements) are valuable, I believe, as Reachers-of-the-Public, in proportion as they are informed by that Spirit of Poetry which is the essence of Reality.

"But Things . . . just the ordinary things that are advertised . . . have no special sense of poetry about them," says some one.

And yet they have when we run across them in the Bible, haven't they? I find thousands of references in the Bible to the commonest things of life: a mustard seed, interest on money, loaves of bread, yokes of oxen, coats and shoes and olive oil and honey and sparrows and houses and fig trees and sheep and vineyards; and each one charged with that sense of mystery and poetry.

Who marked all these things down and made them "common" anyway? Aren't chairs and tables made a certain height and width because God made man a certain stature? Isn't this very sheet of paper on which I write of a certain texture and adaptability and convenience to the size of the human hand? Aren't we touching divine mysteries when we strike a match, or answer the telephone, or add up a column of figures?

---

1. *Charles Addison Parker.* Born in 1873, in London, England. Educated at Whitgift School, Croydon, Surrey, England, and came to this continent in 1891. For a few years he was in the Hudson Bay Company's service at Winnipeg, Canada, and in 1901 moved to Detroit, Michigan, where he joined the Curtis Company, a direct-by-mail advertising agency which became one of the very prominent houses in that field in the middle west. Mr. Parker became widely known for his fund of unusual ideas and has written and created advertising for many representative concerns. Mr. Parker, some years ago, decided to go into free lance writing and is located permanently in New York.

Moreover, the heart of the race recognizes these realities, feels them. The common people have a deep sense of the divinity of common things, are immediately touched at a reference to this divinity, are ready to be touched more than the sophisticated would admit.

What a marvelous heritage that sense of Reality is, too! Who'd ever want to let go of one whiff of it? And how generally and tremendously we all share it!

Pungent Reality! Let the nerveless have Nirvana, but most of us, at least, will vote to go right on gloating over this dear old full-flavored, rough-and-tumble world where fire is hot and ice cold, and water wet, and wind blustery, and night dark, and every dawn a miracle!

Of course we will!

Oh, the foods we've tasted! . . . Oh, that first bite into a ripe Stilton cheese! . . . then our first encounter with a planked steak Sam Ward . . . and our first draught of Guinness's stout along with a dozen blue-points! . . . and lamb and green peas and browned potatoes and mint sauce! . . . and Columbia River salmon! . . . Thou, Bill-of-Fare! Noblest of human documents!

And then the sights we've seen! Castles and waterfalls, valleys and mountains. And the rare and costly fabrics and silks and brocades and velvets we've touched! And the fragrant and beatific odors our noses know! Aye, and the swinging, ringing melodies we've joined our voices in, and marched to, and danced to, and listened to, with the parted lips of entrancement!

What a world! *Reality,* did we say? Nay, let's put the *g* back in, where it used to be in the olden days, and talk about Re-g-ality. For Regality it is, Squires and Dames, that's coming over the hilltops, in this new Golden Age, to bless us all and make each of us a king and queen in his or her own right.

It has always seemed to me that, of all men of the pen, we, writers of advertisements, have, at once, the finest chance, and the strongest urge, to put this deep feeling of reality into these bits of writing we do about Things.

How significant things are to people! The peaty smell of Scotch tweeds . . . the little shoe that a baby has worn . . . a pipe . . . an armchair . . . a clock on a mantel . . . a vase that has held flowers . . . the flowers she put there!

And isn't writing—of which advertising is one department—in itself, one of the most marvelous gifts and powers? And don't the sheep, the loaves, the cloth, the olive trees of life, the coats of many colors, deserve as fine and as vivid and as effective writing-about as will stir folks deeply?

Won't it be delightful when our every-day advertisements are informed by this spirit of worth and charm, so that our magazines and newspapers are dotted and gay with poetical allusions to the furniture and fixings of life and the ways and means of fitting them to our affairs?

Money, too—and the spending of it—is a heart-throbbing poetical affair. Ask mother. She knows.

Here's the little bit of money Dad brings home on Saturday night. . . . To Mother's way of thinking, a dozen kindly enough, but very hungry wolves are lying in wait for it . . . the Butcher, the Baker, the Milkman, and all the other bandits. . . .

"Seems to me I have to pay it all out as soon as it comes in!" she says. All the more reason, of course, why she feels the keenest sense of responsibility that every purchase shall satisfy her wish for the family's life-enrichment. There's so little left over for luxuries. And each luxury—if it's only a pair of silk stockings, or even a jar of marmalade—should have "delight" wrapped up with the package. She's just as keen to understand and improve the spiritual standards of her family life as you are to improve the morale and vision of your business. She *wants* to make right choices.

Someone is going to write a play or a movie about the Pay Envelope one of these days, and we'll all go to see it and get a great deal more insight into what "consumer demand" means, translated into terms of life. Here are tears, sacrifices, sleepless nights; here are thoughtfulnesses, sharp clashes between members of families, disappointments, little triumphs, a constant, never-ceasing series of dramatic situations, more poignant, more inspiring, by far, than any of these pretty little plays we can see, between eight-thirty and eleven o'clock any night on Broadway. So, why not let's make our advertisements, which have all to do with the spending of this precious pay envelope, dramatic, as well as poetical?

Let's even drop several pegs below dear and intelligent "Mother" in the purchasing scale. Let's be, for the nonce, a little housewife in a cheap little Harlem apartment. Today's a big day with her. Six chairs in a very ugly color of golden oak, a table and a hall rack to match, have just been unloaded from an installment house.

"Pretty prosaic picture!" we say. That's only because we're blind in one eye and can't see out of the other. Why, that cheap furniture is mysteriously ennobled for her, and always will be, because her Jim took a job as night-porter rather than lie idle. And it's *his* hard-earned money and *his* boundless affection that's coming up those steep stairs as golden-oak furniture that you and I would light the kitchen stove with. Therefore, shall not the advertising, even of cheap furniture, be written with the pen of feeling? "Make Mary a lady!" has sold lots of pianos.

And how often we advertising writers have fallen over this old stumbling block of a word "Merchandise." This package of rolled oats? . . . this is not merchandise, this is food for six hungry children. This player-piano? . . . this is something for a lonely man to lean his soul against and listen to the melodies she used to play. This bed? . . . why, friends, this is not merchandise . . . this is a sacred thing! Children will be born in it . . . men and women may die in it!

Can't we then, and isn't it desirable that we should, and won't we be happier, if we take thoughtful care, when we write these condensed eulogies, these prose poems about the goods we make and sell—these Advertisements—that we write them in that Dear Language of Feeling that we all can understand? In words that flow from the heart, not from the fountain pen?

"Feeling,"—aye, there's the universal key that fits all hearts. And all pocketbooks.

This very fountain pen of yours, Mr. Waterman, *feels* just about the same in any hand. Your Beechnut Bacon, Mr. Arkell, slips as succulently down a miner's throat in the Rockies as it does down a picnicker's in the Catskills.

Catholic or Protestant, Republican or Democrat, Spinster or Divorcee, Poet or Peasant, give them all the sense, the *feeling* of this new thing of yours being already an old friend. Create that want which tells them that they're missing something out of life so long as they're without it. Write a poem-ad of the pleasure of buying it and having it, and how long will it be before they're going to satisfy that want?

"They?" . . . There I go again, saying "they" when I should say "we," forgetting that we're all just "the Dear Public" . . . and have been since the moment the good old Doc came running, with his little black bag, in response to our first tiny "want ad."

We may all have stopped being other things such as scholars and clerks and bookkeepers and traveling salesmen and Directors on Boards and church-wardens; but we've never once, even in our most romantic flashes, stopped being the Dear Public; have we?

So, let's all agree to can the High Hat and the Lorgnette, at least as far as advertising is concerned, and talk straight American, permeated with Love and Good Wishes for each other.

Let's advertise to each other so that we'll all enjoy it and have a good time out of it. If any of us manufacture anything and want the others to know how good it is, let's get something human across about it, in our first twenty words, and go right on being human about it till we're through.

Expressed in terms of a Want Ad, here 'tis:

WANTED

by the Dear Public!

PLEASE, Mr. Advertiser, be my friend! . . . Then you can advertise to me in a way that will do something wonderful for me. And I'll repay your kind interest a thousand fold!

TELL ME STORIES. . . . Tell me about a picnic on a hilltop and the Girl who put English mustard in the sandwiches because that was the way the Boy liked them. . . . Tell me about Daddy carving a boat for his little boy with the new knife he bought at the hardware store just for that.

Tell me about the small girl who cried every time she brought home her report card, and how pasteurized milk changed her school life into a song.

And about the man who never married because he brought up his widowed sister's children, and about the tear that glistened in his eye when he heard "Dream Faces" on the Victrola. . . .

GIVE ME a lump in my throat once in a while. A little poetry! . . . Life's so full of it and your scrubbed and polished advertisements are so empty of it! . . . Please give me more to hope for, more to believe in, more to love. Don't you know that this is the kind of thing that gets me? You should. . . . Everything I do proves it.

LOOK how I crowd to the movies, paying my way, whereas I stay away from art museums and other places that invite me free because they seem aloof and cold. . . . Look how hard I fall for Will Rogers and Elsie Janis and Norman Rockwell and Mary Pickford and O. Henry; and anyone and anything that'll make me feel ten degrees more human, that'll make me laugh a little, cry a little, take sides a little, that'll give me something I love to remember. . . . Aren't there *any* people like these in the advertising business? People who have lived on my street? . . . People, maybe who came from big families, and did chores when they were little? . . . And had measles, and mumps? . . . And knew what it was to make a mighty small income go a long, long way? . . . They're the kind of people I can understand. They know I am pressed with a lot of cares and worries. They'll delight in starting right in to be human with me in the first twenty words.

Chapter 14

Advertising Copy and the So-Called "Average Woman"

By Mrs. Christine Frederick[1]

The young copy writer sat in his 6x8-foot cubbyhole in the World-Beater Advertising Agency, his unnecessarily serious eyes peering steadily out of his shell-rim headlights.

"I must key this copy to the Average Woman," he muttered, repeating the instructions solemnly given him. "But who and what in the devil is the Average Woman?" Beads of intellectual perspiration (there is such a thing) stood forth on his Woolworth Building brow. Somehow his projector wouldn't work—he couldn't throw on the screen of his imagination this mythical Average Woman.

He took his troubles to his copy chief.

"Get on the train," ordered that Napoleon of Imagination, "and go to Bean Center, Texas; to Paris, Kentucky, to The Fair in Chicago, and to Child's Restaurant. You'll see her, all right."

He did, or thought he did. Just as, no doubt, did Edward Bok, when editor of the *Ladies' Home Journal.* He used to tell of how he once passed by a little cozy house in a small Ohio town and saw standing in the door

---

1. *Mrs. Christine Frederick.* Born 1883; graduate of Northwestern University. Was first to work out application of scientific management principles to home management, embodied in articles in *Ladies Home Journal,* later in *The New Housekeeping,* Doubleday, Page & Co., and now translated into French, German, Polish, Scandinavian, and Japanese. Founder, 1910, of Applecroft Home Experiment Station, Greenlawn, Long Island. Consulting household editor of *Ladies Home Journal* for many years; now household editor of *Designer Magazine* and of Sunday magazine sections of all Hearst newspapers in twenty-six cities. Lecturer; founder of the New York Advertising Women's League. Author of *Household Engineering* and many booklets; consultant for famous advertisers and writer of special advertising copy for food and household articles.

a woman, whom he always afterwards visualized as the average woman for whom he was editing.

Illusion, abstraction, guess-work, intuition—all appear to have their part in creating the average woman for those who are trying to reach her. Can she be more accurately studied? Is there some way to stick her on a pin, like a butterfly and put her under a microscope? We've got to know more about her—"mass appeal" is more and more a necessity, not only via advertising, but even by radio. Psychology tells us something about human beings in general, but Prof. Thorndyke of Columbia University has said there are no really authentic differences between men and women, as far as psychology knows, except possibly a greater emotionality. Which may be true, but we who make a specialty of understanding women certainly know that women have many characteristics purely feminine which must be considered when you advertise to them.

Our heroine, the much-worshipped and sought-after Average Woman, to whom we hope to sell our beans, cold cream, soup, talcum, spaghetti, chewing gum, washing machine or automobile, must at all costs be prevented from going to the store and saying, merely:

Give me a can of beans!
Give me a jar of cold cream!
Give me a can of soup!
Give me a box of talcum!
Give me a pound of spaghetti!
Give me some chewing gum!
I want to see a washing machine!
I want to look at an automobile!

It is our romantic aim, the job we give our waking hours to, that when she enters the grocer's, she may say without the slightest degree of hesitancy:

Give me Van Camp's Beans!
A jar of Daggett & Ramsdell's, please.
Three cans of Campbell's tomato soup.
Etc., etc.

If we are to spend so many millions to reach Milady Average, we should be willing to spend money and time understanding her. The average woman's mind is frequently not reached at all by very expensive advertising campaigns. Some of it is pathetically over her pretty head, and some more of it is well under her pretty feet, so poorly is it aimed. (Nor, as I shall presently show, is it aimed any better at women who are not pretty.) Insufficient time, attention or money are spent to analyze the so-called "Average Woman" herself. She invariably is the result of a fantastic, often distorted picture developed in the mind of the individual who conceives her. The picture is *only* in his mind, and is the result of whatever he can conjure up mentally.

Frankly, now, what does the average business man know about the average housewife? Many do not even pretend to know or to care about finding out. Others make quaint efforts to learn by asking their stenographers or their wives—and getting about as unbiased an opinion, to quote a recent writer in the *Saturday Evening Post,* "as the testimony of a dog owner in a bite case."

Ludicrous errors are made in merchandising as a result; not alone in copy, but in the merchandise itself. I have a junk room in an out-building which I call "the cemetery." It contains devices which during a dozen years have been sent me. It is a weird and mournful collection, and the claims for them no more deceive an intelligent, discerning woman. Many makers of good articles, on the other hand, are hiding their light under a bushel.

Why don't more advertisers make a practical, objective research of women and their reactions to a particular article or plan? Why don't they aim to learn more about the problems and point of view of the average housewife?

Is there really such a thing as an average woman? To flatly and finally say "no" would be one of the most unkind things to do, for what young hero of the advertising world likes to have his illusion shattered, when he has, throughout the years, built up for himself such a beautiful Pygmalion? Would it not be a most deadly shock for him to think, for a moment, that she *will never* come to life? Yet the truth, as woman knows it, must be told:

A woman who comes out of the head of a man rarely is a woman! He either highly fictionalizes her, or endows her with all the romantic qualifications that he believes a woman ought to have. His "average woman" is likely to be a sort of cross between Pola Negri and his stenographer. Of course, he tries to endow her with some home-like, old-fashioned characteristics to make the picture balance a bit—with the result that he drags his poor old mother in somewhere, and the picture, finally, resembles, in its incongruity, something of a beautiful, but highly wicked Parisienne knitting socks for father! How else can you account for pictures of women running washing machines while attired in ball gowns, or women making preserves in the kitchen, attired in flimsy boudoir laces?

The cardinal principle by which to explain womankind is *paradox.* Women want desperately to be different; but at the same time they want to be alike, as the fashion czars know. How can mere man understand paradox? A woman lives it and loves it. Her "yesses" are "noes," her retreats are advances, and she is both kind and cruel, highly practical and other-worldly.

But this is metaphysics—we must keep clear of the sheer mystery of woman and stay by the knowable. Professor Hollingsworth has said that there are greater differences between women than between men. Ten women will be a great deal more varied than any ten men. Have you ever seen ten women together who looked alike? Or twenty—or a hundred, if you like? Still, in one or two particular characteristics women may be bunched together like so much asparagus.

Technically speaking, there cannot be any such person as the "average woman." It is statistically accurate to say that an "average woman" would be *an abnormal woman!* You can't "average" human beings because you can't reconcile their differences with the use of averages. Things that are different cannot be compared. Long, long ago a cloistered old book-worm, Quetelet, tried to find what was an average man—"a man who would be to society what the center of gravity is to bodies." But he couldn't put life into such a conception.

You will see how this is if you study women from the favorite male method of classification—the color of her hair. You can't say the typical woman is dark-brown in color of her hair, even though there are considerably more women with dark-brown hair than of any other hue. Here are the official figures: dark-brown, 40%; light-brown, 25%; black, 20%; "blonde," 10%; red, 5%.

This may be a revelation to men; you can see that the brunettes number 85%. The blondes, who have hogged most of the vampirish reputation, are only 10% in number.

Descending from head to foot, the prevalent size for women's shoes used to be, some years ago, about 4 or 4½ and every woman squeezed and suffered the tortures of the damned rather than admit she had a foot any bigger than a 3. Shoe manufacturers actually falsified sizes. Nowadays that idea is *passé,* and the measure of woman and her ankles and feet is no longer an indication to her character, charm or beauty. The average size of women's feet these days is 5½ or 6—and no disgrace attached to it, either! Clementina's No. 9's do not disqualify her. You have heard the story of the shoe clerk who lost a customer by saying: "Madam, your left foot is *larger* than the other"; and the shoe clerk across the street who gained that same customer by saying, instead, "Madam, your right foot is *smaller* than the other."

How about Milady's Average's bust size? America can hold up her head proudly, for there are actually more "perfect 36's" than any other size. Here is the "inside dope": Size 34, 20%; 36, 30%; 38, 20%; 40, 15%; 42, 10% 44 to 48, 5%.

There is, of course, much truth in the fact that "the Colonel's Lady and Judy O'Grady are sisters under their skins," and on this theory a good many products, particularly those appealing very strictly to the truly feminine tastes of women, have stood a good chance of striking a high average of return. But women are becoming more and more highly individualized, and with this greater individuality, must, necessarily, come a keener study of women as targets for advertising or for the output of special trademarks or brands; a study to classify and group them and thus hit the target of mass appeal more often. *Right classification is the answer,* not lump "averages."

The *real* way to find out about the typical woman for your own particular advertising proposition, is to make a questionnaire survey. That is the true way to determine a "mode." You select the women who are of the kind you deal or hope to deal with, and then you have a statistically sound basis on which to construct your picture of the typical woman *for your purposes.* By carefully seeing to it that you select a proper proportion of all kinds of women who are included in your typical customer list, you avoid a defective picture. The women should be selected from all the levels of wealth you expect to appeal to; from all geographical points you expect to reach; from all sizes of towns and types of living conditions you cater to. They must, in other words, be good "samples."

But even such data must be revised often these days. In the past few years radical changes in wealth and social status, which always affect women more decidedly than men, have occurred and must continue to occur. The changes are taking place so rapidly, that even tomorrow may be different from today. Localities are different; women of various age-levels react differently. You can advertise to fifteen-year-old flappers today, whereas ten or twenty years ago, fifteen-year-olds were still in the nursery, more or less! Now they lipstick, etc.—with the emphasis on the *et cetera!*

Home conditions are also difficult for some people to visualize. Some copy writers talk and think as if all women have servants. They should visit Sauk Center, Minn., where Sinclair Lewis lives! They should respect facts a little more. Ninety-nine per cent of housewives have no servants—a figure which astounds the ill-informed who never move out of their own circle. Yet the immense vogue of vacuum cleaners, washing machines and electrical devices are based on the vast numbers of women who do their own housework. Even wealthy women have moved into smaller houses and have fewer servants.

There are only 2,184,214 women in domestic service. Let us say roundly two million families have servants, because we must allow for families with more than one servant. This was in the 1920 census; our population has increased considerably since then, but not, alas, our servants.

Now let us look at business women, of whom we hear a great deal. The 1920 census showed 8,549,399 women "in gainful occupations," which represents 21.1 % of all women over 10 years of age; 2,439,965 of these were in "clerical and professional work," including the 1,423,658 stenographers and office girls. As I figure it, there are only 1,016,307 women who are above the stenographer or manual labor class in industry—only 11.9% of all women who work—less than 1% of our population, or 3.6% of women over 21 years of age. The other women are working on farms (1,084,074), or in factories (1,931,064). To me it would seem that only about a million women in the United States are "business women" in the real sense of the word; women taking business at all seriously. Everybody knows that the great bulk of women in factory and office are there to add to their dress allowance, get away a little from home discipline, and have more opportunity to meet beaux!

But do not get the idea that I am belittling women's importance in economic things. Oh, no! Women buy 71% of the family merchandise; 48.4% of it they personally select without advice, and in the selection of 23% more they have an important voice. Fifty per cent of automobiles are bought with women's eyes on the goods before signing up. Naturally, women buy 90% dry goods—but what about the 11% of *men's clothing,* which the research shows they also buy, to say nothing of 22% more of it that they buy in collaboration with men. Thirty-four per cent of what you wear, if you are a man, is bought for you by your womankind—if you are a typical man. She spends most of the approximately thirty-five billion dollars expended in retail stores every year—about one hundred million dollars a day, or about twelve million dollars every hour of business!

Your typical woman, then, is a difficult problem to visualize all in one romantic frame. She must be viewed rather from various angles of approach. You have some of the physical facts about her—color of hair and size of feet; you have something about her occupationally, and you know what her spending power is. Her psychology—the "emotionality" Professor Thorndyke attributes to her—is vastly more subtle.

Every woman has about the same reactions when she is in love, when she has a child, and when her feet hurt. Also, she is "average" in her tight economy for all things useful and her lavishness on things decorative of herself. She is a born bargainer; she will not be fooled by inferior goods, no matter how successfully trade-marked or camouflaged. She likes to feel she is different than other women; yet she likes to be doing and wearing what is "the mode." She likes to imitate the "best people"; she accepts authority readily.

She is sensitive, aesthetic, likes cleanliness inordinately; likes delicacy, refinement and tenderness. She is sentimental and fearsome; she is highly practical and personal in her outlook. She is not interested in mechanics or abstract ideas.

Women as Bait in Advertising Copy

If I were to take my ideas of women from many advertisements directed to women, I would most certainly have strange conceptions of what Dr. Johnson called "the sex." I positively assert that women are still used too much pictorially in advertisements as advertising bait.

I shall try to show firstly, that the P.G.[2] as bait in advertising copy is declining and rightly so; secondly, that it is men, and not women, who are appealed to by the lurid use of the P.G.; thirdly, that a great mistake is made in substituting the chorus type of beauty in place of that type of woman who is really more powerfully appealing—the woman who is natural, sweet, intelligent and "homey" but not homely; and lastly, that even when the P.G. is legitimately used in advertising copy, she is often erroneously and misfittingly displayed, creating what I choose to call an "advertising anachronism."

---

2. "P.G." refers to "Pretty Girl."

Now what is the idea that is supposed to be behind the P.G.? Is it that all of us universally never see enough pictures of feminine charm? Is it because *men* chiefly prepare and draw our advertising copy? Could it be because of the poverty of ideas on the part of the advertiser, who, because he can't think of anything else or build up a convincing argument, slaps on a P.G.? Or is it only a half-conscious condition which is slowly dying out because it is unsound and incorrect?

I think it is a composite of a number of these reasons. I think that the development of the "reason why" appeal in advertising has just naturally pushed the P.G. off the stage, and that it, coupled with the rising of general intelligence on the part of the woman consumer, will soon cause readers to see her no more.

Of course we women have helped along the tradition that we are the most beautiful sex; but in spite of this fact, and that we may have encouraged men to use beauty as bait in their advertisement copy in the past, I shall prove that the use of the P.G. in advertising copy is decreasing as we become more sensible. Ten or twelve years ago practically the only way to advertise tire ads., toothpowder, razors, cigarettes, as well as most articles of personal, feminine, and household use, was to catch the attention by slapping a P.G. on to the picture. The P.G. either sat in the tire, or smoked the cigarette, or hugged the article close to her not over-obviously clothed person.

"Ask Dad, he knows"—if he will tell—of those days when the chief reason for buying cigarettes was to get a small photo of Lillian Russell or Cissy Loftus, or a bowery burlesque Queen to stick around his mirror, and when all tobacco advertising vied with its rivals solely on the basis of the vaudeville artists they included in each package. But compare a striking tobacco advertisement of today—"Your nose knows," or "Watch them register—they satisfy"—which leaves the P.G. in mentionless oblivion.

There is a marked lessening of the use of the P.G. not only in the smoking, suspender, and allied men's fields, but in all lines of products either of distinctly women's or for household use. I might perhaps venture to suggest that all women today are so universally beautiful that men do not need to put a headless lady into a shaving brush or buy a package of cigarettes to gaze on extraordinary feminine charms!

There must be *some* reason why the P.G. has disappeared so markedly. Today competition is most keen, and the best business brains are devoting themselves to advertising, so that we are seeing the sense and power of "reason why"—of arguments based on the scientific, fact, utility, economy, convenience, comfort, style and educational "appeal" in the advertising of countless products.

And now for my secondly—I believe it is men, and not women who are appealed to by the P.G. as she is exploited in our current advertisements. *Do pretty women appeal to women?* I admit that women are admirers of female beauty, but the point men never see is, that we are far sharper-eyed critics of our sex than men, and know real beauty when we see it, and when it is not beauty at all. There is no antagonism so pronounced as the antagonism of the average common-sense type of woman for the artificial doll type, for whom man, in his crass ignorance and uncritical susceptibility, so commonly "falls!" Do women admire the "chicken type" in advertising?—No! But this does not in the slightest degree restrain a woman from admiring the really fine and appropriate type of woman, the beauty of Julia Mar-lower, Elsie Ferguson, or Maxine Elliott, when adapted to its setting. All we ask is that our sensibilities be not offended by daubing an advertisement with female pulchritude.

If women were so inordinately fond of gazing at female beauty as the advertising artist would have us believe, you would find that every American housekeeper would subscribe to the *Police Gazette* along with her copy of the *Ladies' Home Journal* or the *Designer.*

As for men, I do not believe they, either, are so titillated at the sight of a pretty girl as is popularly supposed. I think that the tremendous output of the printing presses and the development of the moving picture has made P.G. faces so commonplace and cheap in every crevice of the modern world that the thing has lost its novelty. I admit that in a far-off mining camp or on board a freighter bound for Borneo, men may still ponder deliciously over an advertisement or almanac baited with eyes and hair and cheeks and lips, but men do not need to do it in modern civilized centers where there are millions more women than men.

Most men and women coming out of a movie theater, are so satiated with goo-goos and tar-dipped eye-lashes of the closeup showing the obviously displayed beauty of the movie star in violent action, that when their gaze falls on a billboard or on a newspaper showing an advertising "still" of a P.G. eating Simkins self-winding spaghetti, it leaves them cold and unmoved.

And now for my thirdly—that it is a mistake to substitute the chorus type of beauty for the woman who is really more powerfully appealing and of a higher, finer kind of natural charm.

Judging from the creations which he turns out, I infer that the average advertising artist's habitat is bounded on the North by Midnight Follies, on the South by Greenwich Village, on the West by the Russian Ballet and blockaded on the East by the late Mr. Comstock's society for the Suppression of Vice. No advertising artist seems to have a wife who does her own housework, he never had a mother, and a grandmother of course he never saw or heard of. New York has a copyright on its women. The type of "chicken" which he knows and portrays so glibly, the eyebrow-shaved, massaged, short-skirted doll of anemic New York life is a parasite and oddity to the total population of these American States. He would not find this type in Clyde Ohio, Goshen Indiana, Rock Hill South Carolina, Paris Kentucky, or all points west, and yet it is the consumers in these towns that buy the advertised washing machines, soaps, breakfast foods.

And now for lastly. We know that both actors and producers of plays take the greatest pains to have their characters true to period, to setting, to costuming. Imagine Hamlet wearing a business suit and riding a bicycle, or Marguerite wearing a middy blouse and running a sewing machine! Yet, this is exactly what our advertising artists do—they are so crazed, so obsessed, so held by a "complex" of a pretty girl that they blindly draw a pretty girl as they imagine her and as they see her clothed in city fashion, no matter if she graces an advertisement for poultry food to be used on the farms of Oshkosh. As long as she is pretty she will do!

Recently I noticed a pretty girl in a washing machine ad wearing a ruffled apron, a bewitching ruff on her hair; she was attaching a well-known and most excellent washing machine to the lamp socket. Is she the lady herself who is going to do the washing? Well, not all homemakers wear black uniforms and these accessories preparatory to work. Is she the laundress? Not all laundresses, either, wear a ruff on their hair and a frilly ruffle as a fig leaf. Ah, I have guessed it! This is the parlor maid, the one who takes your card and ostensibly removes the dust with a derelict rooster. Yes, our artist has drawn a perfect, scrupulously exact and charming parlor maid. But—and here is my point—do *parlor maids operate washing machines?* No, never—well, hardly ever, except in the dreams of the advertising artist.

The American woman has no more use for overdoses of female beauty in advertising than she has for old chromos, or the antimacassars of the Victorian era.

And she definitely resents the mere idea of so promiscuously using woman as bait. She sees the all too obvious machinery of the advertising puppet show behind the flaunting of woman in advertising and grasps your desire to steal into her good graces by means of the pass word of the pretty girl.

Broadening the Consumption for Family Goods Through Educative Copy

One of the practical results of some careful analysis prior to preparing advertising to housewives is that family and consumer conditions are often uncovered which can result in important new merchandising slants.

When an advertiser of household goods desires to increase the volume of his sales he has two paths toward growth: (1) increasing the number of families using his goods, (2) increasing the amount of goods used per family. How can he know which offers the easiest road unless he studies the mind, habits and economies of the housewife, on different levels?

I am constantly noticing that advertisers are ignoring the second broad path to greater volume. For instance, some few years ago I brought to the attention of a famous maker of canned soups the fact that his growth had been confined to increasing the number of people buying canned soup, while ignoring a particularly rich opportunity to educate those women who already bought the soups, particularly tomato, to use them as sauces in cooking and serving. I pointed out that ten cans of soup could be used in a family for this purpose to one for soup purposes alone. The result was that I prepared a booklet giving recipes for such new uses of canned soup, and a resultful advertising campaign was begun, with a new and educative copy slant. Great numbers of women now buy canned soups for these new purposes.

Many other articles of household use are susceptible to this consumption broadening process, to a degree which can mean doubling and trebling of sales. Fleischman's yeast is a famous example, but the soup instance mentioned above is more generally illustrative.

Two famous breakfast food advertisers have been making history for themselves along this line—Postum, and Shredded Wheat. A big prize contest conducted by Postum to develop different ways of utilizing Grape-Nuts, and the new copy slants developed from it, have resulted in a wider public realization of the use of Grape Nuts as a general food article as well as a breakfast dish. Shredded Wheat has done the same thing with equally striking results. Over 50,000 women entered the contest, suggesting Shredded Wheat for puddings, salads, cookies, custards, and in combination with meats, cheese, eggs, fruits, etc.

What is needed is a creative outlook on the household market; a more inquiring, open attitude of mind to study the possibilities of a given field. The enterprising advertising writer is usually the one who, does such delving, and usually makes use of expert home economies, experiment and advice. I am convinced that there are not enough practically and theoretically trained women brought into consultation to dig out such broadening-out possibilities. Men are too likely to look exclusively upon the merchandising side of their business and fail to relate closely their article and particularly their advertising to the typical family conditions and possibilities.

If you are selling a food article, especially a semi-staple, the chances are that modern dietetics and up-to-date family practice have opened doors for your article which you may be ignoring—or made others *pass.* The increased per-family income has made unnecessary the rigidly narrow standards of older days. It has immensely widened the range of purchase and of diet. It permits the use of more expensive soaps and more kinds of soap products, for instance. It permits the making of more kinds of pastry and breads, the enjoyment of more manufactured articles, the equipping of kitchens with more devices.

Lines of goods which are being crowded off their perch by the modern higher standards are in real need of such revitalized advertising copy. Codfish, mackerel and salt pork, for instance, belong to an older and more economical era; and today they are being dropped for foods more alluring. The sellers of such articles have need for both vertical and horizontal growth. Other articles have a fairly satisfactory growth along horizontal lines, either through natural increase in population or by dint of sales effort. The one lack is to increase the uses of the product, increase the average consumer's knowledge of the wider applications of the article. There is always a certain especially intelligent, alert group of consumers who are using your product in a wide range of ways, far above the average; and the important thing is to lift a greater percentage of your average users up to the consumption level of your small minority. More than that—you may lift even your intelligent minority's level of consumption to still higher points by securing technical home economics counsel to develop new suggestions for a greater variety of applications of use. There is an ever-growing body of women who are alert to new ideas, and whom you have only to convince of a bright idea to get them to adopt it forthwith. This is not true, of course, of the great mass, who can be educated only slowly; but the educated minority is worth a great deal of special attention; giving them a copy treatment entirely different from the dull level of women.

"Three-in-one Oil" is an example of a household product which has been exceedingly keen for vertical growth; offering prizes for new ideas for uses and constantly educating the public through advertising as to the multi-various uses of its product.

But more particularly I refer to articles which are more or less fixed in the minds of people as good for only one or two uses, whereas there are in reality one, two or three other uses. I do not think it of great importance to discover a few more uses for Three-in-one Oil, to add to its already long list; but I do think it a big idea to educate women to use a disinfectant, let us say, for the ice box, the sick room, scrubbing pail, the bath tub, instead of merely for the toilet or the garbage pail. There is far too little per capita sale of disinfectant because of its narrow use. The same is true of antiseptics, of polishes, of paper towels, of linoleum and a score of other house-furnishing articles.

In the food field there are a great many more examples, of course. Rice is not given its full possible variety on the menu, nor bread, nor crackers, no cheese, nor flavoring extracts, spices, cocoa, gelatin, cocoanut, salad oil, spaghetti, and a long list of other foods. People get in a rut in the use of an article. They use it for one purpose and never for anything else, because it does not occur to them. Cranberries were once reserved only for two days of the year, for some purely habit reason, until a use-broadening campaign was begun.

The American woman is red-ripe for education along use-broadening lines, because huge numbers of women have a longer family purse today than before the war. They can do more things, buy more things, and they are still fascinated with the novelty of experiment. An advertising writer to women should get the sense and the spirit of this.

Advertisers are not all aware, also, that cooking knowledge and general household science has advanced in the last dozen years, and that it is distinctly behind the times to neglect the increased knowledge of the day. Competitors will surely break the new ground first if it is not looked after.

Certain types and kinds of cookery are also neglected because there is no educational advertising in operation. Deep-fat frying, for instance, or casserole cookery, or home candy making—to mention a few at random. Pie-making is becoming a factory and restaurant proposition; whereas pie is the American man's first love. Few advertisers are stressing home-made pie. Not long ago, for a great California fruit-growing association, I developed some new pie recipes which are to be featured in advertising; but this is but one kind of pie. Nobody else is at work boosting home-made pies. There ought to be a pie cook book, for every woman ought to learn this broad path to a man's heart!

Every concern selling family food ought to be aware that it is dealing with an art and science, flexible and full of possibilities, and it should also realize that the domain of the kitchen is rather an alien land to men. Only women can fully grasp what women's needs and opportunities are. I find in very many instances that the typical man's point of view prevails; the "goods" is regarded as so much mere merchandise to be moved and distributed, without a real understanding of the situation *in the kitchen.* One reason why "Crisco" has been so splendid a success is because two years of experiment were made, even in the kitchen conditions of ignorant southern negro women, to make sure both that the article was adopted to women's needs, and that the literature and advertising about it were close to the average woman's understanding and need.

We thus see at work the social changes due to new types of merchandise, new wealth. The farm woman once wore little else but gingham and black alpaca. She buys copies of Fifth Avenue models today, and her daughter, whose face was innocent of aught but freckles, now owns the standard female laboratory of toilet articles.

Food is perhaps the most striking item among the new consumption standards. We spend for meat about seven times as much as we spend for bread; about five times as much as we spend for our public schools; and even ten times as much as we spend for our churches. A rearrangement of our family budget in the direction of more vegetables and fruit and other forms of food is inevitable and is, in fact, taking place. War-time discipline has led to the discovery of new foods, with much resulting benefit.

The family menu will continue to show many changes in consumption habits. Many splendid foods which have never had a good chance are now more widely appreciated. This has notably happened to macaroni and spaghetti, of which there is now a very greatly increased consumption. Such articles of food as the lentil, and the entire pea and bean family, which serve as meat substitutes, are enjoying greatly increased patronage. We are rapidly developing into a fruit- and vegetable-eating nation. New fruits and new vegetables are constantly making new friends, as a result of modern educational advertising, based on close study of home and family conditions.

The American woman's standards of purchase are also higher. *She is more desirous of really good quality than ever before.* It has often been said slightingly of this country that we bought a greater amount of worthless merchandise of poor lasting qualities and of no aesthetic beauty than almost any other civilized country. The war's experience in commodity purchases has taught us that quality pays because it lasts longer and has greater beauty and fitness. There will be fewer houses filled with cheap imitations of period furniture and other miscellaneous "grimcracks." Even our wall papers will be less ambitious, ornate and oppressive.

The advertiser of family goods who aims to understand the modern woman and her home problems will have to do a great deal more digging than talking to his wife and stenographer before he writes copy! Home economics in relation to merchandising and advertising copy is today a well developed science which cannot be ignored.

Chapter 15

Believable Advertising

By O. A. Owen[1]

To tell the truth in such a way that people recognize it as truth is one of the hardest things men set themselves to do. From the time when, as children accused of some other kid's misdeeds, we wept and pleaded to have our innocence believed by incredulous parents and teachers, up to the era when we go into print and tell the public what we know about our canned goods, fireless cooker or shovels, we are constantly aware that all the lies ever told by others have armored average human minds against us. We find, too, that though sincerity has an accent of its own that is popularly supposed inimitable, insincerity can counterfeit that accent with wonderful accuracy.

In writing advertising copy, it is not enough to know that one is telling the truth. That alone will not necessarily make the public give credence. Our knowledge of the product, our enthusiasm and our sincerity will not automatically produce conviction. To rely wholly on them is to make the mistake of the actor who, disdaining all tradition and technique, thought if he believed himself to be Richelieu while on the stage he would act the part to perfection.

There is a technique of believability in advertising.

There are definite things to do with "copy" to make it transfer to other minds the solid grounds for approval of a product which any copy-writer worth his salt regards as a prerequisite to good work.

There is an art of making oneself believed in print, and sincerity alone is no more a substitute for it than anger is a substitute for knowing how to box when a man has to fight.

---

1. *O. A. Owen.* Well-known sales promotional copy writer and copy chief with large publishing houses; has lectured on copy writing and written many ads of all types.

127

I propose to tell such few of the elements of the science of being believed as I have noted in advertising. There are many more such elements than are here set down, and it is quite possible that I shall leave out important ones. The topic has not had as much separate attention given it by writers on advertising as it deserves.

Figures

The front cover of *System,* the magazine of business, carries the titles of two or three of the main articles within, and in addition some such statement as this:

"Also 327 suggestions by 143 writers on how to make sales and reduce costs." The advertisements of automobile tires frequently give results of mileage tests, expressed with what seems to be needless accuracy, as 17,967.32 miles. Ivory soap, as we all now know, is 99 44/100 per cent pure. (I wonder how many million dollars were spent to engrave that figure—and Heinz's "57"—on the American brain?) A certain financier, famous in his time as Bet-you-a-million Gates, made it a principle in the promoting which netted him a hundred million dollars, always to state exact figures in his arguments. If the purchase of a mill was $453,667.12, he would even in his most hurried talk repeat the sum in full.

If *System* should say on its cover, "A wealth of suggestions by a battalion of writers," would it be as convincing as "327 suggestions by 143 writers"?

If the mileage test was described as "exceeding 17,000 miles" would that be as truth-like as 17,967.32? Would "almost absolutely pure" do as well as 99 44/100%? If the promoter had used the round sums that inferior promoters delight in and had said "about half a million dollars"—would he have amassed a nine-figure fortune by his flotations?

It may be set down as a copy axiom always to use figures, when possible, instead of words, and always to use exact figures instead of round sums. This may often make awkward copy, but it is a characteristic of facts that they interfere with smoothness. Reality has a rhythm of its own. Any story of real life, romantic though it may be in places, is likely to possess anticlimax and ugly irrelevance precisely when fiction would not. Perhaps it is because of this that exact figures have a natural believability. Just why one way of telling truth is accepted by the public and another way is not constitutes in many cases a mystery. It is not always possible to understand the why's of faith, nor its occasional inconsistencies.

When a quotation is made from a book, report or other document, not one reader in a hundred thousand will verify it, yet it is eminently worth while to cite the exact volume, chapter and page when quoting. Addresses and even telephone numbers can be given in some cases, where annoyance will not result to an individual mentioned in an advertisement, and will add materially to the credibility of what is said. Figures are the acme of exactness, and exact statement is characteristic of truth telling.

It is an American trait—increasing as life becomes more hurried and complex—to act on surface indications without tedious investigation. If anything "looks good" to the typical twentieth century American he will "take a chance." Advertising, after all, is a series of affirmations by a stranger. It is not physical demonstration nor sworn evidence. No consumer is going to institute an investigation before buying a 50-cent bottle of dentifrice. Believability above a certain point makes sales; below that point it does not. Advertising must make out what lawyers call "a *prima facie* case"—that is, a case that warrants a trial in court. Only, the court in such instances is the consumer and the trial is buying and using the goods. Therefore, advertising, with nothing but printed affirmations as its unsworn witnesses, must learn the peculiarities of human belief, the science or art of creating tentative faith.

Proper Nouns

To say "a great Western city," instead of "Denver," is to create some suspicion. It is, in form if not intention, a species of evasion. "A celebrated judge" is a phrase carrying nothing, while mention of Charles Evans Hughes commands attention. Mr. Rockefeller is conceded by all of us to be the richest American, but if so described, and not named, readers unconsciously score one point against the credibility of the copy. Even further, *John D.* Rockefeller is better copy than *Mr.* Rockefeller. Proper nouns are almost as valuable as figures in advertising.

It is often, of course, forbidden or impracticable to use a many s name in an advertisement, but in such cases the familiar "name on request" helps a great deal.

It is more believable to say "styles now reigning from Rue de la Paix, Paris, to Fifth Avenue, New York" than "styles now reigning from the fashion centers of Europe to those of America."

Reiteration

Years ago in a small weekly I read an advertisement which was headed "A Suit of Clothes Free!"—an incredible statement. Over and over again it was stated that a suit of clothing could be procured without cost. I think the assertion was made fully a dozen times. One did not believe the headline, nor the first or second reiteration, but it is an instinct based on life's experiences to be impressed by repeated and emphatic repetitions of any statement, however extraordinary. So people speak who protest against the unbelief of their hearers. The arrested man who says once, sullenly, "I am innocent!" then stops, is probably guilty, but he who repeats the phrase unceasingly and earnestly shakes the strongest conviction to the contrary.

I was forced, in spite of myself, to answer the advertisement. It contained no clue as to the method which would produce a free suit, but its reiterations bred some belief. The reply disclosed that any one who would sell five suits for the advertiser would receive a sixth for himself as compensation. The advertiser got what he wanted when he received an inquiry, for thereafter he released a follow-up which was, as I remember it, a masterpiece of repetition.

The point is that an advertisement worked up belief in a preposterous claim by merely making the claim a number of times, without adducing any further evidence or explanation.

Modern advertisers understand that repetition, in the sense of keeping on advertising month in and month out, pays, but I doubt whether they sufficiently practice the other kind of repetition, namely, that within the advertisement itself.

Local Connection

If I lived in Scranton I don't know why I would sooner buy oil stocks from an office around the corner than I would from one in Boston or New York, but I would. There are doubtless rogues in Scranton as in a metropolis. Stellite knives are made in Kokomo and sold from a New York branch also. I am going to order one by mail, and I shall order from the New York branch, buying "sight unseen" quite as much as though I sent to the Indiana headquarters.

We inherit a deep-seated trait from our tribal ancestors. Strangers and far-off people are still presumed to be crafty and hostile by the savage who sleeps in our race soul. New Yorkers are my people; Kokomites are outlanders.

Consequently a touch of localism in an advertisement makes it believable. I know a seller of garages whose plant is in Michigan and who for some years has shipped his excellent automobile shelters to every part of the Atlantic coast. Now he is going to campaign in a big way, concentrating his men around towns where his garages were installed. In nineteen cases out of twenty the "prospect" will never go to see the local structures, but the mere fact that one of his own tribe and totem owns one inclines him to believe the salesman's other statements. That trait in human nature is the foundation of this wise garage maker's big selling effort.

If I, from Philadelphia, were advertising a new wall board in Texas, I would refer to a Houston merchant who carried it as my "agent," and I would try very hard to have a bit of the wall board in the Governor's mansion at Austin, and tell of it. That bit would do more for me than acres of wall board in Albany, Hartford, Boston and Harrisburg, for are not these the capitals of the far-off Northmen who eat oysters and wear narrow-brimmed hats?

Testimonials

Some of the earliest things done in advertising have never been improved on. Among them are testimonials, the mainstay of the old and wonderfully effective patent medicine advertising. These are best when the full name and address are given, but even when disguised in initials they have strength. Everything, it seems, can be made the subject of a testimonial, and a well-worded one from an obscure person is sometimes almost as good as one signed by a movie queen. The less they are edited the better. Bad grammar and anything else casting ridicule upon their writers must come out, of course, but if there be, as so often happens, a natural and quaint turn, an artless confession, a colloquialism, an idiom that betrays the layman and unprofessional hand that wrote it, these should be conserved as precious. They are fine gold. They are believable, for the phraseology is internal evidence of genuineness.

Education and Its Lack

There is a manner of thinking and writing innate with highly educated people. I do not mean by this literary excellence, because such people may and often do write dully and at times obscurely. Roosevelt and Grant had different styles, neither being at all equal in literary merit to, let us say, such lesser lights as the critic Heywood Broun, or whoever the current literary god may be. But a thoroughly educated man of the type I mean somehow puts his own picture in whatever he writes. He will not consider what he speaks of as unique in a singularly unoriginal world, for he knows many things like it. His emphasis stops short of over-emphasis. His vocabulary will, as a rule, be rather large. There will be a bookish touch in what he says and more than a few allusions that would not occur to all. The best illustration of the kind of believability that inheres in everything such people say that I can think of was when Senator Proctor of Vermont came back from Cuba and told this country what he had seen there. It was just before our war with Spain—just before, for the simple reason that his sober account resolved America to fight Spain. Proctor was temperamentally the most unsensational man imaginable, a very grave and reverend senior. There were no "winged words" in his story, no epigrams, nothing quotable, but the ring of perfect truth was in every word.

The many reserves and hesitations in his telling would, I suppose, be anathema to a professional writer of advertisements. I don't say reserve and hesitation are good copy qualities; but I do say that if any copy writer had Proctor's intellect, education and character, his copy would have reserve and hesitation at the right places and no other.

The point I am arriving at is that, first, a high degree of education will quite unerringly make believable even amateurish advertising. Second, that a quite low degree will frequently do the very same thing. That is one of the inconsistencies of faith. Occasionally there strays into print the advertising of some man who chooses to write his own copy but who has had scant schooling. His very ignorance, oftener than not, makes his advertising amazingly profitable. One case was an Italian restaurateur who sent out a circular of his own composition, in ludicrous English, that drew customers by scores to his shabby place in a side street. Another was the apparently "corking" copy put out by a laundry-man who employed a high-priced copy expert. He lost trade until he wrote his own ingenuous appeal that brought housewives flocking to his place.

Senator Proctor tells what he saw in Cuba. His education and intellect are high. We, the public, feel that they preclude misrepresentation. He is believed, and that speech drives Spain from our shores. An Italian chef tells about his little restaurant. His ignorance and lack of learning make us smile. But we believe him as we do a child. He has not mind enough to lie, we reason, and his modest fortune is made by his circular.

"Giving Yourself Away"

It is contrary to all advertising doctrine that advertising should admit a fault in the thing advertised. Yet it is among the oddities of faith that we seldom believe a statement which is an unqualified catalog of excellences, just as seldom as we really like a strong man until we learn his little weaknesses and failings.

I will never forget looking at a Fox typewriting machine in a store run by a young Irishman in the Rue Vivienne, Paris. The Fox is an English machine built apparently by a maker of battleships. Every type bar and part is about five times too massive for its purpose. This young fellow did his Irish best to sell it, but was betrayed into the admission, "Sure, it's cloomsy (clumsy) but—"I bought it on the spot, enraptured. I knew it had no other faults, or he would have blurted them out"—sure.

In Chicago once a year there came to my office a collector for a local bureau that spotted and put out of business fraudulent charities. The bureau saved offices such as mine many a toll that would have been levied by swindlers. I was hesitating about making my annual contribution of $10 when this collector burst out, quite in the Paris Irishman's style, "I know we're nothing but beggars." It was just the naïve touch that reminded me what a really honest institution his humble bureau was and he got his money, and we both got a good laugh that was worth $10 by itself.

There never was and never will be a perfect automobile, soap, fireless cooker, breakfast food, burglar alarm, novel, hotel, advertising agency or anything else. You have a deathless affection for a certain chop-house or a certain tailor, but haven't they defects? Doesn't the tailor invariably misfit the vest in front and doesn't your favorite waiter lag with the second helping of butter when you order pancakes? Have you ever encountered perfection anywhere on earth except in advertisements? Wouldn't it be friendlier if they admitted an occasional drawback, as that the automobile was not constructed to climb trees or the fireless cooker to smelt ores?

In every sincere telling there is an element of confession. Until the fly in the ointment is disclosed the story is instinctively known to be too good to be true. The vise advertiser may safely "give himself away" somewhere if only to be believed in the main.

Superlatives

A good many publications will not allow advertisers to apply superlatives to their products. In the beginning this irked many copy writers or their employers, but I believe most of these have since learned that the inhibition helped them by making their story more believable. For a magazine that was unusually strict in forbidding superlatives I once wrote as follows:

"One of our fixed rules is not to admit advertisements that apply superlatives to the product discussed. This rule has cost us many a dollar, for not every advertiser will amend his manuscript. We ask him, 'Suppose, at the same time we print the statement that your machine is the best, some other concern, making a similar apparatus, advertises with us that theirs is the best? Where does that leave us for consistency—we, who guarantee every statement our advertisers make?' The reply often is, 'Yes, but mine is the best!' It matters not that housewives, comparing and pricing the two devices, buy the other as often as his—his is still the best!

"We have never met a manufacturer who said that he made the 'second best' article of its kind! We never expect to. But if such a rare being should turn up and announce his article as second best, the startling, the revolutionary frankness of the thing would sell his goods—because it would establish his truthfulness on such a firm base that in the next breath he might make almost any claim and be believed!

"If one advertises that an article is healing, delicious, economical, light, durable, nickel-plated, antiseptic or anything else definite, the mind can grasp the claim, weigh it and act on it. But what does *best* really mean? Best for whom? For what? Isn't it about as inept as the 'best best' occasionally used by frenzied advertisers?

"You open a magazine at random, see the name of a soap more or less unknown to fame, and are told it is 'the best soap made.' Of all the hundreds of soaps devised by man's skill in centuries, you just happen to have learned of the supreme detergent of them all! You feel as Madame Curie felt when she discovered radium—or, if you are like most of us, you say 'Piffle!' and turn the page.

"The genius who wrote of his soap 'It floats' knew the art of inducing belief better."

Guaranteeing

The reference to guaranteeing in the above reminds me of a curious phase of mass belief. In law, in transactions between trained business men, and when embodied in contract form, the guarantee of anything is the strongest claim or promise that can be made. It obliges the seller to make good financially for the shortcomings of what he sells. A warranty deed is a guarantee of title laying the seller under binding obligations. An insurance policy is a form of guarantee.

But in advertising the stubbornest unbelief the great good-natured public ever shows is aroused by the word "guarantee." This is not an idle statement. The magazine from which I have excerpted guaranteed every advertisement between its covers unqualifiedly. I know, because I received the rare and few claims for reimbursement sent in by readers and my orders were to send checks even if the claim was frivolous or unfair. We advertised this guarantee to readers with a persistency that wearied even ourselves and with every change we could ring upon the language of truth and sincerity. But all to no avail, or to little avail, for a long time. I may say, it took two or three years, or more, before there were signs that any considerable part of our public believed us.

There have been cases where guarantee "got across" more easily, as with the first introduction of Holeproof hosiery, but I think that was because in every case the dealer was asked by an intending buyer as to the sincerity of the promise and gave his personal word in support of it, making its believability rest on other grounds than printed assurances.

I think the public's skepticism about guarantees comes partly from the fact that the word has been used recklessly for years by all sorts of sellers who meant nothing tangible by it, and partly by the fact that the word itself to many people, and especially to women, means merely emphatic assurance and not legal obligation.

I have seen a good many manufacturers, and some publishers, vastly worried when it was first proposed that they embody guarantee in their policies. I have seen them call in their lawyers to scrutinize the wording of the guarantee lest it involve them in unforeseen and huge responsibilities. They were business, men and as such had found guarantee a dangerous thing to play with. I have seen the same men afterwards both astonished and relieved, and still later disappointed, to find out that the American consumer puts no faith in and pays no attention one way or the other to advertised guarantees.

Motives

If an advertiser promises to do something that looks to be rather noble and disinterested he should never omit to explain his motives for doing so, if he expects to be believed. There is always a business reason for doing things of this sort. The public knows that to be the case and looks for the "bug under the chip," that is, some selfish motive—usually making the wrong guess.

The guarantee, for instance, is usually announced with a flourish as of some great public service. This may account for the lack of enthusiasm the public shows for it. Publishers guarantee advertisements in the hope of increasing their pull and so selling more space. They ought to say so. Manufacturers guarantee in order to facilitate and speed up sales. They ought to say so. Theirs is a legitimate motive and nothing to be ashamed of. The explanation would enlist public belief and make the guarantee show results.

There has been an epidemic within very recent times of stores announcing reductions of prices, the asserted object being to reduce the cost of living or some other public-spirited end. The public accepts the lower price but not the motive. I am sure the whole advertisement would enlist more belief and make more sales if the advertiser said—what all of us knew pretty well, as it chances that we read the news columns as well as the advertising—that sales were slow and previous prices failed to move the goods.

The rising vogue for institutional advertising has brought with it a good deal of pompous pretense and a considerable effort to paint the enterprise advertised as a species of humanitarian effort or as the realized dream of an idealist. The average copy writer will take this view, if permitted, as easily and inevitably as the average commercial artist will pick out and paint the one picturesque corner in a grim factory. "It is their nature to," God bless them, seeing that they have, respectively, the literary and the artistic temperament.

Only, it would be so much better literature and art if each faced the true romance of business, a stern romance of hope, struggle, persistence, victory against dragons and monsters that spawn in sky-scrapers and emit poisoned breaths of protested checks. There is plenty of thrill in business, and plenty of beauty in factories. If institutional advertising could let us share the joy of the game as the money-winner feels it, and make us understand why he loves his smoky chimneys like a father, we would believe what he prints—which we don't now.

Various Media Useful

Human nature is so made that if the same news reaches us from different sources we very soon believe it, while it might be repeated from one source many times without winning much added credence. For this reason the believability of any concern's advertising is fostered by its appearance in a variety of media, such, for example, as newspapers, magazines, car cards and posters, or any like combination. I do not know that I can adduce proof of this statement from any particular campaign, but I think many buyers of advertising will recall successes springing from this principle, whether varied media were adopted for that reason or an altogether different one.

Unbelievable Advertising

The division of labor that obtains in modern advertising, and some other conditions that surround it, are responsible for much advertising of the kind that does not command consumer belief and, therefore, pays poorly.

This situation occurs constantly: A manufacturer employs a copy writer, or he employs a manager of some sort who in turn employs a writer, or the manufacturer accepts the services of an agency and it writes his advertising. In any event, the employer is the final authority. He probably is not fitted for the role so well as the agency he hires. Or, if his own man or men write for him, he is the blind leading the blind except in the unusual case that these men are high-priced experts. Even in the latter event they are his minions and will obey him pretty closely.

His business is a part of himself. His personal pride and his pride in the product are closely interwoven. He is pleased and flattered by praise of his goods in print. He can with difficulty be induced to approve a moderate style. His whole experience has been with tangibles. Here he enters another field where intangibles—mass opinion, human nature, literary values—reign. He is out of his sphere and does not realize it. Some parts of advertising, such as the appropriation, the mechanism of circulation, the successes of other advertisers and the personalities of the agency heads who meet him as an equal, are quite in his line and give him the fallacious conviction that advertising is only another phase of that business life where he has been winner so far. His shrewdness even shows him that much of the "expert" counsel offered him is not expert. He leans less on professional advice in advertising than he does in matters of law, architecture or health, where experts self-evidently can guide him.

The net result of his contact with the tangle of pretense, self-interest, error and waste called advertising is, on the whole, an inferior, not very believable and, therefore, expensive kind of advertising, from which only the fool-proof quality of advertising itself can be relied on to yield the frequent profits it does.

There can be no complete remedy suggested, but it lies within the power of any intelligent advertiser to learn what makes advertising believable and then so guide his writers that greater profit results.

Chapter 16

Looking at Copy and Looking Into It

By Harry E. Cleland[1]

Once upon a time—thus the story runs—the so-called "ad writers" were cocks o' the walk and ruled the roost.

Presently some bright genius, who had probably flopped at "ad writing," discovered that copy was not all there was to advertising. He climbed the then tallest building and trumpeted his message to other aspiring "ad writers" whose pens had likewise wabbled in the pinches: "Welcome to our city!"

After a bit, nearly everybody was convinced that copy, far from being the whole of advertising, was something that existed on the southernmost hair of the dog's tail—and was put there to annoy the dog.

Thus this business of advertising see-sawed between this and that with the loudest voiced faddist straddling the center and teetering the board to his fancy. It suffered from growing pains in an up-and-down direction.

Now I submit, with all due respect to the discoverers of new 'isms and to the devotees of whatever the latest cult may be, that one basic fact remains true in advertising.

All that the buyer sees is the finished job. Why it got there or how, why that place was selected for its appearance, how many conferences were held before it was launched, which thoughts were emphasized and which expurgated—all these mean nothing in the ardent reader's young life.

So, you may engross it on parchment and rivet it to the linings of your hats that—

---

1. *Harry E. Cleland.* A writer for many years of technical advertising copy, with agencies and the service departments of the large technical publishing houses. Well known as an expert in technical advertising and at technical copy.

While copy is not all there is to advertising it is all there is to an advertisement.

I include, of course, in the term "copy" the art-work, text and typography.

Industrial Copy

Having established the importance of copy, we proceed rapidly in a northerly direction to a discussion of industrial copy as such.

I take it that this is no kindergarten class in the subject and that all of you know your little book and are able to write copy yourselves or constructively to criticize it. All of us know that there are three things we can do well—manage a ball team, run a hotel and write advertising.

It would serve no useful purpose to bring examples of bad industrial advertising here and point out their defects. That would merely be to pose as an apostle of the obvious.

Nor is there much to be learned from selecting a few good advertisements and indicating their merits. They may not be as fine as they appear when measured in the micrometer of results.

Criticizing adversely single advertisements with no knowledge of the background of them is like condemning the population of a city because a few citizens choose to commit mayhem.

Likewise, bringing a few pages of copy here and holding them up as examples of excellence, will lead to ejaculation of that well-known bromide, "They mean nothing to me—my business is 'different.' "

So I have chosen to discuss industrial copy in its broader aspects. If we get the foundation sound, the superstructure may at least stand up.

Hobby Riding

I believe that industrial advertising has been riding a hobby too hard and has foundered the beast. It has chosen to flock by itself altogether too much on the ground that it is a highly specialized form of advertising which has nothing in common with general advertising. It has proclaimed that there is no kinship between lingerie and line-shafting, that perfumery and pumps are not on speaking terms and that the principal relationship between scented soap and motor trucks is an odor. There is some truth in the allegation, of course, but taking it too literally is not leading to any improvement in the advertising pages of the general run of business papers.

Humanity averages pretty much the same. To assert that business men as such cannot be reached through their emotions is a brave attempt to alter fundamentals, but it won't work. Business men are still susceptible to fear, beauty, blemish, humor, greed, vanity, ambition and a host of other things that mark the difference between mere men and that figment of a playwright's imagination—the super-efficient Robot.

By all means let us be human in industrial copy. A man may be an engineer, yet few of them are afflicted with that deadly thing known as the engineering mind. We are led to believe that most of them have it because it is emphasized by being the exception, not the rule.

A shop-keeper is not so deadly serious about spending money to make money that you have to present your subject embalmed in a sarcophagus. Smile once in a while. Humor is the shock absorber of business.

Ideas are driven home by contrast. It's good drama, good psychology and good advertising to get your effects by light and shade. Not long ago Fred Stone, the comedian, whipped from buffoonery to a serious discussion of religion, and, after the first shock of surprise, carried his audience to enthusiastic approval, mainly by contrast.

Your good salesman knows the method and uses it. Emulate him. Emulate him all the way through your copy if you can and you will never go very far wrong.

It takes three people to produce a good advertisement. Any more spoil the broth. As, you know, they are the writer, the artist and the printer.

I plead for more harmony among them, a more sympathetic understanding of the other's viewpoint. The trouble is each one wants to push his own pet into the parlor. The result is a lack of balance in advertising that makes it repulsive or otherwise inefficacious. I have known printers to suggest lifting entire paragraphs of text to get certain typographical effects. And I've known writers to insist on retaining every last word to the exclusion of white space and any beauty that the printer might have injected into the layout.

Originality Pays

We need more originality in industrial copy. When one can pick a dozen advertisements out of one technical paper and by simply changing name and address and perhaps the half-tone make any one of them apply equally well to any of the others, there's evidence of lack of both thought and ideas. There are only words.

When every first issue in January contains a dozen admonitions to the reader to "begin the New Year right," it's evidence that somebody's harkening to Salvation Nell's song and is "following on."

We need better English in industrial copy. By that I don't mean primarily better grammar. I mean that we should use this wonderful tool with skill and care so that we may inject our ideas into the consciousness of our readers and make them stick.

I remember having hired a writer once upon a single word—and my judgment was amply vindicated. There wandered into the old Hill Publishing Company a man of not over-prepossessing mien who thought he wanted to write advertising copy. He was a newspaper reporter. I gave him a test job. The product was a machine tool. The concern had invented the term "centralized control" to indicate that the operator could stand in one position and manipulate it to perform every operation of which the tool was capable. The newspaper man in a terse sentence described this and then said, "Contrast this with shuttling the operator back and forth." The word, of course, was "shuttling"—a picture in itself. That man became one of the best technical copy writers and last season the Century Company published his second novel.

It was *Sentimental Tommy, I* believe, who lost an essay contest because the time limit expired while he was searching for a word which didn't mean precisely this nor exactly that but was between the two and yet leaned a bit to the latter. Tommy's opponent became a good hack writer. Tommy went on to genuine fame.

Industrial copy needs this same care in the selection of words. It's only when you're making a speech to a defenseless audience that you can afford to be slipshod. And then you shouldn't!

How Long Should an Advertisement Be?

Every so often—and sometimes in between—Mr. Manufacturer rises to announce that nobody reads long advertisements. So the moot question has been and is, "How long should an advertisement be? "Nobody has ever answered that question satisfactorily. Certainly it should be just long enough to carry its objective and no longer. If you can get any satisfaction out of that answer, make the most of it.

One way to shorten copy is to shorten the words. Practice writing your headlines and text in words of one syllable. You'll be amazed at the strength of your copy. All good writing is distinguished by simplicity. It's the essence of strength. For instance, if you wish to indicate that your material handling machinery reduces the working force from ten men to one, you may choose to say in your headline—"Manual Labor Materially Reduced" or "It Took Ten Men to Handle This Job Before" or "Are You Affected by the National Labor Shortage?"

If I had the job, I should say: "In Place of a Gang, a Man!"

They are all words of one syllable and make a picture that almost instantly occurs before the reader's vision.

Fat Phrases

I wonder if you will agree with me that there is too much pomposity in industrial copy. It's usually the result of taking our business too damned seriously. It waddles around like a very fat and very serious old woman. Avoirdupois and dignity may be all right taken separately but they make an alarming combination.

You've all read advertisements full of mouth-filling words and turgid rhetoric with an idea buried somewhere beneath a mass of phrases. I think that the war and excess profits were responsible for this. In any event they seemed to occur simultaneously—with no armistice yet declared.

It was rather discouraging to find that a publisher had lately acquired the habit. He wanted to tell the world that a certain class of men were the real thing and that said world should appreciate the fact. It was a perfectly good and simple theme, but the copy was such that only a very patient reader could dig out the idea.

Now, of course, the answer will be, "But look at the impression we made and the letters we got!" But that reply fails to move me. That particular line of advertising was a form of flattery. You can flatter a man in any language and with any words and he'll come right back and kiss you.

So I suggest greater simplicity in industrial copy. It means greater clearness, less effort on the reader's part, more chance of driving the argument home. Big words and long sentences do not denote strength any more than a 60-inch waistline does. Look at the master writers of English and you'll find that they get their effects by the simplest means.

Who was it that said, "You must forgive the length of this letter. I haven't time enough to write a short one."

Modern Advertising Writers

Witness the master advertising writers of today. Does Fletcher search for words that he himself cannot understand? Not on your life! Yet he makes an imitation pearl seem more alluring than the real thing and a barber shop, by the magic of his pen, becomes a life extension institute. When Jim Henry, salesman, takes his stubby pencil in hand, and chews the end off, does he try to impress by his erudition? Not so that it can be observed! Yet Mennen's went on the map with a bang and stayed there.

I quote these examples of writing from the general field because that is where we must go to find the best. As I remarked at the beginning of this talk, it's time to drop our insular attitude and take a look at the world around us.

Any of these writers whose work we admire could take a highly specialized industrial account and write copy of the same distinctive character.

In our organization we recently established a service department and to get away from that musty old word we call it the Results Department. It was placed in charge of a man who, knowing none of the traditions or precedents of the average business paper, will probably break all the unwritten laws—and thereby make a great success.

I believe that a higher premium should be placed on advertising writing. I don't mean by that that any one should have his salary boosted tomorrow. But make it an incentive to become a writer and stay one. The trouble now is that you develop a first-class man and then "promote" him to assistant manager or club salesman. As a matter of fact such a move should not be a promotion at all. I have never heard of an association of advertising writers, but there should be one. And one of its principal jobs should be to advertise the value and importance of copy.

Ideas Are Needed

We need more ideas in advertising copy. An oil company conceived the idea of publishing in its advertising the exact grade of its lubricant to use in every make of automobile. Naturally every car owner ran down the list to find his baby and the kind of oil that would keep it healthy.

A bookkeeping-machine concern took accounting out from under the shadow of the pen—and showed the pen and its drab shadow in every advertisement.

The maker of a hand shovel—one of the commonest of tools—painted a red edge on his product and it marked a red-letter day in the history of that business.

A paint maker, instead of sticking to the rubber stamp method of naming his product "white enamel," calls it "barreled sunlight."

Those are ideas—for lack of a better name—which show some thought. The advertising writer should daily beseech his Maker, "Oh, Lord, this day make me think!"

The correct writing of copy is not a science nor anything like it, unless common sense be a science. It cannot be guided by mathematical rules nor governed by immutable laws.

Whenever we think we have established some standard, somebody breaks all the measurements—and gets away to a huge success.

Formidable?

However, there are certain things the young aspirant should study. A study of form and balance and decoration to lend beauty—sturdy or delicate—to his layout. A study of grammar and rhetoric, of course. A study of the style of the best writers of English prose—ancient and modern. A close observation and study of human nature, its frailties and strength, and something of the psychology of the crowd.

A formidable program, perhaps, but a necessary one if we are to have our copy in the hands of men who will do their share toward making the advertising dollar worth par.

This advertising dollar is a circle of many segments. One of the largest is copy. Lift it out and you leave a gaping void which cannot be filled by some cheap expedient. There is no substitute for it.

Chapter 17

The Human Side of It

By Wilbur D. Nesbit[1]

You can always get a man's attention by offering to do something for him, or offering to show him how he can be happier, how he can better himself. If we were to say to a man: "You don't want to buy a phonograph, do you?" we would at once suggest "No" for an answer. But if we presuppose that he knows a great deal about phonographs, that the social position of his family demands a phonograph of real beauty as well as of mechanical excellence, and if our headline intimates to him that his own sincere judgment will be in favor of the Blank Machine, we will get much further with him. An advertising campaign setting forth the advantages of canned fruits and vegetables used well, displayed headlines telling that the first canned goods were put up for Napoleon's army. That historical fact jolted the dormant attention of the reader at once. He saw Napoleon planning his great campaigns and depending on cans of corn and beans and peaches to help him win. There are many advertisements of razors and shaving soaps. The first successful safety razor was blazoned to the possible user by the alluring promise of "No Honing, No Stropping." If you desire to instill human interest into advertising a shaving soap or a razor, get down your history and read how Alexander the Great inaugurated the custom of shaving. Historical

---

1. *Wilbur D. Nesbit* began work as a printer. He followed that by newspaper work, as reporter and city editor. As advertising manager of a department store in Indianapolis he began writing jingles, which led to his producing the newspaper features for which he is well known. From that work he turned again to advertising. He is one of the best known copy writers and account executives. He is the author of a number of books, as well as of the highly popular patriotic poem, "Your Flag and My Flag." He is president of the Forty Club, Chicago's famous dinner organization; has been president twice of the Indiana Society of Chicago; formerly president of the Chicago Advertising Club.

characters are always interesting and always attract attention to an advertisement.

The heading of an advertisement is much like the title of a story. Kipling is a master at devising titles. "The Man Who Would be King" arouses our interest and attracts our attention, for example, much more than if it were "An Episode in India." "Barrack Room Ballads," as the title for a book of poems, whets one's curiosity. It brings up a mental picture of a long barracks room, with jovial soldiers lounging about and blending their voices in song. It has color and life in it. If that book had been called "A Book of Indian Poems" it would not have taken such a hold on the public.

One of the prominent magazines published an article about a man who has been a cripple all his life; it tells how this man realized his ambitions and made a success of himself. If the magazine had featured the story as "The Story of a Cripple," it might have attracted the attention of a few sympathetic souls, but when it was blazoned on the cover as "A Wonder Story of Will Power," it grew into something different and greater. Similarly, a magazine article entitled "A Man Who Has Loaned Millions to Other People" puts the glamour of romance about a narrative of a man who organized a new kind of savings banks.

White space will attract attention. A proper margin of white space about an advertisement emphasizes the headlines and the text.

Interest can only be aroused by sincerity. Interest must be cumulative. Notice how a public speaker holds his audience. He does not crowd his climaxes; he does not utilize his strongest points first of all. He begins by attracting the attention of his audience. He opens his address with a statement with which the audience will either agree or disagree. If possible he gets the sympathy of his audience. His next line of thought will be something that increases the interest of his hearers. If he is earnest, if he is sincere, his earnestness and sincerity become contagious. An audience soon loses interest in a speaker who is obviously not wholly sincere, not interested in his own argument. Similarly a reader discerns very quickly when a writer is "writing against space." And once you lose the interest of a reader you lose that reader—that possible customer.

The greatest interest of all is self-interest. If you can plan and word your advertisement so that it is apparently written from the reader's side, it will hold his attention. He will feel that it is a sympathetic kind of advertisement, that it has his welfare at heart. A manufacturer of typewriters was planning an advertising campaign. He was eager to get away from the beaten path, to avoid talking about cams and ratchets and cogwheels and type bars. He reasoned that the buyer and user of a typewriter was not necessarily a trained mechanic, nor was he interested in mechanical specifications. He desired a real selling thought embodied in his advertising, and it must be a selling thought that was obviously in the interest of the customer, for therein lay his great opportunity of gaining the sympathy of his readers. He evolved the idea of showing that his typewriter was so well made that it would stand the hardest usage and still be a good machine after service of a year, or two years, or even three or more years. His advertisements told that here at last was a typewriter that did not need to be bought with the definite understanding that it would be taken in trade later on. With this idea as the starting point it was possible to weave in mechanical arguments without using mechanical terms. Over and over this thought was expressed in his advertising, and as a result of the campaign his typewriter gained a prominence it had not enjoyed before. He attracted attention, he aroused interest, he argued persuasively, and he induced action—he made sales.

The question is often asked: How long should an advertisement be? It has been argued that all that can be told in any advertisement may be expressed in a few terse sentences. An advertisement should be like the story attributed to Abraham Lincoln. It was said that he was asked how long a man's legs should be. He replied: "Long enough to reach from his body to the ground."

An advertisement should be long enough to tell its story. No longer and no shorter. If you will imagine an advertisement as a salesman, telling a stranger about a new product, you can visualize the efforts of that salesman to attract attention, to arouse interest, to present his argument, and to make the sale. A few terse sentences will not suffice. If the salesman were to stand before the customer and bark epigrammatic sentences at him, the customer would be apt to turn on his heel and seek a more pleasing conversationalist. On the other hand, if the salesman were to drift into an interminable harangue, the customer would be apt to excuse himself and go where he would be given a chance at least to think, if not to take a little part in the conversation himself.

For this reason it is better to avoid trying to tell it all in one advertisement. Selling an automobile, for example, is not a matter of getting the prospect's check on his first visit. Patience, the emphasizing of a different quality or feature each time the prospective customer is in the salesroom, is the good salesman's method.

Analyzing the product and its possible market brings out many good selling points, each of which may well be selected as the subject for an individual advertisement.

In time it will be found that one or two of these are the best selling points. Then they will be used as the keynotes and the other points woven in with them. A phonograph, for instance, may be advertised because of its tonal quality. But in time this emphasis will be found to be losing its force. Then the advertising will be changed to bring out the beauty of the cabinet, showing that the musical charm of the instrument is receiving a housing in keeping with its superiority; and so on, point by point. There are few articles which cannot offer at least ten good points—subjects for separate advertisements.

You must consider the people who are to buy the article you are advertising. In writing advertisements of gloves, we may say, you will use a different argument to persuade a woman to purchase a fine dress glove than you would to induce a man to buy a working glove.

In the one case you would appeal to woman's natural love of beauty. You would show how the glove enhanced the natural charm of her hand, how it gave her the finishing touch of being well-groomed. You would mention the fact that the gloves are the last to be put on, that they either make or mar the costume. Then you would tell how carefully these gloves are made, how exactly they are stitched, how they have been designed, perhaps, by some eminent glove-artist in Paris, and so on. And you would never forget to impress her with the fact that these gloves bear the seal of the latest fashion.

But with the work glove you would go about your task in another way. You would show how ruggedly it is made, how stoutly it is stitched. You would tell how long wear and great durability are made into it. You would tell how well it fits the hand, and how it really helps to do better work because it supports the muscles of the hand when they are weary. Your imagination would have you at work, out in the cold, wearing a pair of those gloves and doing the best day's work you ever accomplished because of that fact.

You would make the woman feel that here was somebody who was accustomed to moving in the best society and knew what was the exactly correct mode in dress gloves; you would make the man feel that here was somebody who knew what hard work was and who knew through experience how to select a glove that would lighten that hard work.

Some people, in writing advertisements, either accidentally or purposely omit asking the reader to buy the article advertised. Now, the end and aim of an advertisement is to sell, not just to get the reader mildly interested, so that some time when he is down town he will, if he happens to think of it, go into a store and ask to be shown whatever it was that was advertised. Your advertisement should convince the reader that he is going to be more than satisfied with his purchase, and should put him in a purchasing mood. Often a writer will think it really beneath his dignity to say to his reader:

"Please buy this." He feels as if this puts him behind a counter, serving whoever comes down the aisle. Yet that is just what he is doing, and if he believes in himself, and believes in the goods he is advertising, and believes in the manufacturer of those goods, he is performing a true service when he leads his reader to make the purchase.

If you are writing an advertisement for a kitchen cabinet or a refrigerator, you will not write it as you would one for a piano or for a library table. Pianos and library tables have their elements of beauty; they are to be seen as well as to be used. They are in the higher sphere of life. But the refrigerator is not always a spotless thing of beauty, holding fresh fruits and meats and eggs and other appetizing things. Nor is the kitchen cabinet always standing, immaculate, against the wall, its door glistening and its shelves arrayed with shining jars and glittering knives and things. There are days when both refrigerator and cabinet must be cleaned. A maker of refrigerators and a maker of kitchen cabinets kept this in mind in their advertisements. They told how the refrigerator would keep things fresh and sweet, and how the cabinet would save thousands of steps and lighten the work in the kitchen. But they also told, and told very emphatically, how easy it was to scrub and wash and clean the refrigerator and the cabinet. They told of smooth surfaces—no square panels or corners to catch and hold dust or dirt and grease. They put a "Saturday-night clean-up" atmosphere into their advertisements, and they convinced the women who read them that they had at heart the interests of the women who had to work at keeping house. And their campaigns succeeded.

There is nothing that one man sells and another man buys that does not have its angle of human appeal.

It must meet a human need, satisfy a human desire, or gratify a human whim.

A musical comedy gratifies the very human wish for color and sound; a drama appeals to human sentiment; a story, to human understanding; and a sermon, to human conviction.

The successful advertisement approaches the reader along the same lines.

As we have said, there is no business organization that does not have in it and of it an individuality, whether of one man or a composite of many men.

The greater this individuality the greater the success of the business organization. Advertising is the expression of this characteristic, of this human appeal.

You cannot submerge or suppress it; advertising to be good, must extend the personality of the concern to its prospective customers.

It is just as much a part of the policy and the operation of the concern as is its product.

Good advertising is virtually a product of the house it advertises. It serves the customers of that house.

Good advertising is good nature. Good nature is the greatest human appeal on earth; not "jollying," not lightness of verbiage, but the good nature of sincerity, of friendliness.

That sort of advertising makes people glad to read it. If a man can write that kind of copy, people are always going to stop at the page holding this advertisement, and stop with pleasant anticipation. You can read an advertisement and come pretty near telling what kind of treatment the advertiser will give you. His individuality cannot be kept out of his advertising. If it is his advertising.

Advertising should be the advance agent of satisfaction. It represents the good faith of the house and must be as trustworthy and as confidence-begetting as the guarantee that goes with the goods. Some people buy things because they need them; some buy things because they are curious to know about them; some buy things because somebody else buys them; but all buy things because they want them.

Good advertising creates the want; good merchandising meets it.

Successful advertising is interwoven with successful merchandising and *vice versa*. The successful house, large or small, is the one that makes a human appeal, day in and day out, to its possible and its present customers.

The advertiser who believes in himself and in his goods inspires other people to share his belief.

The man who writes his copy approaches him as do his potential customers. It is for him to acquire the advertiser's enthusiastic belief. If he does that he cannot fail to show it in the copy. This kind of belief projects itself in simple, strong, earnest copy which commands the confidence of the reader and convinces him.

That is human appeal—contagious belief.

Human nature is the same in all phases of life. There has to be, there is, a human side to every advertising problem. Nine times out of ten it is the individuality of the organization whose product is to be advertised.

Put that individuality, that sincere, earnest belief, into it, and there is a natural and willing response.

A good advertisement follows the line of human appeal, which is by way of the heart and mind.

Chapter 18

Copy That Is and Isn't

By Harry Tipper[1]

One of the philosophers has said that the human race only progresses in so far as necessity compels it to do so, and I think that is, in quite a considerable measure, true. When a channel of communication is open, we are not apt to question its efficiency, but merely to use it. Before the war, we were carrying on our transactions with South America in a financial way through London, because there was a piece of machinery in London whereby bills of exchange could be promptly discounted from any quarter of the globe. We were quite content, therefore, to use that channel without finding out whether there was a better way of doing it. Similarly we were quite content, before the war, to take the by-product of coal, in its raw state, and ship it to Germany and get it back in the shape of dyes and chemicals, without considering whether there was some way by which we could utilize that by-product to make those things ourselves. It always happens that in the growth of industry or of any branch of it, precedents, traditions, established methods of doing things become so inherently a part of the customs of the industry that we fail to realize their proportionate values until some revolution, some abrupt change, some panic or some financial readjustment compels us to go over the whole phase of the industry with a new mind and a new light.

---

1. *Harry Tipper.* Born in Kendal, England. Educated at Kendal Science School. Experience in engineering, sales and advertising. Formerly: President of the Association of National Advertisers; president of the Advertising Club of New York City; president of the New York Business Publishers Association; at one time advertising manager and member of Sales Committee of the Texas Co. At present General Manager, General Motors Corporation Export Company. Author of *Human Factors in Industry, Discussion on Labor, The New Business, Advertising, Its Principles and Practices, Advertising Campaigns.*

In advertising, as in the rest of business, we must examine our work with the object of cutting out the waste, and I think we must realize that economy, that is, wise. expenditure, which is the real meaning of economy, is a matter of education and not a natural quality. It is observed always that the most ignorant people are the least careful in their expenditures. It is observed that people, who do not know, fear most to depart from precedent, because they cannot analyze the situation so as to take a new path wisely.

Therefore, in considering advertising, what is waste and what is efficient and wise expenditure in advertising, we must reckon with the fact that it will take a great deal more intensive concentration, analysis and consideration of the details of advertising in order to expend the money wisely and eliminate the waste and not the useful portion.

That means that we have to make every unit of advertising a little more efficient, do a little more work, and do that work with less waste, less delay, and with less weakness in its operation. One of the important ways of making each unit of advertising more successful is in a study of the copy that we are to use in filling the units of space that we occupy with advertising, whether that space be on a letterhead, whether it be in a pamphlet, whether it be in a publication or upon a signboard. All our work is confined within limits of space, and we must measure, therefore, our wise expenditures by the value of the unit of space, as completed and used.

I think that the question of copy is of considerable importance to the advertising man, a little more important today than at any other time, because, in times of prosperity, when buying is easy and therefore intensive selling not so acute, it is difficult to determine whether we succeed because of an expenditure or in spite of an expenditure, and I fear that our conclusions are frequently clouded by the general success and include as measures of success lots of things which would in other circumstances have become measures of failure.

So, in taking up the question of advertising copy, I do not believe that it is necessary to make any apology for considering it as important. As a matter of fact, the only thing which connects the advertiser with his public is the character of his copy. Everything else is simply a vehicle by which the copy can reach the man to whom the advertiser addresses himself, and, therefore, while copy is but one thing out of many, copy can exist and can work with little or no attention to the rest of the matter, but the rest of it cannot exist and cannot work unless attention is paid to copy.

It seems that copy is a matter which escapes definition. It refuses to be confined within adamantine limitations. It has nothing in common with mathematical formula or standardization, and it must be so when, in writing, we use a method of communication which can weave words so that they represent, as one writer has put it, the adamantine rigidity of a statue or can so liquefy words that they can coalesce individual opinions into a general sentiment. When a thing can be used for the limitations of the most mathematical and specialized operations, and at the same time be used to bring enthusiasm into a group of men on the most intangible and metaphysical of sentiment, such a medium can hardly be the subject of one definition or be expressed in a set of specifications with the possibilities of a standardization. In fact, it is necessary in considering such a subject to have recourse rather to the statement of what cannot be done than the statement of what can be done, for out of one hundred ways of saying a thing, ninety-nine ways may be the ways in which it should not be said.

In approaching the subject of copy, therefore, I do not propose to dwell upon those intangible platitudes with which you have been bombarded for nine or ten years, indicating the attention value, the interest, the conviction and the action contained in copy, because even though those platitudes may be true, they mean nothing when we are through with them, but I do propose to talk about four elements which copy must contain and which mark the success of copy in accordance with the degree with which they are used, and I name them in the order of the importance which I would attach to them: Knowledge of the audience. Knowledge of the subject. Knowledge of the language. Sincerity of purpose.

Walter Raleigh in his book, *On Style,* says that the speaker automatically provides his own audience. "One touch of the archaic in his words, and the doors are closed and the people are assembled in the seclusion of the quiet drawing-room, while a single turn of peasant speech or a rustic meaning given to a word which is not allowed in genteel parlance, and the roof is blown off the villa, and the inhabitants are set wriggling in the unaccustomed sunshine"; so that the man who writes makes his own audience, and if he does not understand the audience that he wants to reach, he will not reach it, whether he has ten million circulation or not, and whether he uses the best media that the country provides or not.

And yet we know audiences very little and study them, as advertising men, somewhat less.

You, of course, know of the historic advertiser that Frank Holliday so enjoys telling about, who has been advertising rubber boots in Texas for a number of years, when the country people in Texas wear leather boots and the city people wear rubbers. You have seen copy which has been sent out by the advertiser, with the same type, with the same surroundings, with the same illustrations and with the same sentiment expressed, appearing in the *National Geographic* and *Vanity Fair* at the same time, without any change. In fact, I have seen copy going to the technical engineer, to the merchandising dealer, and to the layman, who had no interest in either of the other two, without a single change and from the same place.

And then, think of the generalities which must occur when you don't know your audience, because if you cannot speak the language of the people, you are confined to those generalities which, meaning so little, cannot be criticized. We have some adjectives that have been so thoroughly worked out that we cannot use them ourselves. They have been misplaced and misused to such an extent that we can't even consider them.

I took about fifteen pieces of copy advertising one type of product, cut off the illustration and the rest of the identifying material, and then a couple of days afterwards tried to remember which was which. It was almost impossible. The remarkable unanimity of statement and the almost complete generalization of claim made it practically impossible to find any individuality.

Let us grant for the moment that advertising is successful from the mere reiteration of the name—as Matthew Arnold said, "beating it upon our weary brains like a hawker"—and that from mere familiarity and identification we can impress to a degree the audience of indiscriminating laymen, yet at what an expense of waste that must be, at what a tremendous inefficiency!

We are so inefficient in advertising that if we get 2 per cent returns from a magazine in inquiries, when we go out directly for inquiries, we are getting something to be really proud of, and if we get one-quarter of 2 per cent in orders from the inquiries, we are again elated, which means that we are getting just one-half of one per cent of the possibility of our work.

But that is not the only way in which we fail to study our audience. We fail to study the language of the specialized audience that we must reach. I would not be a bit surprised but what the failure to secure the proper results from specialized publications lies largely with the failure of the advertising man to get in and understand the audience that reads those publications. I question very much whether you, any more than I did, find it possible to study the audience of a particular medium through its editorial columns, as you should. If you are receiving a hundred and fifty magazines every month—and of course you don't look through them all at the office—how many of them do you understand editorially—I mean, not the editorials but the people who read them? And if you don't understand those people who read them, how are you going to write to them effectively?

Passing on from that element to the second one—knowledge of the subject—I think we have gone a long way from this question in the last few years. In fact, I have heard it stated in some quarters that a writer is better off if he doesn't know a subject. It is true that there are some men, and they are reasonably scarce in this world, who are provided with such a facility of language and such a capacity for adaptation, that they are able to seize upon the essential features of a possibility and present it to an audience with a very superficial acquaintance with it. But the average man is neither eloquent nor discerning unless he knows his subject, and I don't believe that the average man is any more eloquent or discerning in his written language than he is in his spoken language. We are working, in the advertising business, with the average man. We have thousands of copy writers, we have thousands of people who must write to this public that we reach, and they can't be all of that scarce character of genius which has a native capacity for adaptation of language. Yet we say it is not necessary to know the subject. That perhaps is another reason why we have such a lot of glittering generalities about a product.

The machinist knows that no two machines made from the same patterns, machined and measured with the same micrometers, gauged to the same gauges and finished in the same assembly shop are quite alike, and any man who has worked with machines for weeks at a time, as I have worked with them, knows that you must humor one machine a little differently from the other. And no two products were ever quite alike. And certainly no two business organizations that produce those products were ever quite alike. If it is not possible for the advertising man to know his subject well enough to seize upon the individuality of his own product and present it to his audience, his work is undoubtedly inefficient and he has lost the large opportunity of his purpose. Knowledge of the subject should be absolutely *a sine qua non* in advertising.

It is true that every man who knows his subject does not necessarily know how to write about it, but if a man have the first primary quality, which I have stated before and regard as of the most importance—the knowledge of his audience—and follow that with the knowledge of his subject, then, indeed, he can write, and write so as to express eloquently to his audience the possibilities that lie within his own grasp.

Knowledge of the subject, to my mind, is something which we have sadly neglected in almost all of our advertising. Why should you insult an engineer by addressing him as a layman? Why should you pretend that a merchant who is merchandising his goods cannot be reached in merchant language and with the merchant individualities of your product? Why should you think that the man who reads the *National Geographic* reads it from the same angle and expects the same language as the woman who reads *Vanity Fair*? Why is it that we can't spend more on the individual piece, wisely expend in time and money and make the individual piece really count for a much larger percentage of actual action?

Some people asked me a few years ago how it came about that in the outdoor advertising of the Texas Company I succeeded in getting so many head-on signs, particularly at the curves of the road, Well, it happened for just one reason: because I knew I didn't know anything about billboards; and, knowing nothing about them, and knowing that I wanted to use them, I decided to sit in the driver's seat of the motor car and find out what he could see and where he could see it and how much his vision varied under different conditions. I spent three thousand miles in the car, fifteen hundred just making general observations, and fifteen hundred with a little circle inscribed on the wind shield and cross lines to it, so that I could measure a little bit. Then I decided that the only things that I wanted were certain signs in certain places, and it didn't make any difference to me whether they were a little more expensive, because I knew that in total effect I would get four or five times the individual return.

Now, that is the way that business progresses, not perhaps by spending more upon the individual efforts, but by gaining so much more out of the individual effort that the total expenditure of effort and of time and money for a given return is less.

It is an increase of the unit value of space that we are after. Just look at the advertising yourself next time you pick up a magazine and compare that advertising with some of the old mail-order and patent medicine copy that we laugh at, that was set in six-point type and had no surroundings at all, and pulled to "beat the band." Notice the human difference between the way the one writer appealed to the audience and the way the other writer is appealing to the audience. It is true that we must know the surroundings, we must know why a certain kind of type represents an angular, square, constructive definition, and why another style of type represents an artistic and elusive proposition, and why a certain type of border belongs in the material side of things and another type of border attaches itself to the sentimental. We should know those things from the history of type and from the history of decoration, but all of that is simply to heighten the very message we have to give, simply to lend additional force by the physical appearance to what we have written, and not to support the egregious blunders that we make in the actual writing.

Further, this matter of knowledge of the subject goes a little deeper, for unless we know the organization that we are dealing with and the product that we have to sell, we will not only find it difficult to reach the audience, but we will find it difficult to understand the whole business of advertising in that connection, for human nature does not discriminate, according to our values, with our products; it does not view them in the same way that we view them. The outside, general human nature has nothing in common with our ordinary point of view as manufacturers, and it is not steeped in the endless operations that belong to that product. It views them from a different point of view, and, therefore, we must know something of the subject, as well as something of the audience in order to translate what we know into what they will understand. Unless we know it, how can we translate it?

The third point that I want to bring out is knowledge of the language. I have counted fourteen different automobile advertisements that were either "superior," "the most beautiful" or "the smartest" (or some other word of that kind) "car in America." Now, surely, there is something more about that wonderful construction, "the automobile" of any particular make, than that kind of a statement. Why, it embodies the brains of wonderful engineers, it has taken thousands of men to make it and has all kinds of separate and distinct parts in it that are themselves a beauty because of their strict usefulness. Can't anything be said of that but a mere word, that it is "the smartest," a superlative that means less than anything else, a qualification that does not qualify and a statement that really doesn't claim?

And yet perhaps we are a little bit like the man whom Walter Raleigh talks about, who, "being introduced to a language of a hundred thousand words that quiver through a million of meanings, is tempted by the very wealth of inheritance to be careless and is content if, out of those million highly tempered swords, he can construct a few clumsy coulters." For language is something which cannot be used by the careless. It is like putting an inefficient workman in charge of the finest of instruments, which must be handled by the most delicate of craftsman's hands, for it has grown up through the centuries, expressing at every stage some additional values of human emotion or human activity or human operation that have accrued to it, that have invented new combinations of letters to express themselves; it is in itself an epitome of human progress from beginning to end. If we knew how to use it, we should be able to write it. If we knew the language we should then know something of the audience itself, for it has expressed within it the whole gamut of human emotions. But we know so little that the average man's vocabulary is not more than between five hundred and one thousand words out of the hundred thousand that are possessed by us, and even of those words only about three hundred are ordinarily used, because in conversation, as a writer put it, in the ordinary flow of talk, not accuracy but immediacy of expression is required, and one passes on with his inadequate expression lest he be left in the belated analysis as the tide of talk flows past him. He wants to be immediate and not accurate, because he knows that his sympathetic hearer will infer from his own poverty what he himself could not express.

But for us who attempt to reach thousands to millions of people at one time, such an inadequacy of expression cannot be countenanced, and it is impossible in written language to allow the inferences which may be allowed in conversational tones, just as it is impossible to stand up on a platform and say the things as they would be said if the platform were not there. So we cannot afford to know language as little as the people that we reach. We must know language at least well enough to be simple, and it is astonishing how much knowledge it takes to be really simple. It is a curious thing about all mechanical arts, that they have progressed from crude complication to simplicity, so that they represent now in any one single machine more beauty than they ever did, because of the fact that the superfluities have been cut away. It is true that it has taken thousands and thousands of men to reduce one of those superfluities, and that it has taken more and more parts to make the operation more simple, just as it is true that it takes more study to understand language and it takes more words to arrive at a simple definition, more knowledge of words. You cannot expect to be lucid unless you know sufficiently of language to know why a word should not be used in a particular connection.

But back and above all this estimate of some of the fundamentals that are required in good copy and some of the things that we ought to do and do not do in copy, lies the one feature which must be a part of the writer's equipment, if he is to reach his audience, and that is sincerity of purpose. It is particularly true of the written word, what is true to some degree of the spoken word, that no man carries conviction unless he himself be convinced, for the written word has a way of carrying its own insincerity upon its face, of measuring to the cold eye of the man who reads it, without the atmospheric surroundings that help the speaker, of measuring to him the fallacies and the lack of conviction of the writer. So that we are able to say, as we read the books that have been written, that a writer here was playing for effect, that he was not convinced, that he was just constructing a frame work for a particular purpose, and that it didn't flow out of the fullness of his heart, as thoroughly and firmly convinced of the desirability of action.

And how, I ask, are you to be convincing if you don't know the audience, if you don't know the subject and if you don't know the language?

People say to me sometimes, "You know, I have an idea if I could only express it," but they forget that thought is born in language and that thought does not exist without words, and that anything which cannot be expressed is not. They forget that consciousness only begins with a spoken communication, and that there is no such thing in the world for useful purposes as an idea that cannot be expressed, and the very usefulness which we have is limited to the possibilities of our expression. There is little use in being sincere if we cannot translate.

I stood in New York the last day that Marshal Joffre was visible there, and I managed to hear a few words he said, but my French is not very good, and he spoke French rather rapidly, and it didn't connect. It was undoubtedly very beautiful, very fine, but it made no impression upon me, because I couldn't understand it. And why should you talk to people in Louisiana in phrases which are not known beyond the boundaries of the Eastern States? Why shouldn't you get down, when you talk to Louisiana, to the language that they know at home, the particular phraseology they use there?

I remember that some of the most successful copy I ever made for the State of Texas was written in Houston, Texas, in my office there, and six weeks after I got back to New York I couldn't write it. I had lost just the touch of the local atmosphere that was necessary to make the difference between ordinary copy and unusually efficient copy.

Finally, of all the things which man has to do, there is nothing quite so great as that of impressing other people or expressing to other people in writing. The whole of the accumulated knowledge of the world is compassed in a few books, because it is written. We have progressed in the mechanical arts, we have progressed in those other arts that are not yet purely mechanical, because we have been able to gather into our books the thoughts and the operations of thousands upon thousands of brains, doing a little, improving here and there and all over, and have brought that down so that in a few years a new generation can accumulate all that is necessary of what has gone before. There is nothing quite so great as the possibility of expressing to your people in written language.

While this is but one of the operations of advertising, and while it is not always the most important operation of advertising, I believe that a thorough knowledge of the fundamentals of copy will so illuminate all the rest of the advertising problem that a study of it will make us even better business men than we are, and certainly much greater advertising men in the time when our efficiency must be increased.

Chapter 19

The Sales Power of Good Copy as Demonstrated in Book Advertising

By Helen Woodward[1]

There is no doubt that the book-buying public in the United States has increased very much in the last few years. But this increase has been very small compared to the increase in the users of other luxuries—for instance, the users of fine silk stockings, good perfumes, automobiles.

There are many reasons for this comparatively small increase in the number of books sold; some of these reasons have to do with the kind of books published, their distribution, etc.; but one very important reason comes directly under the heading of advertising.

As a whole our publishers have not seen the opportunity and the possibilities of building up a new book clientele. There are a certain number of people who regularly buy books, and to these people, as a rule, publishers appeal exclusively. There are millions of people in the United States hungry for books, eager to be trained and shown how. These statements are not merely a matter of guesswork.

Years ago there existed, distributed among many now unknown publishers, a very large sale of sets of books on installments. These books were sold at most exaggerated prices. They were never sold on their merits—that is they were never sold on the reading matter that was in them. They were sold on the idea that there were 9,000,000 people who had already bought them and that volumes standing end on end would climb Mt. Everest and that volumes side by side would encircle the globe, or almost anything except the actual contents of the books.

---

1. *Helen Woodward.* Famous for her highly successful advertising copy for books and sets of books. Her advertisements for Mark Twain's and O. Henry's works brought quite remarkable direct selling results and set a new standard for book advertising of that type.

As a consequence this installment book business wore itself out in a very few years. It was never sound. There were a great many failures among these publishers and the book business was quiescent for a number of years.

At that time it occurred to one of our leading publishers that if books were sold at a fair price on installments and if they were sold for their contents by means of advertising copy very carefully prepared, rather than for their bindings, a solid business could be built up. This idea was carried out successfully by the *Review of Reviews, Harper & Brothers, Scribner's* and a number of other well-known publishers. And today after a number of years, an honest business that is substantial has been built up, and the names of some of our best American writers, such as O. Henry, Mark Twain, Richard Harding Davis and some others, have been placed higher than they ever had been.

It is important to notice that this sale is built almost exclusively on the idea that all books are sent on approval; therefore you have to have a satisfied customer and the only way to have a satisfied customer is to tell in advance what he is actually going to find in the books. There is no use telling him that O. Henry is the greatest writer that ever lived if he does not care for O. Henry's kind of book. If there had been any doubt in my mind about this it was very sharply dispelled by an experience of my own a few years ago.

One of our publishers had among their writers one of the most distinguished of American novelists. This writer appeals only to the very cultivated few. An attempt was made to sell the works of this writer in similar fashion to Mark Twain and O. Henry. The orders came in heavily but the books came back from customers almost as quickly as they went out. People had bought expecting to find something as popular as the advertising copy appeared to make it. Instead they found in the books a subtle and beautiful style for which they cared nothing. All this has a bearing on the advertising copy used for current new books.

Our publishers, as a rule, have a feeling that if they tell the public that John Jones has written a new book, that the public ought to rush to grab that book. There is, no doubt, a certain limited public that enjoys the work of John Jones and buys it as soon as it appears; but there are vast numbers of people that would like John Jones if someone would just tell them about John Jones and what he writes.

It is preposterous to think that in this country today there are only about 30,000 who buy the works of the three English novelists, who, with one exception, are perhaps the greatest living writers in the world. It appears to me certain that good advertising copy could make vastly more readers for these masters.

To go back once more to the installment book business. When we began, in this revival, to advertise O. Henry, we naturally picked out so-called literary magazines, but we have learned in the course of years that our big sale is not from these magazines. We have discovered dozens of media of which the publishers of new books know nothing at all. We should have to close shop on this installment book business if we should stick to the usual recognized literary media.

What does this mean? Simply that there are several million people in this country ready to buy books if someone tells them about them in the right way. To this there comes at once an objection on the part of most publishers which could be put thus: "Suppose we publish a new book by James Smith. James Smith sold 30,000 copies of his last book, therefore we can spend perhaps $2,000 on advertising his new book, altogether; otherwise we cannot get our money back."

There is no question that as a rule it would be impossible to get any real money back on a single book. It is possible that James Smith is a writer who will never appeal to more than 30,000, but if the author has a popular appeal I will venture to say that it is quite possible to increase that 30,000 to 100,000 or 250,000.

To do this the publisher would naturally have to be certain that James Smith was going to stay with him as an author and not go to some other publisher; in other words, he would have systematically to advertise James Smith as though James Smith were a fine pair of gloves, with the idea of his building up a permanent demand for James Smith.

One of the commonplaces of literary criticism is the wonder at the popularity of Harold Bell Wright. Yet there is no mystery here. It is simply a startling example of what can be done by systematic, organized advertising and publicity work. A great reputation has been built up for many by this method, and such similar sale could undoubtedly be built up for many another American and British author, if the publisher had the foresight to invest the time, money and thought, and use advertising copy which would produce a real understanding of the author, and consequently desire for his books.

In all my experiences in the advertising of other kinds of business I have never found any advertiser who approaches the sale of goods by advertising as the publisher does. Suppose we have a new soap to put on the market. Do you think for one moment that we would pick out simply two or three newspapers in New York, two in Chicago, one in Boston and one in Philadelphia, put two or three advertisements in each and sit back and say, "Now let's see how many pieces of soap we are going to sell? Suppose at the end of three weeks we found that we had sold 1,000 cakes of soap and perhaps in the course of the next year we sold two or three thousand more. We haven't much margin. We made perhaps $500, so let's spend $100 on a new kind of soap."

Of course this is a far-fetched case. The circumstances are not the same as those in the book business, but there is some similarity. The publisher puts out a new book, and as I said above, he advertises in two or three newspapers in New York, perhaps one in Chicago, one in Boston and one in Philadelphia and sits back. Except for literary reviews this money is practically wasted. But don't forget that these reviews are read only by people who are interested in reading books and are in the habit of buying books.

The vast millions of people in this country who read newspapers or magazines, but never read a review, will buy books if they are told how.

We have proved this on books sold on installments. If you can sell an author like Robert Louis Stevenson in popular style, you can certainly sell a new thriller by a popular writer of today.

The trouble with the publisher's approach to the advertising problem is fundamental and persists throughout his approach on all publishing problems. He insists, as a rule, on advertising as though he were producing literature. And most books published today have no relation to literature. There should be no attempt made to sell the average book to literary people. They should be sold for what they are—entertainment and a few pleasant evenings, a good story—a good cry or two and a good laugh or two. A large number of people would buy this kind of book who don't want to buy George Moore or Edith Wharton. But such people must reach conviction and appreciation through advertising which is done in a manner worthy of the task and its results.

In other words, there is a possibility for the publisher to build up a huge clientele for at least some of his writers if he would approach his product as a manufacturer would, and merchandise it and advertise in similar fashion.

My suggestions, therefore, are three: First, that the publisher advertise books for what is in them rather than some literary measure of forty years ago; second, that publishers appeal to a new public; and third, that publishers invest in a non-literary author with the same foresight which a soap manufacturer might invest in soap.

Chapter 20

The Copy Writer's Work Bench

By John Starr Hewitt[1]

The more one sees of the difficulties of copy writing, the deeper grows the conviction that really great copy depends even more on seeing and feeling than it does on writing.

The man who sees truly and feels deeply can hardly help writing sincerely.

Even at that, his writing will always give him trouble enough.

The truer and more ample the sight, the greater the difficulty of getting it *all* on paper.

And to express fully a fine, deep feeling calls for a writing skill possessed in the highest degree by only a few in each generation.

* * *

Some of the greatest writing that is being published today—and also much of the worst—is being printed in the advertising pages.

Probably the immature and the superficial are to be found in the other arts, also.

It may be too much to expect that advertising, which in its modern sense is hardly more than twenty-five years old, should have already reached the serene standards of maturity.

But it so happens that the copy writer owes a special obligation to his times.

---

1. *John Starr Hewitt.* Born in Burlington, New Jersey. Educated in private schools of Burlington and Philadelphia. Editorial and literary work with J. B. Lippincott Company, 18971907. In 1907 attracted to the advertising field by the copy writing genius of the late George L. Dyer and joined his organization in that year. Since 1911 Chief of Production for the George L. Dyer Company. A Director of the Company since 1912, and Secretary since 1923.

He has taken on himself voluntarily to give voice to the messages of commerce.

This commercial responsibility is no light thing.

Commerce is mature, substantial. It is the full-fledged expression of the peculiar spirit of our age. It is calling forth the highest creative genius of today.

This mature, self-conscious commercial genius will not forever put up with being weakly interpreted or misinterpreted in its advertising.

So it behooves the copy writer to grow up, get his work-bench in order, and learn to practice his art as a mature and conscious craftsman.

In every job that he undertakes is implied the promise to make a contribution to a commercial success.

No other writer assumes the same responsibility. The only obligation of the novelist, the poet, or the essayist is to interest a group of readers who are already predisposed to interest in the sort of thing he writes.

But the advertising writer promises his client not only to interest the reader, but to stir him up to positive buying action.

* * *

The copy writer who means sincerely to develop into the mature craftsman, may well stop here and take stock of where he stands now.

Perhaps he has already produced a considerable volume of acceptable copy. If he has any contact with the client, he has seen the results at first hand. On the surface of things, he might perhaps feel pretty well satisfied with himself.

But let him ask himself in all humility whether he owes his success to the merits of his work, or to the suggestibility of the American citizen.

The alert eagerness of the American mind is one of the marvels of the human race.

An enormous mass of superficial advertising gets by, simply because this alert consuming mind meets it more than half-way, reading into it a rich human meaning that the copy writer never put into it.

Let him take no comfort from the fact that the public is eager to buy, and so almost any kind of publicity may "make sales."

This eager buying mind is not a crutch for a weak, superficial performance. It is a challenge to the deepest, truest work that is in him.

His obligation—voluntarily assumed—is to express the full content of his client's business. *All* of it.

Not merely the physical facts of the merchandise, but all its human associations and meanings.

Not merely the human meanings of the merchandise, but the vision and ideals of the manufacturer.

And not merely the vision and ideals of the manufacturer, but his authority and leadership in his industry.

The whole American public is his audience.

All the hopes, and strivings, and ambitions of human nature are there for him to work with.

To the writer who has real love for merchandise, there is open a richness of writing material that will last him his life long.

In every industry, factory and technical process is contained a human drama waiting for the writer who can see it and give it authoritative voice.

The ideals of the manufacturer are the truest thing in his life. He puts them into his merchandise; but it is up to the copy writer to express them for him in words.

An opportunity for the copy writer if there ever was one—to make articulate the innermost dreams of a man's life! A challenge to insight, sympathy, understanding, and a call for the highest technique of the craft of writing.

There are four essential tools for the copy writer:

Sympathetic understanding of plain folks.
Genuine appreciation for the human facts about merchandise.
Sensitive feeling for what words mean to the other fellow.
Sincere respect for a commercial ideal.

The copy writer's job is to understand both the manufacturer and the public and to bring them together on the ground of mutual belief in each other.

He has committed himself to express the rich human meaning of his client's business in terms of the specific, concrete human life of the reader.

He has no personal opinions whatever. His work is to understand the hopes, and likes, and ambitions of the Mothers and Fathers of this country.

Only the writer, who can feel in his own being something of the full, overbrimming content that a woman puts into such thoughts as "Home" and "Baby," will ever write great advertising copy.

Then let him tag around the house after her as she does her chores. Let him get all the meaning she reads into "Ironing," "Cooking," "Clearing up."

Let him get a full insight into what the word "Rent" means to the average man. What is this citizen thinking about and hoping for when he helps out in the kitchen after dinner—or plays with the children—or tinkers around with hammer or paint brush—or weeds his backyard patch of string beans?

What is it that makes so many men downright stingy in buying for themselves, but prodigal in spending for their families?

The highest and truest advertising copy is always pitched to the specific *here* and *now*.

This sense of the here and now is one of the first things for the copy writer to acquire.

Aimless blazing away in the advertising pages (and there is still plenty of it) has no excuse today. There is no room in the commercial world for slighted responsibility and opportunity thrown away.

If any copy writer finds himself in doubt how to go about a professional job of writing, he need only study the able, professional copy being published. Any man who will, can find it. There is no mystery about it. Its principles and methods are plain to be seen.

These principles are easily stated:

1. Every piece of merchandise has its specific concrete appeal.

2. This appeal is organic to the nature of the merchandise in its relations to the human life of the consumer.

3. What the consumer thinks and feels about it depends on the *time*, the *place*, and the state of the public mind about that *kind* of merchandise.

4. Every kind of merchandise goes through the same three stages in the public consciousness:

(a) A pioneer invention. A new and untried human relation. A few bold buyers take the plunge.

(At this stage it is the business of the copy writer to sell the human meanings of the new invention. And more than that—to begin now to establish the authority of the pioneer manufacturer.)

(b) Word gets around that there's something in it. Greatly increased public acceptance. Other manufacturers enter the field. Wide choice in styles, grade and price is offered the public.

(Now the copy writer has to reckon with a new set of human reactions. True, there is still a large section of the public to be sold on the desirability of this *kind* of merchandise. But the pioneer manufacturer no longer has the whole burden of doing this. All the other manufacturers are also doing it. But the big job now is to consolidate the authority of the pioneer manufacturer as to *style, price* and *money's worth.)*

(c) Everybody now takes this kind of merchandise for granted. It has won its place in the life of the nation. Thousands are buying it. Hundreds are manufacturing it. This is the stage of acute competition.

(The responsibility of the copy writer now is to strengthen the competitive position of his client—not only with the consumer, but with the dealer. It calls for all his understanding of human nature—and all his ability to present the human meanings of style, price, money's worth, and the authoritative leadership of the manufacturer. Everything he writes, even to the consumer, must strengthen his client's position with the *dealer.* In this competitive stage, strong relations with the best dealers are of utmost importance. He is the man who passes the merchandise along to the consumer, and every manufacturer is competing for his trade.)

The above is but one example of the constant changes that are always taking place to affect the copy man's approach to his work.

This particular change happens to be a standard trade situation.

Other possible changes that he will have to look out for are shifts in public opinion—the most subtle of all the situations the copy writer is called on to meet.

Such shifts of the consuming mind may have to do with style—with price or money's worth—with balancing this whim of taste against that demand caused by a fundamental need.

They may take their rise in any twist of human nature, and assume any one of a hundred forms.

The man who cannot sense these shifts of public opinion, and base his copy on them, has not the makings of a great copy writer.

But nearly everyone has at least a little native inward spark of such understanding.

He may not even be aware of it now. But he must have it—or he never would have been led to express himself through advertising.

If he has the persistence to take this spark; nurse it; feed it with human contacts; fan it into the glowing flame of all-comprehending human sympathy, soon or late he will find himself a true copy writer—often when he has just about given up hope of ever writing any copy really worth while.

* * *

As to methods in copy writing, each man makes his own.

One who should watch a master of copy writing at work for a month might come away wondering if he had any real method at all.

In a mechanistic sense, he probably has not.

For one campaign, a whole flood of captions may come rolling from his pen before he writes a word of the text.

At another time it may be the "dealer paragraph"—or a legend for an illustration—or the description of a piece of merchandise.

But one thing will be found universally true:

He always grasps the *most significant thing* first, and uses this to fix the *key* of his whole advertisement or campaign.

This "most significant thing" is the human relation of the merchandise to what folks are thinking about here and now.

This is the reason why a really great advertisement is always so convincing.

It starts with what is in the reader's mind.

It grows *organically* from this root. It has the inevitable ring of solid and substantial truth.

Copy written in this organic way takes on all the modes and forms of human thought and emotion.

It may start with the simplest situations of a woman's everyday housekeeping, but always sympathetic, and always interpreted in the terms of the merchandise.

> Things iron better when they are quite damp. So in the Hotpoint Iron, the *point* is made *even hotter* than the rest of the iron. . . .
> You get the *maximum heat* where the iron first touches the damp material. Your clothes come out fresh, crisp and delightfully smooth.

Or it may call on all the resources of a poetic handling to present the scientific facts that give the Elgin Watch its dominant timekeeping authority.

> Elgin takes the time from the stars and puts it in your pocket.
> Out in Elgin, Illinois, there is a spick and span little building standing all by itself on a little knoll.
> This is the Elgin Time Observatory—for the sole purpose of recording the exact time from the passage of the stars across the meridian.

The astronomer makes 110 star records in each night's observations—and the time is correct within a few thousandths of a second.

Now to put this precise time in your pocket.

This is the function of four master clocks.

These clocks are checked and corrected day after day by the star observations. They transmit the exact time second by second to the Elgin Laboratories and Timing Rooms.

The Elgin Watch you put in your pocket or clasp on your wrist was checked hour after hour, day after day, through all the critical processes of adjusting and timing, against the star time observed by the astronomers in the spick and span little building standing all by itself on the little knoll.

And in the United States Rubber advertisements, it takes three highly technical discoveries, throws them against the rich, colorful drama of a world-wide industry, and presents the whole in all its human relations to the user of rubber products.

If the United States Rubber Company had not established its own Rubber Plantations *fifteen years* ago—

This Company owns Rubber Plantations totaling 110,000 acres in Sumatra and on the Malayan Peninsula. It has over 5,000,000 rubber trees, with almost limitless opportunity for increased production as more trees are planted. Furthermore, each year the trees now bearing yield larger and larger quantities of latex—the milky liquid that flows from the rubber tree when it is tapped. A sure and increasing source of rubber latex of the highest quality.

Within the past few weeks, the United States Rubber Company announced to the users, merchants and manufacturers of Rubber Goods of all descriptions three new and basic developments—

Sprayed Rubber

Web Cord

Flat-Band Method of Building a Cord Tire

In the light of these advances, the forethought of this Company in establishing its own rubber plantations, and *insuring its supply of rubber latex,* seems almost prophetic.

If this Company had not been growing its own rubber for years, working clear through from the *latex* to the finished articles of manufactured rubber, two of these discoveries—Sprayed Rubber and Web Cord, might never have been made at all.

The New Sprayed Rubber

Instead of coagulating rubber out of the latex with smoke or chemicals—the only methods known heretofore—latex is sprayed as a snow-white mist into super-heated air. The water is driven out of it—nothing else. Pure rubber alone remains. . . .

The New Web Cord

Web Cord also starts with the latex.

The technicians of this Company discovered that pure rubber latex has a strong natural *affinity for cotton cord.*

Here was the clue to something that cord tire makers have been hunting for years—how *to impregnate cord tire fabric with pure rubber—to* get away from using chemical solutions of rubber which injure cotton cord. . . .

Tires without a Weak Spot

The Flat-Band Method of building a Cord Tire *does away* with practically all the *flexion resistance* within the tire. . . .

Every cord in the tire is kept at the *correct length,* lies at the *correct angle,* and takes its *proportionate* part of the load. . . .

* * *

To the copy writer who thinks in literal terms, the human relations of such things as the Elgin Time Observatory and the United States Rubber Plantations might seem somewhat obscure.

If he feels this way about it, it is a sure sign that he does not understand how the American mind delights to thrill over the romance of merchandise.

In spite of his seeming sophistication, the American citizen is naive, fresh, essentially childlike, full of generous enthusiasms and capacity for wonderment.

His everyday life is pretty dull. Get up—eat—go to work—eat—go to bed.

But his mind is constantly reaching out beyond this routine. This is one of the reasons why the American is such a great fiction reader—moviegoer—talking machine and radio fan.

He compensates for the routine of today by the vision of what his life is to be tomorrow. It is the vision of getting ahead.

Everything he buys comes as a partial fulfillment of this vision. A man will dream for months before he buys his first motor car.

What he is dreaming about is not a mechanism of chassis and wheels and engine.

It is himself, and his wife and children. Their social standing, health, enjoyment, convenience.

To him, what the manufacturer has achieved exists for *his* gratification.

And in the manufacturer's leadership he finds confirmation of his own astuteness in recognizing the superiority of the manufacturer's goods.

So it is with everything else he buys. No one ever in his life bought a mere piece of merchandise—per *se.*

What he buys is the satisfaction of a physical need or appetite, or the gratification of some dream about his life.

It need not even be an important purchase. Everything he buys represents to him a conscious choice in molding his life to his vision of it.

Even with such an everyday thing as a new kind of breakfast food, a woman will read a vision of her family taking a step forward—if the copy writer will give her half a chance.

There is the expectation of new and delicious flavor—the pride in being among the first to discover the new and better thing—and the emotional gratification of seeing her family like what she provides, and thriving on it.

All small things, perhaps—but it is the ability to handle these intimate points of view sympathetically that tests the powers of the copy writer to the utmost.

What he has to do is to interpret these intimate human dreams in terms of his client's merchandise.

He will feed the dream with every element of fact and imagination.

He will school himself in true and ample seeing, concrete thinking, deep feeling.

He will never lack for things to write about. His field is as broad and deep as human nature.

As this growth takes place within himself, he will find his writing style purifying itself with his thinking. Fewer adjectives. More nouns and verbs—the words that express concrete *fact* and *action.*

He is apt to find his vocabulary growing smaller—sloughing off a lot of vague, general words that used to clutter up everything he wrote.

What he has left are a few thousand vivid words that express the true universal thoughts and emotions of everyday life. Simple words, most of them—many of only one syllable.

His writing takes on a new *vocal* quality. It is as satisfying to the ear as to the eye.

This vocal quality is a thing to be worked for. It is not merely "worth" acquiring. It is vital.

Until a piece of copy has this vocal quality it is not pulling its full load. It reaches the reader only through the eye. The highest, finest writing gets to the reader through the ear, also.

This is not a writer's trick, it is a basic human fact.

Nearly everybody, when he reads, pronounces the words to himself. The sound of the words floats into the brain through the ear, while the shape of the words is entering through the eye.

So the impression is doubled.

When a piece of copy won't "read right," the chances are that it is full of long words. So the sounds get all jumbled up.

It is the short, simple words that make easy reading copy. They vocalize. Mostly these words are of the oldest heritage of the race. They are polished by long use until they slip easily from the tongue and snuggle themselves into the ear.

They are apt to arrange themselves kindly in the sentence. They offer the widest range of vocal color.

Soothing words—bustling words—and words that ring like a gong.

Broad vowels—flat vowels—full-bodied, portly vowels—and the high pitched sharp vowels that cut a sentence off like a knife.

And the consonant sounds. The soft "b's" and "d's," and "m's" and "n's," and "r's" and "l's." The hissing vigor of "s" (but one has to look out for too many "s's" in a row—they may trip the reader's tongue even in silent reading). And the shock of the "t" sound and the "k" sound at the end of a sentence.

Fortunately, the writer who schools himself to see amply, think truly and feel deeply, will find himself picking the right word by instinct.

This is a faculty that grows by use.

His words will be chosen not only for what they mean, but for their associations.

His writing will deliver the full content of the thought and emotion.

He finds himself with a new sense of intimate contact with the inner life of the reader.

He becomes conscious of true power in expressing the ideals and authority of his clients.

Instead of writing long academic words about the little details of merchandise, he is expressing the great human things of merchandise in short simple words.

That is, he is writing great copy—at last.

Chapter 21

The Psychology of the Printed Word

By A. Holmes, a.m., Ph.D.[1]

Whatever by-products, spiritual or material, advertising may distribute to its makers and buyers, its prime purpose, and sole and solitary reason for being, is to secure buyers for the products advertised. This it may do by direct appeal to buy; or by indirect methods preparing the public or the individual mind by education, or otherwise, eventually to buy. Its end and purpose is action—specific and directed action. It appeals for orders; it, like all salesmanship, wants the name on the dotted line.

In this respect advertising is entirely in harmony with man's nature. For the end of man, as far as psychologists and philosophers can make out, is action. He is not primarily, but only secondarily, a thinking animal. His mind is not a mere reservoir for hoarded knowledge. If he is an encyclopedia, he is a *walking* encyclopedia, and the information he has should tell where to go and how to get there. That is the function of the printed word everywhere. Its power lies in its ability to inspire and direct—to tell where to go and how to get there, what to do and how to do it.

To attribute such power to cold type seems absurd. And it is. The power does not lie in the lines of ink or paint spread on a surface. It

---

1. *Arthur Holmes.* College pres.; b. Cincinnati, May 5, 1872. Educated at Bethany (W. Va.) Coll., 1894–5; B.A., Hiram (O.) Coll., 1899; a.m., U. of Pa., 1903; Ph.D., 1908. Ordained Disciples of Christ) 1899; pastor 6th Ch., Phila., 1899–04; Memorial Ch., Ann Arbor, Mich., 1904–5; religious and ednl. dir. Pa. R. R. Dept. Y. M. C. A., Philadelphia, 1905–8; instr. psychology, 1908–9; asst. prof., 1909–12; asst. dir. Psycho-Clinic, 1908–12, U. of Pa.; dean gen. faculty Pa. State Coll., Sept. 191218; pres. Drake U., Des Moines, Ia., 1918–22. Mem. Am. Psychol. Assn., Am. Genetic Assn., Sigba Xi, Phi Kappa Phi, Theta X. Author: *Decay of Rationalism,* 1909; *The Conservation of the Child,* 1902; *Principles of Character Making,* 1913; *Backward Children,* 1915. Joint Author: *When to Send for the Doctor,* 1913.

lies in the power of those words to make their appeal to human nature. To exercise any power whatever, they must be attended to, read, and acted upon. Nobody puts up a sign warning *animals* off the premises, and a campaign of advertising amongst illiterate human beings would be a sad waste of money. The printed word must have power to attract attention, power to hold attention long enough to tell its story, power to move the prospective customer, power to direct the customer. These powers it must have mediately or immediately; or else the advertiser's money is wasted.

Such powers rest upon the nature of man. He reacts to any stimulation whatever. "Impressions produce expressions" is the fundamental law of man's psychic nature. He can no more help that than a nervous woman can help jumping when a window falls, or the mouth of a tramp help watering when he smells frying chicken, or a healthy baby help kicking and grabbing. Man must act, inside or out; spasmodically and haphazardly as in reflexes; purposively without knowing why, as in blind instincts, and purposively with full knowledge of what he is trying to accomplish, as in voluntary, rational or ideational actions. All of these varieties of actions—reflex, instinctive and purposeful—are subject to arousal by advertisement. None of them should be left out of consideration by the framer of productive appeals. How each one operates we will see in the next few lines.

First, let us take the simplest form of human action, the reflex. It is a simple, unconscious action aroused by some object or idea or feeling. The winking of the eye is a good example. The ordinary action is due to an impression of dryness and is performed unconsciously. In the same manner is much of our seeing done. A million objects affront the eye, and how many of them make any impression on our minds? Nobody knows for certain. But it is certainly true that many which seem to make no *conscious* impression, do, however, make an *unconscious* impression. Later on, those unconscious impressions may arise and dominate an action. Sidis and Goodhart in their book on *Multiple Personality* give most interesting instances of such cases. For example, consider the case of a patient who could not feel pain in, say, his hand. If the hand was pricked several times with a pin, he felt nothing. But upon being asked to guess the number of times he was pricked, he did so and guessed right every time. A most amusing story is told of an American traveler who, in a small town in France, saw suddenly a street-scene entirely familiar to him. He was astounded. Never before by any possibility had his eyes rested upon that actual scene. He had never been in France before; never out of America; hardly out of his native city. Yet there stood a perfectly familiar street before his eyes. The puzzle weighed upon his mind till, after returning home and getting back to his own familiar room, he stood wiping his hands before his wash-stand, when his eye happened to fall upon a picture on the wall above the basin, and there he beheld the pictured scene he thought he saw for the first time in France. He had looked with unconscious eye upon that picture thousands of times. Something had remained from each look, something obscure, dim, unknown, but something that, upon proper stimulation by a more energetic demand upon attention, could arouse in him a sure sense of familiarity. How many millions of times is such an experience repeated by the readers of street-car advertisements? How many riders can recall what they have read on any morning trip to work? Yet what an infinite amount of influence have those signs exerted all unknowingly upon every one who cast even a casual glance at them? If nothing else has been done, the first small step toward making the goods advertised "old and reliable" has been taken in the reader's mind by making him, all unconscious to himself, familiar with those goods.

But there is much more in even the reflex action of men. At the very beginning, for example, of any salesman's work, mass- or individual-salesman, writer or talker, the attention of the customer must be attracted. That may be an entirely reflex matter. No baby can resist following with his eyes a light moving in a dark room. Hardly any grown person, off his guard, can help doing the same thing. Any moving object caught out of the corner of the eye, jerks the eye around for one full look at that thing. All moving signs depend upon that inborn reflex to attract attention.

But further, if the message of the sign is to be consciously read, the attention must linger a moment. Again laws of reflexes come in to hold the observer's eye or repel it. Movement will attract the eye, but *not hold* it. The eye muscles weary too quickly. Therefore, no reading matter ought to move. It ought to stand still, and stand still long enough to be leisurely read. That additional attention must be secured and can be secured in many ways.

The most usual way is to secure it by color. Here again certain reflexes play their part. For, in looking at anything on earth, even by the merest glance, always two results are obtained by the beholder: First, he secures a sensation—a color, shape, size, something called a sensation; then, secondly, he also has aroused in him a feeling either agreeable or disagreeable. If it is disagreeable he removes his eye from the object as quickly as he can, and goes in search of something agreeable. If it is agreeable he lingers. This law holds for every look a man or woman ever gives to anything. Sometimes the intensity of the feeling is so keen that the looker is clearly conscious of it. The charm of some objects is irresistible, as the young man understood who measured his girl's good looks by asserting that when she came into a street-car every bit of the advertising became a dead loss. Sometimes things are repellent, as the executive understood who wanted a typist not too difficult to look at.

Colors vary in their attracting and holding power. White, red and yellow attract but do not hold. The causes are many, but the most fundamental reason for this is the effect such colors have upon the eye. Each eye is furnished with certain cells which are affected by certain colors. Whenever any one looks at anything these cells are worn out, just as a muscle is when it is used. If it is worn out faster than it is built up by the nutritive processes of the body, then a feeling of disagreeableness, of boredom, of weariness, and finally of pain, comes on. White, red and yellow have this power. They tear down the eye-cells faster than the eye cells build up. Hence, nobody wishes to dwell long on any spaces covered by these colors.

However, because of its long associations with man's tragic experiences, red has a wonderful power to attract the eye. Red stands for danger because it is associated with blood, with fire, with burning suns and scorched waste-places of the earth. Consequently it may be used judiciously to attract the eye, but no skilled sign-writer or artist will ask the eye of any one he is trying to please, to dwell long upon its glaring and disturbing power.

On the other hand, since man's eye has been built up in the rest periods of sleep in the dark, since it awakes under the blue sky and is surrounded by the green verdure, these colors ease the eye and give to the spectator a feeling of quiet, serene and calm pleasure. For his eye-cells are now building up as fast or faster than they are wearing out. Therefore, words printed in blue letters on blue backgrounds have been long ago recommended by German scientists for children's school books. All skilled artists understand the handling of colors to produce effects, but not all of them understand that human nature and that human physiology which underlie their practically gained knowledge. Much more lies behind these simple statements about reflexes, but enough has been said to show that all the time, each and every instant, the power of the printed word in color depends much upon its suitability to the fundamental constitution of man's nature.

When we consider instinctive actions we must not for a moment forget that they are complex processes having both an inward and an outward aspect. Instinctive action is blind action. The agent does something and does not know why he does it. That is the part of instinct that usually attracts the most attention. But inside the actor there is a world of feeling. He does what he does because he feels like it. That is the immediate inner instigator of his act. But more, he feels like it because there has appeared before him some object that arouses the feeling, or the object suggests some idea that arouses the feeling. To see the object he must pay attention to it. That attention itself is the result of instinct. Any advertiser can see from Professor William McDougall's definition of an instinct, in his *Social Psychology,* the vast practical importance these inborn traits in man possess for the advertiser's art. He can see that the ordinary man is fashioned almost fatally to become a mark for his skill. "'We may then define an instinct," says the great psychologist, McDougall, "as an inherited or innate psychophysical disposition which determines its possessor to perceive, and to pay attention to, objects of a certain class, to experience an emotional excitement of a particular quality upon perceiving such an object, and to act in regard to it in a particular manner, or, at least, to experience an impulse to such action."

Here, born in man is all the explosive mine laid ready for the advertiser's match. Notice, instincts are born in a man. No advertiser needs to *create interest.* Such an attempt is not only futile but utterly needless. Interests are already there, a whole reservoir full, waiting to be tapped and drained off to the commodity for sale. The advertiser is merely building the conduit for bringing that huge hoard of inborn interest to his own product. It is a disposition, too. The customer is already *disposed* in certain directions; disposed to read, disposed to buy. And he is *"determined"* to perceive. It is impossible to keep the crowd back, hopeless to prevent them from looking at advertisements. And equally they *will pay attention.* Why sweat and labor and be discouraged about securing attention? They *will* pay attention. Likewise, they will feel an emotional excitement. That is putting it strong, but this is a staid Harvard professor who is writing, and he knows his field. The action follows sure and soon; or, if the onlooker is in a street car, and cannot act immediately, he experiences *at least an impulse to act."* What more can any advertiser ask? All the materials for a sale are before him in the form of instincts, inborn and innate, in his prospective customers. They form a veritable gold-mine waiting his pick and shovel, or, more literally, the point of his trenchant pen to prick them into active life.

Here, of course, enters the advertiser's art. Notice that all this internal commotion leading to action is aroused only on the presentation of *"objects of a certain class."* Aye, there's the rub! Objects of a certain class! Some advertisements fail utterly in entrance to that aristocratic class. Some enter as if to the manner born.

What is the difference? Careful analysis of the two kinds of advertisements, I believe, will show that one was written with no consciousness of this huge force, instinct, in human affairs; or else, did not make the proper appeal and so had no power; while, on the other hand, the successful advertisement knocked at the door of the reader's mind with the Chesterfieldian instincts of a born gentleman and found ready and eager entrance. No lady could refuse its advances; no gentleman could rebuff its insinuating address. It did this because it appealed properly to instincts.

Make no mistake. Man is not ultimately a rational animal. His inborn desires determine what he wants; his reason tells him how to get it. But the innate tendency is the final arbiter. "The human mind," says McDougall in the same volume, "has certain innate tendencies which are the essential springs or motive powers of all thought and action, whether individual or collective." Instincts move men to think and to act.

Now for a moment let us look at some of the applications of this knowledge of instincts to the art of investing the written word with irresistible fascination. We have seen above a few suggestions about color and other attributes, and there are many more in the same line. Skill and common sense will discover them. Right now our problem is a little more complex, just as the instincts, as we have shown, are more complex than the reflexes. For, in the first place, there are many instincts, as Professor James pointed out in his *Principles of Psychology*. They are hard to classify, as many scientists have discovered who have attempted it. They combat each other at times. Some of them play large parts in human lives, while others appear on the stage only occasionally and then for minor parts only. Those which are most permanent are concerned with the maintenance of life in the individual. Self-preservation is the first law of nature. Food preserves life; so hunger has been counted the most fundamental of all instincts.

So absolute is the ruling power of food-getting that were it not for competition in selling food, no advertisement for it would ever be needed.

So the art of the ad writer is not satisfied by merely announcing food-sales, but in dressing up the appeal to human appetite for food in such luscious, delicious and fascinating furnishings that the appeal to man's primary instinct is irresistible for that particular food. Nowhere does the art of the advertising fraternity exhibit itself in such glowing colors and with such a fine sense of appeal.

Next to the self-preservation instinct is the reproductive instinct with all its varied, complex, baffling and intricate direct and indirect appeals to sex. Such a world of feeling is impossible to treat in a scientific treatise, much less in a paragraph. For the advertiser the sex-interest, with all its consequences of dress, ornaments, homes, schools, churches, institutions, laws, customs, habits, and with all the complexity of other instincts following in its train, related and interrelated with it, furnishes nearly his whole quiver of word-empowering shafts. Possibly it is an overworked appeal. Certainly it is too often misused. Always it is as dangerous to use it as to neglect it.

One or two concrete illustrations will enlighten more than many words of dissertation. Sometimes the sex-appeal is lugged into the advertisement by the neck and heels and produces in the reader a reaction worse for the expenditure of so much extra money. For instance, the observer's eye is suddenly assaulted with a dusky female taking up nearly the whole foreground of expensive space on a sign board. It is hinted, by the usual artificial and dead-in-the-wood palm-trees, that she is located somewhere in the tropics. The lapping of green waves in the distance leads one to suspect that the scene is laid on an island. But these are entirely minor impressions. The major attention is drawn to this husky, mahogany, white-toothed, strong-limbed, female figure in the foreground. Now, what in all the possible realm of salable products do you think such a figure advertises? It might be anything. As a matter of fact, such an advertisement is common almost to the point of nausea. It misses its whole point by its commonness. It illustrates good money thrown away because its appeal has no pith or point. As a matter of fact, one such advertisement used the figure to sell an ordinary edible.

Note the mishandling of human nature in such an attempt. First, attention is supposed to be attracted by an appeal to one instinct—and a powerful one. The method of doing that may or may not have been tasteful, pitched on a low plane or a high plane, well or illy done. For the moment we are not considering these items. We are looking at such an appeal from the cold, hard viewpoint of dollars and cents. The appeal was made to customers to buy something. That something, in the case just mentioned, was a delicate morsel, supposed to be good to eat. Here was a scantily clad girl dragged in by the hair and heels to arouse one instinctive interest, in order to sell an article that appealed to an entirely different instinct. Why not leave out the girl and appeal at once to the hunger-instinct? That would save money and make more sales.

But let us take even a more concrete case. Suppose George, riding home at night, is idly going over the street-car signs. One catches his eye. Again it is the over-done appeal to sex in an under-done state of habiliments—a vaudeville girl this time, or circus girl, or dancer, or any girl whose vocation might lend a weak excuse for thus exposing her, scantily clad, to the drafts in a public conveyance. George's eye idly roaming about stops with her; exploits the picture; has some of his interest aroused, and quite naturally, by the laws of association, drifts over to the reality of the picture and rests finally upon the idea of going that night to see a good show. That idea tickles him so much that he goes home, gets dressed, takes his best girl to a show and lavishes upon the evening five times as much money as the cost of the article advertised.

What was that article? Oh, we will say a pair of suspenders. Why the incongruity of the young lady? Obviously she needed no suspenders for supporting her slight investiture. She was thrust in to attract attention, and, unfortunately, did it. So the money spent for that printed word was worse than wasted. It not only failed to sell suspenders, but it did sell something else. It not only ruined a suspender sale, but it used up the prospective customer's money on another enterprise. Such advertising is business suicide. Upon this side of handling the instinctive appeals I have dwelt for some time, for such appeals furnish such temptations to their use and so often end in misuse. Let us now turn to more constructive uses of them.

One of the best uses to which inborn instinct can be put is in building up sales sentiment. A sentiment is a complex construction built up in people out of their inherited feelings, impulses and emotions by environment and education. The education is not book-learning alone, but includes all those factors which bring ideas into mind. A sentiment is then a large affair. Its base is inborn instinct, and it rises like a pyramid in consciousness, to an idea at the apex. It is all knit together by time and experience. Therefore, it is one of the stable and durable structures in each human being. It appears in the forms of love for any person, or love for country, or the sentiment of religion. It is always directed toward an object, a person, or an idea. In general, all sentiments can be divided into those of love or of hate, taken in their broadest sense. Such a classification reveals immediately how challengingly important they are to the man who sells by the printed word.

For this reason a man will do as he thinks. That is, an idea which dominates in a man's mind will have its way. It will initiate and direct action. It is unlike a reflex which explodes in disordered action, and unlike instinctive action, which goes toward a goal without seeing it. Ideational action knows just where it is going. It is rational, reasonable, justifiable, sensible. In short, all states of mind lead directly to action. "Some states of mind," says William James in his *Principles of Psychology,* "have it more than others. Feelings of pleasure and pain have it, and perceptions and imaginations of matters of fact have it. . . . It is the essence of all consciousness." We all know pain has power to move a man—the school-boy who sets a pin in a teacher's chair takes advantage of that law of nature;—but it may have escaped the attention of men that ideas, as well as other parts of consciousness, also have that power vested in them.

The reason why that fact escapes attention is because of the numerous and the various ideas which a man may have in his mind at the same time, or close following one another. He thinks of buying; then he thinks of the cost; and the two ideas work against one another. He thinks of buying and thinks of the price, and his stinginess—a feeling—may hold back his hand from putting his name on the dotted line. He thinks of buying for the sake of his wife and children, whom he loves, and the love supports and bulwarks the idea "Buy!" But immediately he feels fear of the future, fear of sickness, of losing his job, or some unexpected calamity, and that fear opposes both love and the idea "Buy!" What he will eventually do, will be the resultant action from all the forces working upon him, forces immediately belonging to feelings, instincts, perceptions, ideas, all of them urging, pushing, hauling this way and that way, one against the other, or some against the others, like cliques and factions in political circles, milling around like undecided and startled cattle, knowing not which way to go, until One Supreme Idea takes possession of the mobs of feelings and ideas, and tells the whole mass where to go; as, on that terrible day in France, when the seething mob, swaying and swirling, suddenly took direction and purpose from the cry "On to the Bastille!" Such a mob, swayed by a purpose, is the picture of what we have called a *sentiment* in the mind of a buyer. Instincts, feelings, emotions, all suddenly organize themselves behind an idea and give to that idea, besides its own mighty impulsive force and its supreme skill to direct, the irresistible momentum of their own innate power to action. Such is the psychology of a sales-sentiment.

Sentiment may be *for* a thing or *against* a thing. It is not altogether feeling. But one of its important ingredients is feeling. Hence, it is most important for the advertiser to set his material appeal to the eye in the proper surroundings to arouse agreeable feelings. This matter we have treated above. Next, sentiment also includes, as part of its complex constitution, instincts as fundamental constituents. Therefore, it behooves the wide-awake advertiser to know human instincts. This also we have touched upon above. Finally, he must know how to organize these around the sole and single idea in which he is interested: "Buy *my* goods!"

Again a concrete illustration may be of help to clarify the matter. Suppose a real estate man wishes to sell a house in a suburb. He puts out a great sign-board. On it he paints a facsimile of the house itself, just as it stands—alone, empty, windows dark, with no human near it. Now what would be the first reaction of a beholder of that sign? A bad one. Instantly a number of feelings would well up. "Lonesome! Gloomy! Ghostly! I'd hate to live there!" A nervous woman might even shudder. All of this welter of ideas, feelings, instincts and emotions, is the sentiment that would be aroused by such a picture. Out of its "Don't buy that!" would come the controlling idea with startling distinctiveness and irresistible sales-opposition.

Now, why? Any one with common sense knows much of the reason. Possibly he does not see all of it. Therefore, it may be that in that part which the common-sense man does not see, lies the success of the skilled salesman of real estate. That part is probably the instinct of gregariousness. People live in flocks, in droves, in families, tribes, nations. This is an inborn desire. Its opposite feeling is "lonesomeness," one of the most powerful emotions to which men are subject. So, first of all, the picture of the house must be made to overcome lonesomeness. It must look "homey" at least. Light must stream from the windows, suggesting that the folks are in.

A glimpse through a window at the well-known fireside, under the evening lamp, etc., etc., etc., with all the skill the real estate man knows so well how to exercise, must forestall any feeling contrary to the gregarious instinct in people. A suggestion of another house by means of a paved street, or the gable of another house, helps the matter.

Then, too, advantage may be taken of another factor due to sentiment. The sale-sentiment for this particular domicile may be placed within the larger sentiment already developed in favor of suburban residence. People who live in the suburbs usually have children. Their sentiment for their children can be appealed to. "Healthy and happy children" is a sentiment to which an appeal may be made by the words themselves. A mere mention of such words makes a genuine human feel good. "School-house within a block. No street-car crossings between." Again there is the appeal to sentiments:—love for the children; parental fears for the children. "Thirty minutes' ride from the business section of city." This is an appeal to the sentiment for father. "Shopping district within easy reach"—for mother. All of this illustrates concretely the fact that an idea "Buy this house!" can be vitalized by having switched into its being the current of sentiments already in existence.

In our emphasis upon sentiment, which suggests to the reader the thought of feeling, we may have obscured the thought of ideational or volitional action. We must not forget the supreme part which an idea plays in the construction of a sentiment. The idea stands at the apex. It *directs* the action aroused by the instincts, the perceptions of objects and the emotions. Its immediate duty in the art of securing a sale by means of the printed word is to send the reader to some particular place to buy some particular article. Usually this idea, "Buy this'", is conveyed through the words on the sign or in the advertisement. The rest of the material is put there for the purpose of attracting and holding attention long enough to secure the reading of the rest of the message. That reading depends upon attention. The attention must not only be attracted in the first place, but also held.

Will the crowd give attention? Here we come to that bugbear—for people unacquainted with psychology—called the "Will." It assumes that men have the power to say "Yes" or "No" to an advertisement. The assumption is only partly correct. A man has power to decide in the first stage of the game, not in the last. The game is not in the arrangement of the advertisement, nor its matter, nor its style alone. The game is to be found in the play of those forces upon the man's nature. If the advertisement does not attract him, he can say "No." If it attracts him, and he does not pay attention to it long enough to break away from his usual line of thought, then he can say "NO." But if the printed word can seize his attention, hold him chained, drive from his mind all other thoughts except the one "Buy this'", standing at the head of an organized sentiment from which every opposing idea, perception, feeling, instinct and disposition have been driven out or smothered to death, then *he cannot say "no"!* His will is dead. The only place where his will can come into play, according to William James, is in paying attention. If he pays attention, if he pays attention long enough, the outcome is as fatal as standing still long enough under a falling brick.

Many are the illustrations that might be given of this power of ideas to decide and to direct action. It is shown in all its luminosity in hypnotism. There ideas rule. That can be seen from the process of hypnotizing a person. He simply concentrates his attention upon some attractive object, say, an electric light bulb, or a revolving mirror. He forgets everything else. Then he forgets what he is looking at, or falls into a kind of sleep. While in that sleep the operator suggests to him some idea. Since that idea is the only one he has in mind, he does according to the direction of the idea. That is the process. In it there is no new law, as Bramwell in his *Hypnotism* well says. The ordinary laws of every day life are in force. Only the situation in which they work has been simplified; extraneous factors have been eliminated, and the whole matter reduced to a simple situation which thus exposes to view the working of a power which operates every moment of our conscious life. The law expressed by William James says that the action represented in mind by an idea will immediately follow upon that idea *unless* the action is stopped—not by physical force, or an act of the will—but by another idea. Popularly stated, what a man thinks that he will do. This is the foundation of the advertising business. Were it not for that law advertising would be *non est*.

The whole end and purpose, then, of an advertisement is to lodge an idea in the mind of the beholder and make him pay attention to that one idea until all opposing thoughts and feelings are eliminated from his mind; or, at least, until all the opposing ideas with all their opposing hosts of supporting feelings are overcome. We have pictured the situation under the figure of a pyramid, illustrating a sentiment, with the idea at the apex; or, as the mob advancing upon the Bastille. We have seen the part which reflex actions, and simple feelings of agreeableness and disagreeableness, have in that sentiment; what huge and important part instincts play in it; and finally how the idea caps the climax of the pyramid of sentiment and directs the person in his action. The power of the printed word thus lies in its ability to take advantage of human nature constructed as it is; to make its appeal to the various factors going to make up action, and to transform that power into sales. In general it may be summed up as the power to make sales-sentiment *in general;* and in particular, it is the power to make sales-sentiment for the *particular* commodity advertised.

Chapter 22

Simplicity in Advertising Copy

By Humphrey M. Bourne[1]

Simplicity in advertising has most to do with the printed message—the copy—the last word in the advertising plan. If it fails, all fails.

So please let me open with the advertising man's prayer:

"O Lord, make me short on words and long on ideas."

Elbert Hubbard used to say, "The copy's the thing." However fine the product, clever the merchandising plan, shrewd the advertising committee, well selected the media, if the copy doesn't measure up, then the rest tumbles, like a row of dominoes when the end piece falls.

It is so easy to discuss abstractly advertising without having due cognizance of advertising policies. The thing to be sold may be one of many: good will, confidence, service, the institution, or a definite article at a definite price.

Yet whatever it is, that thing, so far as the advertisement is concerned, is the product, and the copy should set out to sell it.

And that calls for the finest kind of simplicity—the straightest line between the writer's selling thought and the reader's buying interest.

It must picture it well, tell it simply, and make them want it.

Good advertising isn't hard because it has to be hard, but because it must be simple.

No advertisement can serve five masters. It must decide quickly to sell one of five things:

---

1. *H. M. Bourne* started in the Copy Department of N.W. Ayer & Son, under his old chief, J. J. Geisinger. Was Advertising Manager of Buffalo Specialty Company, Copy Director of Erwin & Wasey Co., Chicago, and more latterly, Copy and Art Director of Gardner & Wells Company, Inc., New York. Now Advertising Manager of H. J. Heinz Company, Pittsburgh, Penna.

The artist.
The writer.
The engraver.
The typographer.
The thing advertised.

Take your choice.

If it is a work of art, and nothing else, it isn't a good advertisement.

If the selling message is lost in admiration for the writer's style, it isn't a good advertisement.

If some bizarre engraving effect comes between the eye and the message, it isn't a good advertisement.

If the typographical arrangement tries to out-shout the message, it isn't a good advertisement.

But if the advertisement starts out to sell something and keeps on selling it while being helped by the other four factors, by reason of their very unobtrusiveness—then you have an advertisement, for before all else an advertisement is intended to sell what it advertises, and not the mechanical elements that comprise it.

That, you will say, is obvious, elemental, the taken-for-granted rule of advertising.

True—but the obvious truth is too often disregarded. The simplest rules which gave advertising being are too often threatened by the smothering influence of abstract ideas, writer's ego, and a far-fetched style which would never stand the across-the-counter selling test.

Advertising isn't something to play with. It is something to work with, and to work hard with. We can wander as we may from the path of simple straight-from the-shoulder copy, but the longer we have to do with advertising the more certain do we find ourselves returning to time-tried simple effectiveness just as we find ourselves returning to the simple prayers we learned at mother's knee.

While it is true that people, especially the people of America, have become advertisingly educated, it is just as true that for that very reason they must be appealed to *with* reason, simply expressed.

A fine picture, a "catchy" headline, rare style and novel type arrangement may make them exclaim, "That's a clever ad," without their being able to recall the name of the product after turning the page.

If many a full page advertisement were written with the same painstaking care, and lack of unnecessary, fanciful trimming, as the sixty-line mail-order advertisement which must go out into the cold world and bring back its cost many times over, there would be far fewer "clever" ads and many more sales.

Heaven preserve us from the "clever" ad.

The first thing, then—does it pass the page-turning test?

We're a quick thinking, quick eating, quick talking, quick reading nation. When we go to the movies we don't want anything to come between us and our picture, any more than we want static in our WEAF.

We see so much advertising everywhere that we're not hunting it with a microscope.

If we can't take it in at an eyeful, then we don't take it in.

So, it should first pass the page-turning test. Remember, the advertisement is fighting for attention among a thousand others—and, oh, how thick the issues are getting!

The picture should tell the story.

The headline should dramatize it.

The copy should explain it simply and effectively.

The store window, store entrance, clever salesman combination, so to speak.

Yes, people will read a long message when it is really necessary to tell it. Simplicity doesn't argue against that. But the advertisement should first "bull's-eye" something so that when a legion of page turners see only the picture, the name of the product and an active headline, then the advertisement—and the message—will have registered.

Make the test yourself. Thumb through any magazine. Give each page ten seconds. Then name six of the advertisements you saw. Now turn back and analyze them. You will probably find the six built along "poster" lines. The display tells a story whether you read the finer print or not. They are not ashamed to be called advertisements because they are not too proud to work.

It's a treat to read an advertisement that follows a straight line. Your eye and mind gravitate to it naturally. The very set-up helps you to read. It may be a stunt to dodge the message in, out and around some design; but that's all it is—a stunt—and more than often fights off the reader than attracts him.

There was a time when the very novelty of advertising attracted people to it. But that time is past. People have not only become advertisingly educated but by the very necessity of their busy-ness and the increasing number of pages, have become page turners.

Simplicity in advertising must have that in mind always. Tell as short or as long a type story as you like, but let the display deliver a message that the page turner will get. Otherwise it is literally lost in the shuffle, along with the money that went into it.

When it stands the page-turning test the advertisement has a good flying start. If it doesn't, then all the men of the king's English won't rescue it.

Then the headline:

If the people won't come into the store after they've seen the shop window, they won't buy.

The picture may be the shop window of the advertisement; but the headline is the shop entrance.

The window attracts them. The headline is the way in.

If it takes an hour to write the advertisement—spend another half hour on the headline. That may sound trite; but a headline well thought over, gets over.

Make it a lead line—with a long e—a lead that will compel a reading of what follows. If it's service you're advertising, don't just say "SERVICE." Many an otherwise good advertisement has been killed deader than a doornail by a headline like that. Far better to say even "How we served Bill Jones right" than to use that abstract, dead to the world, one-word headline which doesn't say anything.

A good headline is half the battle. Lazy headlines are hazy headlines.

A headline that shouts without saying anything is like a loud speaker in a deaf and dumb academy.

A headline that plays on words instead of making them work is like a man in a treadmill.

Plays on words put few selling ideas to work. And, remember, you're paying about twenty times as much for headline space as you are for text space. You must boil your idea down and then serve it up so that readers will like it—and come back for more.

Don't let headlines patronize or proclaim the reader's ignorance. A simple fact simply stated is far better than an academical theory pompously propounded.

Then comes the message proper. Here simplicity must rule, or the finest ideas will go galley west.

One of the greatest leads in copy, as in editorial writing, is the reference to experience.

Brisbane, I think it was, said that the most effective editorial is one that tells readers something they already know.

A man may *believe* you when you tell him something he doesn't know; but he's doubly convinced when you tell him something he *does* know, and will react to it accordingly.

Tell him that Sirius is a thousand light years away, and he'll believe you. Tell him Edgewater Beach Hotel is four miles from the station and he'll say "Right-o, call a Yellow." He knows.

Eversharp made its point by referring to the experience of writers with pencils without a point.

Rubberset by referring to the experience of shavers with bristle-shedding shaving brushes.

The self-filling pen to the experience of those with ink-scattering pens.

Safety razors to the experience of men who couldn't shave at all with the old style razor, or couldn't shave properly.

Reference to experience, adroitly handled, has a double edge. It sells the prospect on the thing you're advertising, while unselling him on the thing he's now using.

And that's important. You may sell him on the thing you're advertising, but if you don't unsell him on what he's now using, you're interesting him but not *convincing* him.

Say it *humanly*—say it *simply*—say it *convincingly*. Bring the reader's own experience to your aid and he'll bring his buying inclination along with it.

One reference to experience makes your readers kin—they warm up to it like a brother or sister—and no pocketbook ever opened to a cold, abstract appeal.

Keep the message alive.

We've all visited a lumber yard and heard the droning of the buzz saw, when, suddenly the saw rang all over the yard and we listened in afresh. That was the roughage in the log—the knots that relieved the monotony by sounding a new note every so often.

So, keep the roughage in the copy. A sentence that brings the attention up with a jerk is better than one which puts it to sleep with studied rhythm and featherbed words.

A successful salesman is successful because he sustains the interest in what he is selling. A new tack here, a rising inflection there, a different appeal to reason—and the prospect finds himself listening in with new interest.

Successful mail-order copy never sleeps. There isn't a yawn from headline to coupon. It gets and holds attention and stirs the reader into action.

Don't make the advertisement ashamed of *being* an advertisement. All the clever writing in the world wouldn't fool anybody on that. Set it to work and keep it working. Never mind if the boys at the round table don't call it "a clever ad" so long as the returns say it is.

Keep the roughage in and the ego out. Too much smoothness and so-called "cleverness" have killed millions of dollars' worth of advertising. Don't sing them to sleep with your story. Keep them awake with your message. Lullaby copy sells only itself.

Now a few words on technical or trade paper advertising.

Of course, a technical advertisement must keep its scientific feet on the ground. But it can be humanized for all that.

Those who read technical publications are human beings, after all, and can be approached as such. A little of the "you" will appeal just as readily, and often more so, than *xyz*.

Technical paper advertising has improved wonderfully in the last few years. What a somber, solemn array it used to be! Yet a great many advertisements in the technical field still need only a mourning border to complete their dreariness.

Can't we take the technical knowledge of these readers for granted in order to "humanize" a little more? Can't we write it so that it will appeal to the man on the job, or the foreman, or the superintendent, without minimizing its effect on the big chief? They're all human.

The trouble with so many of these advertisements is that they try to be hard instead of simple.

The flesh-and-blood salesman may know all about stresses, specific gravity, and all the other gravities; but to get a hearing he must first be human, and to be really human he must lead to the prospect's own humanism.

Peary may have reckoned it in latitude and longitude; but to the schoolboy Peary discovered the North Pole, which holds far more dramatic interest for the average mind than mere talks of compasses, sextants, false horizons and all the other paraphernalia.

I have wandered back over some old, time-worn paths. Yes, but the thing about these good old paths is that we're too inclined to forsake them for new roads which so often lead up blind alleys or into deep ditches.

I love the word "simplicity" as applied to advertising. Many a time in my early advertising days did I turn to the dictionary for some new, difficult word to build a message around. Now I'm more inclined to see if there isn't some well-known word of less than four letters that expresses it.

And there, by the way, is a job for some bright publishing house—to produce a dictionary of three-letter words for advertising men.

Don't make it clever; make it simple. If you make it simple you make it doubly clever.

I repeat advertising isn't hard because it has to be hard, but because it has to be simple. That's the really difficult part for the advertising man, and the easy part for the reader.

To summarize:

Make it stand the page-turning test. Paint a human-story picture.

Dig hard for the big selling factors, and then present them simply—in as many or as few words as necessary.

In short, picture it well, tell it simply, and make them want it. Never forgetting the advertising man's prayer: "O Lord, make me short on words and long on ideas."

Chapter 23

What Makes Good Retail Copy

By Ruth Leigh[1]

My contact with large and small merchants over the United States has convinced me definitely that the reason their advertising does not produce better results is that it lacks a plan or policy. I have put this question to hundreds of retailers: "What are you trying to accomplish with your advertising?" and invariably, I get the same reply: "To sell more goods." But obvious as it may seem, that answer means nothing more concrete to the average merchant than just what it says.

To such questions as: "What kind of audience are you trying to reach?" "How wide is your trade territory?" "How big is your appropriation?" "How are you dividing it?" I get, for the most part, vague answers that indicate a palpable lack of thought or planning.

To the question, then, "What makes good retail copy?" my first answer is: a definite plan, a merchandising plan, that enables a retailer to know exactly where he is going with his advertising, whom he is trying to reach, where his customers are, and how he is going to reach them.

This means that at the beginning of the year it will be practical for him to decide approximately how much he can spend for advertising

---

1. *Ruth Leigh.* Born New York, 1895. Early training in business, with experience as retail research worker, trade investigation work. Writer of retail advertising copy for several leading high-class New York department and specialty stores. Author of *The Human Side of Retail Selling,* and *Elements* of *Retailing,* both of which were selected by the Educational Committee of the Associated Advertising Clubs of the World for use through local advertising clubs in conducting courses in retail selling and retail management. Both books are used as texts in the public schools of New York, Baltimore, Omaha, and other cities. Member of Store Research and Educational Division, Grand Rapids Show Case Company; traveling throughout the United States studying store arrangement and lecturing on retail salesmanship and store management. Consultant to large stores and national advertisers on retail sales and advertising problems.

during the coming year, whether the bulk is to be spent in newspapers, or divided between newspapers, the mail and other media. It means, further, that a dealer must outline for himself, as nearly as he can, what his merchandising plan will be for the coming year, so that he can build his advertising policy around his selling schedule.

For example, a typical merchandising calendar used by one large store for a year was planned in the following manner:

Advertising and Merchandising Schedule

January White sales. Pre-inventory sales of furs and ready to wear. Annual rug sale.

January 19 February furniture sales begin.

January 20 Midwinter drug and toilet articles sales.

February Continuation of furniture sales. Semiannual housewares sales.

February 24 March sales of china and glassware begin.

March 1 Silk week. Spring ready-to-wear sales begin.

March 15 Veiling week.

March 25 Pre-Easter sales begin.

March 31 Easter sales (week of Easter).

April 1 Diamond and jewelry sales.

April 6 Gingham week and cotton goods sales.

April 18 Lace and embroidery week.

April 27 Hosiery sales.

April 28 May white sales begin.

April 28 Spring and apparel sales begin.

May Continuation of May white sales.

May 1 Home Sewing Week; sale of notions.

May 15 Luggage Week.

May 26 Bedding Week.

May 27 Decoration Day sales.

June 3 Sales of pearl necklaces.

June 5 Sales of bridal gifts, including silverware and linens.

June 10 Graduation Day sales begin.

June 12 Pre-inventory sales begin. June sale of glassware.

June 15 Baby Week.

June 18 Vacation sales begin.

July 1 Fourth of July sales.

July 7 July sale of sheets, pillow cases and bed coverings.
July 10 Clearance sales of summer shoes
July 12 Clearance sales of outdoor and summer furniture.
July 20 August furniture sales begin
July 26 Summer fur sales begin.
August 1 Final clearances of summer apparel begin; August fur sales.
September 1 Sales of china and housewares.
September 6 School opening sales begin.
October 11 Columbus Day sales.
October 18 Umbrella Week.
October 19 Bedding Week.
October 30 Sales of fall goods begin.
November 1 Election Day sales.
November 18 Blanket Week.
November 24 Thanksgiving sales.
November 29 Christmas sales begin.
December 15 Reductions on toys and other gift articles
December 27 After—Christmas clearance sales; end of year

Some progressive stores carry out a similar plan in daily advertising. For example, one Southern store based its copy on the local buying habits of the public, and knew beforehand that:

On Monday it was best to feature piece goods and dressmaking accessories, including notions, trimmings, laces, embroideries, patterns, etc.

Tuesday is a popular visiting day in department stores, and it is considered profitable, therefore, to feature novelties such as leather goods, jewelry and small wares.

Wednesday is a good day for featuring household goods, kitchen utensils, dishes, blankets, linens, silverware and domestics.

Thursday is frequently a visiting day, and stores find it profitable to feature novelties, art goods, yarns and stamped articles. Thursday is usually a popular day for demonstrations and for instructions given in art goods departments.

Friday is a good day for featuring home furnishings and household goods, including curtains, draperies, pillows, and articles of home decoration.

Saturday is the big ready-to-wear day on which sales are greatest in apparel sections.

Of course, such a schedule is based exclusively on the buying customs of a given locality, and illustrates the thoroughness with which some retail advertising is planned to get best results.

Successful retail copy, if correctly planned, therefore, is based on the needs and habits of the public, and renders a service by featuring timely merchandise. To secure the interest and attention of the woman reader, a good retail advertisement talks in terms of *her* interests and *her* needs, and timeliness, based on the woman's interests every day, week and season, produces the most satisfactory contacts.

This bring up the second answer to the question: What makes good retail copy? I believe that the ability of the writer to put himself in the reader's place, and to describe merchandise from the viewpoint of a prospective buyer, is one essential secret of preparing good advertising copy.

Theoretically, this may be easy to do, but I believe many retail advertisements fail because store copy writers look at merchandise with too close and shrewd a merchandising eye. After all, to a retailer and to his writers such an article as a raincoat is a piece of merchandise with profit tied up in it. It is an article hanging in the dealer's stock rooms which he desires to sell, but always, to him, it is merchandise." Unless he is practiced and skillful in writing retail advertisements, his copy is likely to smack of too much store atmosphere.

The customer, on the other hand, views such an article as a raincoat from a fundamentally different point of view. To him, it is never "merchandise"; it is a garment he needs to give service, to protect his health, to give him comfort, to bring about economy by protection of his clothes.

Unless a copy writer is able to forget his store viewpoint, to forget that he is writing so many words to sell so many articles of merchandise, he is totally unable to think of the goods in terms of a customer's needs and desires.

As a matter of fact, many advertisements fail because the writer assumes that the public is more interested in the store than it actually is. People are essentially selfish, and an advertising writer who believes that Mrs. Smith is interested in his store *because* it is his store is greatly mistaken. Mrs. Smith is loyal to a store and its merchandise only until her pocketbook is touched, and there her loyalty and interest cease.

She thinks in terms of her own wants, *her* family, *her* life, *her* home, *her* children, *her* needs, and a skilful copy writer must be aware of the woman reader's point of view as she picks up a newspaper. If he wants to sell her a raincoat, he must forget his store's viewpoint of that garment as a piece of merchandise, and think of it in the terms of health and service, as does Mrs. Smith.

A third consideration that produces good retail copy is the absence of too constant bargain appeal. Many retailers forget that they cannot make the public believe that they can constantly prosper while selling everything at low cost.

As a matter of fact, the public today is fed-up on sales, and has, because of too frequent stressing of the bargain appeal, become more or less suspicious of the sales offered. The public is oversold on sales; it has been too much jazzed by the hysterical sale mania that has overtaken the retailers of the country. Today, almost everything is a sale; we have Men's Sales, Women's Sales, Anniversary Sales, Inventory Sales, Big Sales, Remarkable Sales, Extraordinary Sales, and so on.

I believe that *the wisest thing any retailer can do today is to sell his public staple merchandise at fair prices,* instead of trying to make that public believe that he is giving something for nothing. Indirectly, he will be helping himself, because this sales mania has caused the public to demand sales, and has really hurt the distribution of good merchandise sold at fair margins of profit. In my opinion it is the absence of a bargain appeal that makes retail advertising distinctive today.

Too much exaggeration is a fault of many retail advertisements, and a copy writer who can make moderate, straight-forward statements, without talking in too many superlatives, is pretty sure to get his copy read. Perhaps this exaggeration is the outgrowth of too much jazz in advertising. In any event, the public believes today that advertising claims more than it can deliver.

Pick up any newspaper and see how the advertisements claim to have "the most wonderful merchandise," the "finest assortments," "most excellent candies," "most amazing values." Today, retail advertising is about ninety-nine per cent bombast, and the avoidance of this bombast is a fourth consideration of good retail copy moderate restrained statements in honest, straightforward style. The retailer who constantly cries "wolf" by talking in continual superlatives will find himself unbelieved when he really wants to make an important announcement in his advertising. We need less exaggeration in our retail copy today and more restraint.

Fifth, we find that an element of good retail advertising today is the ability to avoid saying too much and to avoid featuring too many articles. A merchant who attempts to tell about all his merchandise in a small newspaper space is as unwise as the merchant who follows the English style of showing almost the entire merchandise stock in the store windows.

We find a merchant urging the public to "come in and see our extensive stock of lamps for every purpose—boudoir lamps, living-room lamps, nursery lamps, office lamps, in many styles, varieties and prices." The reader's mental impression is hazy when he finishes reading this copy. Obviously, a merchant would do better to follow the simple, old-fashioned rule that we often give to unskilled writers of small-store copy. When in doubt, *give picture, description, and price, of one article or one group of similar articles.*

An advertisement calling attention to "a group of boudoir lamps, ivory finished, with pink, blue or gold colored shades, strongly made, and simple in design, priced $4.50," will obviously leave a more definite impression in the mind of a reader than a general, haphazard description of twenty different styles of lamps.

Open or indirect "knocking" of retail competitors characterizes many retail advertisements, and this is always poor policy. The most effective retail copy today makes no mention of competitors and their merchandise. To acknowledge the existence of competition weakens a store advertising. Far better to let the advertising stand on its own merits, and the values to speak for themselves than to attempt to compare it with the goods of other stores.

It is seldom good policy for the retail copy writer, no matter how inexperienced, to attempt to imitate the style of advertising used by other stores. This results in creating an artificial atmosphere around the imitative copy, and seldom achieves the essential purpose of all good retail advertisements—to create an individual, a personality around the store and its merchandise. The personality that the retail copy writer builds in and about his advertisements is a precious thing if it can be carried out in all the store's publicity.

Too many retail advertisements lack news value. Retailers attempt to imitate the advertisements of others, instead of preparing new, original material about their merchandise that answers such questions about the store and merchandise as: Who, What, Where, When and Why?

Although there are many who disagree with this suggestion, I believe that the best thing any retail copy writer can do to study a popular, successful type of retail copy is to give close attention to the well-known mail-order catalogs, to find out how they answer these questions of Who,

What, Where, etc. They follow the homely formula of Picture, Description and Price on which so much successful retail copy is based. For accurate detail in describing merchandise, choice of fitting words, talking from the reader's point of view, the writer of retail advertising can find no better example.

A retail advertisement only half serves its purpose if it is considered finished after it appears in the newspaper. The next step in the preparation of good retail copy is to inform the sales people of what is being advertised and the talking points of that merchandise. A store's sales people are entrusted with the follow-up of the advertising—personal contact with the store's customers. Unless they themselves are thoroughly sold on the merchandise that is advertised they will not be able intelligently to sell it to the store's customers.

A typical form of preparation for an advertised sale used by a Detroit department store in preparation for its August Linen Sale is shown below:

A. Merchandise thoroughly shopped by Comparative Shopping Bureau Report: No competition.

B. Sales force:

1. Quota increased from 11 to 21.

(a) Survey of departments by means of qualification cards.

(b) New sales people placed in department two days before sale.

(1) Introduced to department members.

(2) Instructed in stock.

(c) Quota of sales force filled by contingents on first morning of sale.

C. Arrangement of merchandise; all stock arranged on tables and shelves in the department on the night before the sale.

D. Merchandise meeting with sales people, held by buyer 8:40 A.M., first morning of sale, August 1st.

1. Merchandise:

(a) Location; (b) Materials; (c) Style; (d) Quality; (e) Sales; (f) Prices; (g) Report of shopping.

2. Throughout the buyer displayed, as well as talked about the merchandise, thus showing how best to handle it.

3. Older sales people in charge of each stock pointed out, in order that questions might be directed, thus saving time.

4. Each girl supplied with pamphlet containing all the items with prices on sale.

5. New girls directed to go about the department and familiarize themselves with merchandise. Later in the day, each girl assigned to definite stock. Girls had privilege of selling throughout the department.

E. Result: Before customers entered the department, the sales people had been

1. Introduced to members of the department; 2. Given help on:

(a) System;

(b) Merchandise.

Quota aimed at for the day, $2,000. Amount actually sold, $3,340.

Chapter 24

The Art of Visualizing Good Copy

By Ben Nash[1]

Primitive selling was a simple exchange of one necessity for another. It needed no imagination because every man knew what he needed and he knew what he had. So he exchanged the thing he had for the thing he needed.

When the art of selling progressed from this primitive exchange of necessities to the stage where the use and value of merchandise was not at once obvious, imagination was brought in.

Imagination since has been the most valuable member in the construction of the successful selling plan.

It is true enough that in many a successful selling campaign imagination has been intuitive. Nevertheless it has been the vital factor without which the plan would have failed.

In order to insure success in a campaign, imagination should be recognized as a vital fundamental. If there is imagination we can organize it and know where we are getting with it.

This enables us to make imagination effective in selling in every stage from manufacturer to retailer. We may measure imagination by a number of well-proven rules in every stage of visual selling—in research, plan, copy and in every visual expression.

The language which everybody understands is visual symbol of color, texture, form and arrangement. But you must know how to talk to

---

1. *Ben Nash.* Advertising counsellor, New York, creator and developer of the "vizualizing" function in advertisement preparation. Was for years with large advertising agencies and constructed many well known campaigns. By speeches and writings on advertising art and layout he has influenced the adoption of the term "vizualizer" as part of advertising agency function.

the eye. You must understand the rules of "visual expression" to attain effective reaction.

Think of the numberless vehicles for using this art—and to a more practical end if used scientifically. Type, color, white space, textures, pictures, in every printed medium; merchandise, window displays, billboards, packages, demonstrations. At every glance of the eye—a skillfully directed incentive to direct selling actions.

Selling through advertising in any of its various forms is accomplished through three processes: (1) through the conception of sales-making ideas; (2) through the effective conveyance of sales-making ideas; and (3) through the conviction brought about by the sales ideas.

We receive impressions or messages through sight, hearing, feeling, tasting and smelling—but sight is more important than the others combined.

Color alone has a definite effect upon our emotions and actions, the use of which is still undeveloped for the transmitting of advertising messages.

Our study is for the purpose of determining what part of the selling job can be accomplished by way of the eye.

We are dealing with the way to get the most effective visual results.

We are dealing with the most receptive "gateway" to the mind. We can keep that gateway open or swinging free and clear. We can bar the gateway with visual irrelevancy and pay the price. We can have our buying public climb the wall or unlock the rusty locks if we are willing to pay for this waste.

We are dealing with *an Art.*

We are searching for "the Art of getting results which being built on visual psychology are harmonious and effective." Art is not pictures—a picture is only one form of art. *Art is the skilful and systematic arrangement of means for the attainment of a desired end.*

In considering any visual expression, then, in regard to the definition "art" we must first clearly think of the "desired end" and of the symbols of color, texture, form and arrangement which are relevant to it.

In every advertisement, for instance, the end is to sell a service or product. Accordingly, so far as each advertising presentation is concerned, it must be considered as more than a picture merely; it must be considered as a positive force. For in the business of advertising, where every dollar must be efficiently used, there should be no place for a single element which does not carry directed power enough to offset the sales resistance to the product advertised.

Every product, product display or piece of advertising material should be a unit. A unit, to which nothing can be added, and from which nothing can be taken without destroying its meaning—a unit in which every element is harmonious and consequently fully effective.

Every element which goes to make up the harmonious unit has its values, uses and limitations and when these are recognized and understood they produce order. Through an understanding of the forces at our command and an orderly use of these forces we can attain our results with the least output of time, energy, money and materials.

A vast amount of selling through the eye has been done during the carrying on of advertising. An equal amount of ineffective presentation has found its places in the advertising archives. Good and powerful sales conception has been thwarted by ineffective presentation to the eye.

Through an easy control of the fundamentals, creative talents can have a wider range of freedom of expression.

Through this control advertising expression will reflect greater character, individuality and harmonious effectiveness because the essentials will be automatically taken care of when the process of creating is going on.

The forces which are applied to impress the eye are:

CONCEPTION; in other words *THE IDEA:*
- Part of an idea
- The whole idea
- Direct idea
- Indirect idea or impression

CONVEYANCE; in other words *THE MESSAGE:*
- Color
- Texture
- Form
- Arrangement

CONVICTION; in other words *THE RESULT:*
- Relevancy of Color
- Relevancy of Texture
- Relevancy of Form
- Harmonious unity of the whole

Idea

The forces found in the Ideas which can be conveyed to the eye have definite characteristics. They can be Direct Ideas; they can be Indirect through inference or general impression; they can be but a part of a Composite Idea, or they may be the Complete Idea.

Message

There are four physical forces which are used in the advertising message. Whether the advertising message is an advertisement, a product, a package, a window display, a piece of printed matter, etc., these four forces are at work.

First, *color*—Color talks immediately. It speaks before the eye or mind has had an opportunity to absorb any other detail of structure, form or arrangement. Color is a sensation. We respond to its stimulation in accordance with psychological laws. Every color causes a reaction, and the reaction should be reckoned with in the advertising expression.

Second, *texture*—Texture, like color, talks in terms of sensation. Its power can be applied to aid in the presentation of a message. It is like the stage setting for the actor's lines. It is the harmonious environment from which the message is delivered.

Today's reproduction processes and the advancement in the paper industry along texture and color lines afford an opportunity for a wide range of expression. Texture should harmonize.

Third, *form*—Every form used in an advertising message is a symbol. Every symbol has a meaning, definite or remote in varying degrees. The forms with which we work are pictures, ornamentation, type. Each of these forms can do different kinds of work.

Pictures: Pictures should talk. They must be relevant. They can convey a part of the message or an entire message. Frequently they only establish a setting or an environment for an advertising message when they might have done a more complete job.

Ornamentation: Ornament has a language, a meaning. Ornament can embellish and create an atmosphere or environment. It should be applied only when it is essential to the desired result. To be in good form it must be historically correct and relevant to the message.

Type: Type is a series of symbols evolved from the early picture writing. The individual type letters are read in letter-group form or word symbols.

Long before (3000 years B.C., the Egyptian wrote in sign-group symbols. Today's type symbols, as a result of the development of type faces, give us an opportunity to convey our thoughts with fuller meaning. The various styles of type can convey the same words in different styles and create different impressions, atmospheres or environments. Type should be relevant and express the idea and spirit of the advertising message.

Fourth, *arrangement*—The arrangement is the force which can give character to the advertising message. Arrangement is the force which gives sequence and emphasis to the various parts of the message.

There are two fundamental arrangements—Balance and Movement, which have innumerable applications.

Arrangement should be relevant and harmonious.

These four forces have thousands of applications in their various combinations:

In the advertisement, the judicious selection of the symbols that get over the exact idea, the skilful juxtaposition of the various parts into a harmonious and effective arrangement offer a field of visual expression which is without limit. A study of the outstanding examples of skilful advertising presentation will show that, though produced intuitively, the laws of visualization have been maintained.

Coming now to the relation between the visual approach and the text part of the advertising message, we must first view the "message" itself; then, by disintegrating it, discover its component parts and find what relation each part bears to the others.

This process has been accomplished in numerous ways by various psychologists and various writers on the subject of advertising; but as we are now only interested in problems to be met in every-day advertising practice, we will break our "message" into the four parts which experience has shown to answer every question:

1. PURPOSE
2. FACTS
3. TONE OR MANNER
4. APPROACH.

We have selected these four specific divisions because they constitute the backbone of the advertising message and are related in a manner calculated to build an advertising message with the greatest possible directness and in its most logical order.

Proceeding through these four factors in this order the message will be logically built. If we reverse them in order we shall have our advertising message as the reader gets it:

4. APPROACH. This brings about an appeal to the reader (or making effective contact with the reader's mind) and by attracting him helps to carry him through in a particular

3. TONE or MANNER or SPIRIT. This brings about a state of mind with the reader and makes possible the most effective absorption of our

2. FACTS. These, if they possess in themselves qualities of advantage and are convincingly stated, should cause the reader to so act as to accomplish our

1. PURPOSE.

The advertising man should arrive at definite judgments regarding each of these four component parts in an advertising message before he can apply his tools—the visual symbols, which, when properly used, become effective visualization.

In other words, he must crystallize his ideas in thinking (or mental visualization) before sitting down with an artist with the idea of arriving at the physical visualization, which will illustrate or symbolize the advertising message. For if he does this with only an indefinite conception in his mind there is bound to be a quite unnecessary picture waste or ineffective presentation.

If the advertising man, however, determines the PURPOSE, seeks out the salient FACTS, determines the TONE and the APPROACH as a matter of advertising strategy, if he adopts the attitude which in fact would be necessary if he had to sell his goods in person, then he has reached the point where he is ready to apply his visual symbols in the direction of bringing about the speediest presentation of his message. The visualization will then be a harmonious evolution, distinctive in character and fully effective.

Chapter 25

Old and New Days in Advertising Copy

By John Lee Mahin[1]

My first experience in writing copy was in selling advertising space in the Muscatine, Iowa, *Journal,* which my father edited for over fifty years. The local merchants in the early '90s wanted something "catchy." They particularly liked such expressions as "Columbus discovered America in 1492, but Bill Jones discovered how to sell the best groceries at the lowest prices in 1875 and has been doing it ever since."

Everybody was happy if some customer would say to one of our merchants, "That was a clever ad you had in the *Journal* last night."

Our rates for display space were so low we discouraged frequent changes of copy because type-setting was expensive.

We could get 80 cents an inch for "locals" against 5 cents an inch for display, so we concentrated on selling locals.

There was very little opportunity for me to make any more than bare statements of new goods and prices.

Occasionally I had a chance for a "write-up"—when a merchant moved, put in a new store front, or a new store was started—or an old one changed hands. Then I followed the method of writing in which I was trained by my uncle, A. W. Lee, as a reporter. His instructions were to tell the story in the simplest and fewest words in one paragraph—as

---

1. *John Lee Mahin.* Born in Muscatine, Iowa, December 14, 1869. Wayland Academy, Beaver Dam, Wisconsin. Night school course, Chicago College of Law, one year. City editor and manager of *Muscatine Journal,* 1887–90; became connected with Advertising Department of *Chicago Daily News,* 1891; later advertising manager, the *Interior Press,* Mahin Advertising Company, Chicago, 1898–1916; Director-at-Large, Federal Advertising Agency, New York City, since 1916. Author: *Mahin Advertising Data Book; Advertising and Salesmanship,* 1916. Has lectured before University of Chicago, University of Wisconsin, Northwestern University, etc.

that might be all the space that the managing editor would consider it deserved—and then elaborate the facts from as many different points as would be interesting to the greatest number of readers and then in the headlines attract as many people as possible to the important features of the story.

After thirty-five years' experience I am still convinced that this is a safe, sound method of procedure, and the young copy writer had better stick to it until he knows he is safe in making any deviations. This method is dependable, day in and day out, when the advertiser himself has a clear-cut conception of his message and can visualize the kind of people to whom he wishes to say it. It gives the copy writer opportunity to show his skill over a wide range of responsibilities.

The copy writer must remember that good advertising is essentially reiteration. He must avoid hackneyed, worn-out expressions. He must continually express the *same ideas* but constantly develop *new ways* of doing so.

In one of William Allen White's books, he says one of the problems of the editor of the society column in a small town newspaper is to describe the same dress several times during the season and give the reader who was not present the impression that each time the lady wore a new dress.

My first conception that advertising copy could be more than letting the reader know what the advertiser wanted him to know—that it could be really creative in its character and especially so in its reflex on the advertiser himself—was given me by a subscription solicitor who was ambitious to become an advertising man.

This man's name was John A. Jelly. He owned a farm about twelve miles from Muscatine. He was assessor in his township and had the "itch" to visit people.

My suspicions are still strong that the farm itself paid best during his absence, under the management of his wife and son. He was a wonderful solicitor for subscribers, and he and I knew from frequently consulting our maps of Muscatine City and Muscatine County the name of every family that did not take the *Journal;* and, what was more important, *the reason for not doing so.* From Mr. Jelly's reports, many ideas were put up to the editorial department for both elaboration and soft-pedaling, and a most accurate line kept on the value of our "features."

One evening Mr. Jelly asked me to let him solicit advertising *in the city.* This seemed so revolutionary that I was sure it was impossible, but I thought the best way out of it would be for Mr. Jelly to try it and quit himself when he found he was not adapted for it, of which I was sure. So I told him to try it out by calling on a very successful music house conducted by two brothers who were highly educated Germans. I had never been able to write anything about music that they liked, which would bring them any business.

Mr. Jelly brought me next day an advertisement scribbled on a piece of wrapping paper, which he said he had read to the Schmidt Brothers and they had authorized him to print it. The headline I recall distinctly. It was "Why Do the Boys Leave the Farm?" The text developed the thought that if a farmer wanted to keep his boys and girls at home he ought to make his home attractive, and then asked the question, "How can you do so better than by having one of Schmidt's pianos or organs in it?" Then the text suggested that if a farmer bought a piano or organ, the Schmidt Family Orchestra would go out and install it, and the farmer could invite his friends and "have a pleasant evening."

There was nothing in the copy about the technique of music. I do not recall that even the names of the pianos or organs were mentioned. The ten-strike, of course, was the Schmidt Family Orchestra. It was Mr. Jelly's idea to use this orchestra directly in merchandising. Everybody knew there was such an orchestra, as these brothers and their children were passionately fond of music and frequently played together. No one had yet suggested that this orchestra go out to a farm house. The Schmidts adopted the suggestion so quickly that I should not be surprised to have heard them say a few years later that they had originated it.

It is needless to say that this piece of copy "pulled." It sold pianos, it sold organs, it sold sheet music. Now just a word about the writing of this copy. Mr. Jelly's spelling and construction was like Ring Lardner's. His copy was always rewritten without in any way changing the purpose of the appeal or eliminating any of his colloquialisms. Merchandising the advertising—which is the reflex effect on the advertiser himself and his employees—was initiated, as far as I am concerned, by this incident and others that followed.

When I went to Chicago in 1921 I met for the first time the advertising manager who wrote his own copy. I was particularly fortunate in working with George L. Dyer, who was advertising manager for Hart, Schaffner and Marx, in initiating the national magazine advertising for this house.

Mr. Dyer started the printing of style books and selling them to the dealers. He was the first to have an illustration of a man wearing clothes with the natural wrinkles in them when the wearer was in a comfortable position. He never wavered in his conviction that the purpose of advertising was to get people to think the way the advertiser wanted them to think and that the best work was done by the advertiser when people thought the advertiser's way, but believed they were thinking that way because of the exercise of their own unaided judgment.

He once said to me, "I am never complimented when a man tells me I am writing clever copy, but when he asks me if we are really making as good clothes as our advertisements claim, I know I have sold him the idea and it's up to the salesman to do the rest.

Joseph Leyendecker was getting $4.00 a week at J. Manz & Co. when Mr. Dyer discovered him. Mr. Dyer told me that Leyendecker would be a great artist, but an advertising man should use an artist only *as an artisan.* It was his theory that the artist should be consulted only on how to express the message of the advertiser and never on what the message should be. When I went to Italy and saw the ceiling in the Sistine Chapel that Michael Angelo lay on his back for four years to paint, I saw additional proof of Mr. Dyer's theory that genius is not debarred from development by obstacles.

One of the current fallacies is that the style of the writer or the artist or the organization is more important to an advertiser than the services of experts who believe their best work is done in developing an individual, distinctive style for the advertising itself.

It is hard for any man to see the credit of his work accorded to others. Mr. Dyer was human. An incident in his career will show that he did not lose anything by sticking to his convictions.

Mr. Dyer and I both realized that Mr. Schaffner started into national advertising with great caution. For two years he was in a position to stop and say he had made the experiment in the interest of his dealers but had found a better way to help them.

Finally an interview appeared in a trade paper in which Mr. Schaffner was given the entire credit for the advertising idea and its development. Mr. Dyer's name was not even mentioned.

Mr. Dyer was furious. He poured out his wrath to me. I argued with him that Mr. Schaffner, in permitting the article to be published, was paying the greatest possible compliment to Mr. Dyer. It was sincere proof of the success of his work.

Mr. Schaffner was definitely committed to continue national advertising. Mr. Dyer's job was secure as long as he wanted it. I told him that I was sure that in three months he would have an offer from a competing house because competitors have a way of sizing up each other at their real value. I was sure that men who knew Mr. Schaffner had not originated the national advertising idea would want to talk to the man who had, as soon as Mr. Schaffner was willing to accept the credit.

My prediction came true. The Kirschbaums, of Philadelphia, employed Mr. Dyer at a salary of $25,000 a year. Advertising history should know the story of his experiences with them. When they pressed him for copy as good as Hart, Schaffner and Marx, he said he could not write it until they made their clothes as good as Hart, Schaffner and Marx made theirs. Mr. Dyer, I firmly believe, maintained that professional stand until his untimely death. He would not write copy that he did not believe to be true.

My personal experiences with Ralph Tilton, John E. Kennedy, J. K. Fraser, B. J. Mullaney, Witt K. Cochrane, Wilbur D. Nesbit, J. M. Campbell, Elbert Hubbard, and Dr. Frank Crane, and my observation of the work of other copy writers, convince me there are three clearly defined types of writers. Elbert Hubbard and Dr. Crane know how to write the language the masses like to read. Arthur Brisbane and Herbert Kaufman both have this power which, I believe, is a product of natural gifts and persistent application with a little shade in favor of endowed talent.

These men write in their own way and their style is unmistakable to those who know them, whether their names are signed to the advertisements or not. Forest Crissey, B. J. Mullaney, Wilbur D. Nesbit and Witt K. Cochrane can tell the story that big men, like J. Ogden Armour, Thomas Wilson, Samuel Insull, E. A. Stuart, and Henry C. Lytton ought to tell the public in a much better way than these men could possibly do themselves.

These writers use the vocabulary and the ideas of the men whose story they are telling. They reveal these men through the written word as these men express themselves in their spoken word. In my judgment this is the hardest test of writing technique—to tell the story so that it reads as if the advertiser wrote it himself.

J. K. Fraser and W. B. Swann are of the type of men who have most largely made advertising what it is today. They are honest, earnest, painstaking, careful, courageous and accurate. Neither would thank me if I said he was a brilliant man. Mr. Fraser originated "Spotless Town" for Sapolio and seems desirous of having every one forget it.

John E. Kennedy belongs to a different school. Mr. Kennedy originated "Reason Why Copy" and was violently opposed to space being used for "mere publicity." He argued that if such advertising paid the advertiser, this made the waste just that much more culpable because it was putting a premium on mediocrity.

An instance of the way Mr. Kennedy operated may be illuminating. After being extensively advertised as the $16,000 copy writer for Lord and Thomas, Mr. Kennedy started out as a free lance. He offered to write ten advertisements for $2,500. At that time, Armour & Co. were clients of the Mahin Advertising Company, and we bought a Kennedy campaign for them. Mr. Kennedy started in by reading all the literature he could lay his hands on relating to hams, bacon and lard. He collected a list of facts that when stated by him were indeed most interesting. He went down to the stockyards and, starting with the live hog, followed all the processes until lard, ham and bacon became merchantable products. He worked at his home and when his campaign was ready I made an appointment with Mr. T. J. Conners, the Armour General Superintendent. Mr. Conners had E. B. Merritt and B. J. Mullaney at the meeting. Mr. Kennedy read his ten advertisements. Mr. Mullaney interposed some suggestions. Mr. Kennedy handed Mr. Mullaney several affidavits signed by advertisers to the effect that he had largely increased their returns with the terse command "You—read these." Mr. Mullaney read them, looked at me with a twinkle in his eye and left Mr. Kennedy to Mr. Conners' tender hands.

Mr. Conners had been P. D. Armour's secretary in his youth. He had a direct way of settling matters when he spoke, although he was a good listener. Mr. Kennedy's copy was based on the assumption that Armour & Co. would drop what Mr. Kennedy called the meaningless "Star" as a brand name and substitute his coined word "Epicured." Mr. Conners said, as P. D. Armour had originated the use of the word "Star," it would not and could not be dropped, and no one would even discuss it with J. Ogden Armour.

Mr. Kennedy and I left. Mr. Kennedy spent two hours telling me that the packing business was one in which initiative, imagination and talent were not permitted to develop. He commented on Mr. Conners' mental and physical characteristics in anything but a complimentary manner. He characterized Mr. Merritt and Mr. Mullaney as "Yes" men—apparently the lowest depth to which an advertising man could sink.

He went home and came back in three days with ten of the finest advertisements I ever read. Everyone was pleased with them. He told the story of the wonderful epicured process of curing hams and bacon and how the Star—P. D. Armour's insignia of quality—was placed on only the products of one out of every fifteen hogs.

Another case where the obstacles placed by the obdurate advertiser apparently assisted rather than retarded the expression of genius!

So far I have said nothing about the artist as a producer of copy. When I was a solicitor for J. Walter Thompson under C. E. Raymond in Chicago in 1893, Oscar Binner dominated the copy for Pabst. His Egyptian black and white illustrations were the most discussed appearing in the magazines at that time. Later, Emery Mapes with his Cream of Wheat negro initiated the "Minneapolis Style" of copy used so long by the Munsing Underwear Co. and Washburn-Crosby Co. At Copelin's Studio I made an actual photograph of a Kohlsaat waiter and induced Emery Mapes to substitute it for the one he was using to advertise Cream of Wheat, which inaugurated the famous "Cream of Wheat" Negro chef. I also photographed underwear on living models for advertising Munsing Underwear.

Today, the term "copy" covers specialized skill and training in the search for and selection of the idea which shall be expressed in the advertiser's campaign. Copy must take cognizance of both the extent and limitations of readers' interests, incomes, tastes, habits and methods of buying.

Copy must compete for attention with many other appeals for the readers' free dollars. A man who takes a trip around the world will probably not buy an automobile. A man may buy a radio and get along with last year's overcoat; children may go to a movie instead of spending their money for candy. The width, depth, height and extent of the problems are too vast to be even sketched here.

Some copy must merely furnish leads for personal salesmen or mail order follow-ups to complete the sale. Copy that tells the whole story here handicaps rather than helps the salesmen. Some copy must sell the dealer, some must sell the consumer, some must sell confidence to the advertiser's organization.

But, any way you consider it, copy is the inner key to success in advertising.

www.ingramcontent.com/pod-product-compliance
Lightning Source LLC
Chambersburg PA
CBHW030835300326
41935CB00036B/170